HOW INDIA WAS WON BY ENGLAND

UNDER

CLIVE AND HASTINGS.

HOW INDIA WAS WON BY ENGLAND

UNDER

CLIVE AND HASTINGS

WITH A CHAPTER ON AFGHANISTAN.

BOURCHIER WREY SAVILE, M. A.

GYAN

Published by

Gyan Publishing House
5, Ansari Road
Daryaganj, New Delhi-110002
Phone: 011-47034999, 9811692060
E-mail: books@gyanbooks.com

Distribution Network
gyanbooks.com
India, USA, Canada, UK, Australia, France

ISBN: 978-81-212-8826-2 (PB)
First Published, 1881

2nd Impression 2023

Printed at: Gyan Press, Delhi.

HOW INDIA WAS WON BY ENGLAND UNDER CLIVE AND HASTINGS.

Author: Bourchier Wrey Savile

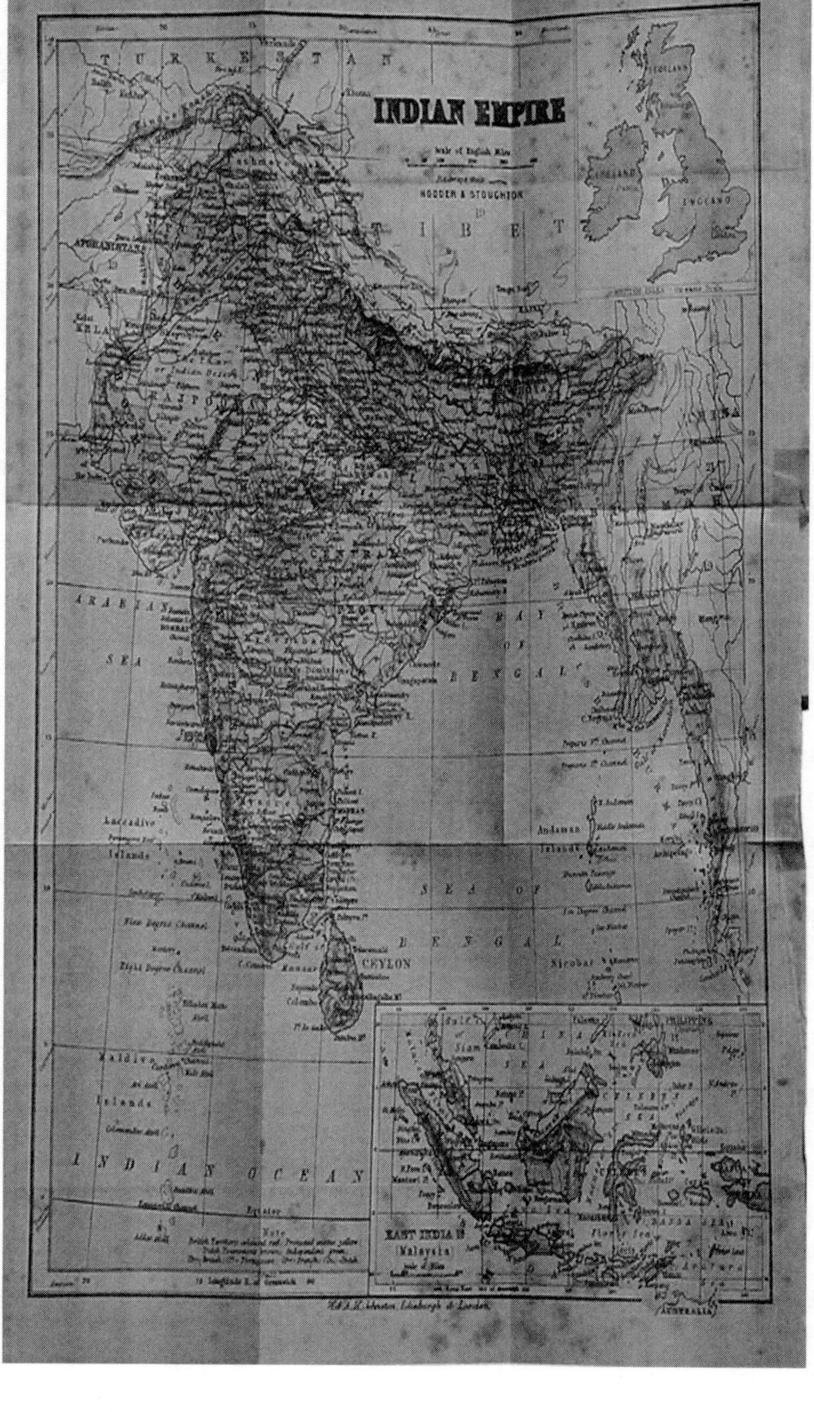
INDIAN EMPIRE
HODDER & STOUGHTON
TURKESTAN
TIBET
AFGHANISTAN
SCOTLAND
IRELAND
ENGLAND
ARABIAN SEA
BAY OF BENGAL
Laccadive Islands
Andaman Islands
SEA OF BENGAL
CEYLON
Nicobar
Maldive Islands
INDIAN OCEAN
EAST INDIA IS
Malaysia
AUSTRALIA

How India was Won by England

UNDER

CLIVE AND HASTINGS.

WITH A CHAPTER ON AFGHANISTAN.

BY THE REV.

BOURCHIER WREY SAVILE, M.A.,

RECTOR OF SHILLINGFORD, EXETER,

Author of "The Truth of the Bible," etc., etc.

"A people which takes no pride in the noble achievements of their ancestors will never achieve anything worthy to be remembered with pride by their descendants."

MACAULAY.

London:

HODDER AND STOUGHTON,

27, PATERNOSTER ROW

MDCCCLXXXI.

PREFACE.

THE object of the following story is to show how the Indian Empire has been won by England, mainly, under Providence, through the skill and genius of two eminent statesmen, LORD CLIVE and WARREN HASTINGS, who may be regarded as the respective founder and builder up of the British Empire in the East. If to these two—amongst other distinguished statesmen who have governed India—must be awarded the chief merit of having established our Empire in Hindostan, it is universally admitted that it was preserved during the Sepoy mutiny of 1857 through the skilful rule of the late LORD LAWRENCE, the great pro-consul of the Punjaub, which happily for us was entrusted to his care at that most important crisis in the history of England. It was he who succeeded in conciliating the recently conquered Sikhs, and in converting them into our staunchest friends, by which means he was enabled at the supreme moment of the rebellion to send the much-needed assistance to our sorely pressed army at the siege of Delhi, when there was no means of increasing our forces to the strength sufficient for the purpose, as Sir Henry Barnard, the general in command, had already every available soldier quartered in that part of India. And against that gallant little army had gathered all the mutinied regiments of Sepoys above Cawnpore, nearly 90,000 strong, as well as crowds of undisciplined and lawless soldiers, who had thronged together for plunder and a final effort to re-establish the ancient kingdom of the Great Mogul.

"In this crisis," says Meadows Taylor in his "History of India," "Sir John (now Lord) Lawrence trusted the Sikhs, and was trusted by them; and yet for some time the condition of the Punjaub was as desperate as any other portion of Upper India; and it was only the cool and determined will of its chief ruler that saved it, and made it the turning point of eventual triumph. Contrasting the utterly inadequate force with which Sir Henry Barnard invested Delhi with that which took it, the undying glory of assistance rests upon Lord Lawrence. Under the domination of his powerful will, Sikh levies, Goorkhas, the troops of Sikh rajahs and feudatories, the powerful siege train, supplies, money, and English soldiers had successively reached the camp on the ridge, and one and all contributed to the result, while the dauntless bravery of English and native soldiers crowned all."

From the many testimonies which have been

borne to the worth of one of England's greatest men in the present day, it would be difficult to find another, after the late Duke of Wellington, who has left behind him a loftier reputation, or rendered greater services to his country;* for we owe it, as the *Times* justly remarked on his death, "in great part to Lord Lawrence that *we have an Indian Empire to concern ourselves with.*" I will content myself with quoting three of these testimonies. "When," said Lord Granville, "our children's children and men of our race—all the world in future times—shall read the story of our rule in India, there was no man whose career they would look back to with more justifiable pride than that of Lord Lawrence; when they learned how in the great crisis of that terrible mutiny, by his force of character and strength of will, combined with the warmth of his heart, he turned the hearts of the brave soldiers he had conquered into faithful, devoted, and trusted followers, and won by the wisdom and

* The Dean of Westminster relates an anecdote concerning Lord Lawrence, which well displays his lofty sense of honour, as well as the good influence which he exercised on inferior minds. During the conduct of some important cause for a young Indian rajah, the prince endeavoured to place in his hands under the table a bag of rupees. Instantly the Viceroy addressed him: "Young man, you have offered to an Englishman the greatest insult which he could possibly receive. This time, in consideration of your youth, I excuse it. Let me warn you by this experience never again to commit so gross an offence against an English gentleman." Very different was the conduct of some of the members of the Indian government of the time of Clive and Hastings in the last century, as will be seen in this sketch.

justice of his rule the respect—and not only the respect, but the affection—of the people who were tempted to rise as one man to cast off our alien rule. But that was only one of the great deeds done by that great and brave Englishman."

"Lord Lawrence's whole life," writes Sir James F. Stephen, one of the highest authorities on such a subject, "was devoted to the establishment and maintenance of the Indian Empire. He rendered to it services of unsurpassed value by organizing the Punjaub, and in the suppression of the mutiny. These are facts known to all the world. Most of those who had the honour and happiness to know Lord Lawrence personally know that he was unsurpassed by any man of our day in those simple cardinal virtues which enable men and nations of vigorous and healthy frames to rule over others, and which made that rule a blessing to the subject, and a crown of glory to the ruler."

Last, but not least, I record with pleasure the just tribute of praise paid to the honoured name of Lawrence by Lord Lytton, the late Viceroy of India. On the news of his decease reaching Calcutta, the Governor-General in Council published the following order in a special Gazette on Monday, July 7th, 1879. "*No statesman since Warren Hastings* has administered the government of India with a genius and experience so exclusively trained and developed in her service as those of the illustrious man whose life has now closed in fulness of fame, though not of age. He bequeaths to his country a bright example of all that is noblest in the high qualities for which the civil service has justly been renowned, and in which, with such examples before it, it will never be deficient. The eminent services rendered to India by Lord Lawrence, both as ruler of the Punjaub, in the heroic defence of the British power, and as Viceroy, in the peaceful administration of the rescued Empire, cannot be fitly acknowledged in this sad record of the grief she suffers by his death, and of the pride with which she cherishes his name."

If we contrast the several monarchies which have been founded in India during the last three centuries, *e.g.*, that of the Great Mogul by Babur in 1526, or that of the Mahratta Confederacy by the Emperor Sivajee in the seventeenth century, or that of the kingdom of Mysore by Hyder Ali in the eighteenth century, with the British Empire as founded by CLIVE, ruled by HASTINGS, and preserved by LAWRENCE, as it exists at this present time, may we not adopt the language of the ancient prophet, and exclaim, "What hath God wrought!"

It will be well for us to remember the great responsibility which the existence of the British Empire, especially its Indian portion, which constitutes a far greater empire than that of ancient Rome at the zenith of her power, imposes upon us as a people towards the millions of heathen who own our sway. Professor Monier Williams, in his recent work on Modern India, justly bids us ask ourselves the following questions :—

"Have not we Englishmen in particular, to whose rule India has been committed, special opportunities and responsibilities, brought as we are here into immediate contact with these three principal religious systems—Brahmanism, Buddhism, and Islam?

"Let us look for a moment at any modern map of India. The first glance shows us that it is not one country, but many. Nor has it one race, language, and religion, but many races, languages, and religions. Its population now exceeds 240 millions. Of these, 185 millions are Hindus. Then nearly 41 millions are Mohammedans; so that England is by far the greatest Mohammedan power in the world, so that the Queen reigns over about double as many Moslems as the representative of the Khalifs himself. . . .

"For what purpose, then, has this enormous territory been committed to England? Not to be the *corpus vile* of political, social, or military experiments; not for the benefit of our commerce or the increase of our wealth; but that every man, woman, and child, from Cape Cormorin to the Himalaya mountains, may be elevated, enlightened, Christianized."

The foundation of England's greatness is dependent upon her adherence to the true principles of the Protestant religion; as Chillingworth tersely expressed it in his famous canon, "The Bible, and the Bible alone, is the religion of Protestants." As long as her power rests upon that secure foundation, she is safe. Like in the Greek fable the giant Antæus always triumphed by standing firm on the earth from which he was said to have sprung; Hercules, learning the secret of his success, managed in a wrestling match to lift him above the strengthening touch of his mother-earth, and thus crushed him to death in his arms: even so England is safe as long as her national greatness rests upon the principles of primitive catholic truth. Nothing shows this more clearly than in contrasting the difference between Spain as she was upwards of three centuries ago, when the thoughts of Englishmen were first directed to the East in the reign of our Protestant king Edward VI., and Spain as she is now, and by comparing her with England at those two respective periods.

The present century has witnessed a wonderful increase in the efforts of the Church of Christ to make known the glad tidings of the Gospel in all parts of the world, and more especially to the teeming masses of our Indian Empire. Prominent among the many agencies at work with that object in view may be named the Church Missionary Society, as faithfully representing the Reformed Church of England; the missions of the Free Kirk, under the guidance of perhaps the most distinguished missionary of modern times, the late Dr. Duff, as worthily representing the Church of Christ in Scotland ; and that devoted band of United Brethren known as the Moravian missionaries. These, together with the efforts made by our Nonconformist brethren, are beginning to tell in our dutiful attempt to evangelize India, notwithstanding the great hindrances with which our missionaries have had to contend, not only in the former opposition by the ruling powers at home, but also in the cold apathy or marked indifference on the part of many who appear to be ashamed of their religion, or rather, who show by their lives how entirely ignorant they are of its principles and requirements.

The testimony of Lord Lawrence on this head is most valuable. At a public meeting in 1870 he expressed his opinion respecting missionary efforts in India in these memorable words :—

"I believe, notwithstanding all that the English people have done to benefit that country, that the missionaries have done more than all other agencies combined. They have arduous and uphill work, often receiving no encouragement, and sometimes a great deal of discouragement, from their own countrymen, and have had to bear the taunts and obloquy of those who despised and disliked their preaching ; but I have no doubt whatever that in spite of the great masses of the people being intensely opposed to their doctrine, they are, as a body, remarkably popular in the country. I have a great reverence and regard for them, both personally and for the sake of the great cause for which they are engaged; and I feel it to be a pleasure and a privilege to do anything I can in the last years of my life to further the great work for which they have done so much."

On the eve of the great mutiny of 1857, one of the leading papers, called *The Friend of India*, by no means fanatically disposed towards Christian missions, thus speaks of the slow but sure progress of the Gospel, as seen in the decay of Hinduism, and the probability of its being supplanted by genuine Christianity: "There is more wisdom shown in the selection of men for the purpose of preaching the Gospel of Christ. Special missions are about to be organized in the half-educated class which calls itself, and perhaps is, the hope of Bengal. Dr. Pfander, long engaged in efforts among the Mussulmans of upper India, has been selected for the Mussulmans of Turkey. The native simple Germans, with their handicraft and medical skill, are selected for the jungle missions. But the greatest hope of all remains in this: our schools and colleges, among the thousands they turn out, may yet produce a native apostle. He will ring the knell of Hinduism. We chatter about caste and prejudice, as if Chaitongo had not flung caste to the winds, and died with eight million followers. A Christian Chaitongo, with the clear brain of a Bengalee, the knowledge of the West, and faith tending to asceticism, would have thousands round his feet. We have ourselves seen two thousand natives losing all their apathy, jumping, screaming, gesticulating at a song. The power of preaching among such a race has yet to be understood."

An interesting episode in the history of how we won India has been recently made public in the fourth volume of the life of that illustrious statesman, the late Prince Consort. On the occasion of the transfer of the sovereignty of Hindostan from the East India Company to the British crown in 1858, the Government of the day proposed, in the proclamation of the event, to ignore the claims of Christianity altogether. When the draft of the proclamation was laid before the Queen, we are told in the biography that it excited much dissatisfaction both in herself and the Prince, as "it did not seem to be conceived in a spirit, or clothed in language, appropriate to a state paper of such great importance." Hence we find the Prince writing in his Journal, 'It cannot possibly remain in its present shape." The Queen also wrote to the Prime Minister as follows:—

"The Queen would be glad if Lord Derby would write it himself, in his excellent language, bearing in mind that it is a female sovereign who speaks to more than a hundred millions of Eastern people on assuming the direct government over them, and after a bloody civil war giving them pledges which her future reign is to redeem, and explaining the principles of her government. Such a document should breathe feelings of generosity, benevolence, and religious toleration, and point out the privileges which the Indians will receive in being placed on an equality with the subjects of the British crown, and the prosperity following in the train of civilization."

One most objectionable phrase in the proposed proclamation spoke of the power possessed by the British Government "for the undermining of native religions and customs." The Queen remarks that "the deep attachment which her Majesty feels for her own religion, and the comfort and happiness which she derives from its consolations, will preclude her from attempting to interfere with that of others." And she expresses a wish that "the proclamation should terminate by an invocation to Providence for its blessings on a great work for a great and good end."

The result of this royal appeal, so just and proper in every sense, was that Lord Derby recast the proclamation, which was thus happily saved from the shame attached to it, had it gone forth to India and the world that England ignored the true Christianity which has been for so many ages her glory and her shield; or that the sovereign had forgotten that she rules, like those honoured kings of Israel, David, Hezekiah, and Josiah, *by the grace of God*, and is the acknowledged "defender" of that only true faith "whereby we must be saved."

Thus it happily came to pass that the revised proclamation appeared in a far more lofty and noble spirit, and more suited to the character of Protestant England. "Firmly relying ourselves on the truth of Christianity," says the Imperial manifesto, "and acknowledging with gratitude the *solace of religion*, we disclaim alike the right and the desire to impose our convictions on any of our subjects. We declare it to be our royal will and pleasure that none be in anywise favoured, none molested or disquieted, by reason of their religious faith and observances, but that all shall alike enjoy the equal and impartial protection of the law; and we do strictly charge and enjoin all those who may be in authority under us, that they abstain from all interference with the religious belief or worship of any of our subjects, on pain of our highest displeasure."

To these noble words were added, at the suggestion of the much-loved and lamented Prince Consort, the following sentence, which fitly concludes the finest and most becoming state paper ever issued by the British power: "And may the God of all power grant to us, and to those in authority under us, strength to carry out these our wishes for the good of our people."

The utterance of such Christian sentiments in a public proclamation was a bitter disappointment to the infidel party of that day. The *Saturday Review*, with its accustomed scorn for religious truth, which has earned for itself the appropriate soubriquet of the *Saturday Reviler*, assailed it for what the editor termed its "menial language," proving its disloyalty as well as its hatred of spiritual religion by speaking of the Queen's avowal of Christianity in the following offensive way: "We are plunged into the cant of the conventicle; Mr. Spurgeon himself, in his most unctuous moments, does not condescend to talk of the solace of religion." This must be taken as sure proof that this infidel writer knows nothing whatever of the power of the Christian religion, or he would not have committed such a blunder as well as falsehood in interpreting the sentiments of the great Nonconformist minister in the way he has done. And then with execrable taste this miserable scorner of all that is best in our fallen humanity wonders that the Queen's Government did not at once make her Majesty say, "Being, as I am, in the habit of *sitting under the solace of religion!*"

From such unworthy taunts it is a relief to know how this reviled proclamation was received by men of a nobler nature, and more capable of judging of its good effects upon the natives of Hindostan, who had thus become subjects of the British crown. Lord Canning, the illustrious statesman who had successfully ruled India during the horrors of the Sepoy mutiny of 1857, and who had preserved his calm serenity when others were trembling through fear, on learning that he was to add the title of Viceroy of India to the dignity of his office as Governor-General, wrote to the Queen to say "that so long as this high function shall be in his trust, he hoped that it would be administered in a spirit not unworthy of your Majesty; and that when he shall deliver it again into your Majesty's hands, it would be found to be without spot or stain from any act or word of his."

Even the natives approved of that very sentence, which so angered the infidel party at home, that whilst owning there was to be perfect toleration in India, as throughout the British Empire, Her Majesty herself reposed in the consolation of the Christian religion. At a public meeting held in Calcutta, a native merchant declared, "I have read the proclamation with great pleasure, and with tears when I came to the last paragraph [the Prince's own]. A nobler production it has not been my lot to have met." Such was the very just rebuke administered by a heathen to the sneers of such opponents of Christianity as the *Saturday Review* and other papers of that class have ever proved themselves to be.

May we not therefore conclude that it is the part of truest patriotism to follow the example set by her gracious Majesty and her illustrious Consort, to give Christianity its due recognition as having served to raise England to be, what was predicted of Israel of old, "chief among the nations of the earth"? Such was pre-eminently the case with the greatest of the viceroys of India, one of those "unanointed monarchs of the East," as the *Daily Telegraph* justly termed the late Lord Lawrence on the occasion of his honoured remains having been committed to their last resting-place in the national mausoleum, Westminster Abbey, though without those public honours which ought to have been accorded to so illustrious and great a man. But as it frequently happens, neither Clive, Hastings, nor Lawrence was rewarded in proportion to their merit; nor in the same degree to that which many men, vastly inferior in every respect, received for their services to the British Empire in India.

Nor should we forget that it is the bounden duty of every one whose conscience tells him that Christianity is the only true religion, to promote the evangelization of India to the utmost of his power; since it is by the aid of the Gospel alone that we can hope to retain our hold over the teeming millions of the British Empire in India. But with consciences satisfied with the discharge of duty, we may say with the Psalmist of old, "Jehovah is the strength of my life, of whom shall I be afraid?" A sense of duty pursues us ever. It is omnipresent, like God Himself. "If we take to ourselves the wings of the morning, and dwell in the uttermost parts of the sea," our obligations are still with us, for our happiness or our misery. We cannot escape their power, nor fly from their presence. They are with us in this life, will be with us at its close; and in that scene of inconceivable solemnity which is yet further onward, we shall still find ourselves surrounded by the consciousness of duty, to pain us wherever it has been violated, and to console us so far as God may have given us grace to perform the same.

B. W. S.

March, 1881.

SUMMARY OF PRINCIPAL EVENTS

Relating to the British Empire in India, together with the dates when the various territorial additions and annexations were made.

A.D.

1553. Earliest expedition to the East in the reign of Edward VI.

1600. First chartered company for trading with the East by Queen Elizabeth.

1613. The earliest treaty of Surat between the English and the Great Mogul.

1615. First embassy sent by James I. to the Emperor Jehángeer.

1623. The massacre of Englishmen at Amboyna by the Dutch.

1634. Second chartered company for trading with the East by Charles I.

1646. Establishment of the first factory at Madras.

1654. Amalgamation of the two companies.

1661. Cession of Bombay to the English crown on the marriage of Charles II.

1674. Trade of the East India Company extended to China.

1690. Establishment of a factory at Calcutta.

A.D.

1702. United East India Company under Queen Anne's charter.

1746. Madras surrendered to the French.

1747. Madras recovered from the French.

1749. First appearance of Clive at the siege of Devicotta.

1751. Clive captures Arcot: his wonderful defence of the same.

1756. The Black Hole of Calcutta.

1757. The victory of Plassey—foundation of the British Empire in India. Twenty-four *pergunnahs* taken from the Nabob of Bengal.

1758. Musilipatam taken from the Nizam.

1758. Clive's first government of Bengal.

1759. War with Hyder Ali.

1760. Sir Eyre Coote's victory over the French at Wandewash.

1760. Burdwan and Chittagong taken from the Nabob of Bengal.

1764. Sir Hector Munro's victory at Buxar.

1765-7. Clive's second government of Bengal.

1765-7. Bengal, Bahar, and Orissa taken from the Emperor of Delhi; the Jagheere of Madras from the Nabob of Arcot.

1766. Mutiny of English officers at Mongheer and other places, checked by the fidelity of the Sepoy troops.

1772-85. Warren Hastings' government of India.

1775. The zemindary of Benares taken from the Vizier of Oude.

1776. The island of Salsette taken from the Péshwah of the Mahrattas.

1778. Najore taken from the Rajah of Tanjore, and the Northern Circars from the Nizam.

1779. General Goddard's grand march across India.

A.D.

1780. Sir Eyre Coote's victory at Porto Novo over Hyder Ali.

1782. First Mahratta war.

1792. Malabar taken from Tippoo Sahib.

1793. Pondicherry surrendered, and the French driven from India.

1799. Siege of Seringapatam. Fall of Tippoo Sahib.

1799. Tanjore taken from the Rajah of that name.

1800. The kingdom of Mysore taken from the Nizam.

1800. Indian troops sent to Egypt to fight with the French.

1801. The Carnatic taken from the Nizam, and Bareilly from the Vizier of Oude.

1802. Bundelkhund taken from the Péshwah of the Mahrattas.

1803. Second Mahratta war. Battle of Assaye. Kuttuck and Ballasore taken from the Pakah of Berar.

1805. Guzerat taken from the Gaíkwar.

1806. Mutiny of the Madras Sepoys at Vellore.

1816. Kumâm and Gurhwal taken from the Goorkhas.

1818. Kandeish taken from Holker; Ajmere from Scindia; Poonah from the Péshwah; districts on the Nerbudda taken from the Rajah of Berar.

1824. The Burmese war.

1829. Abolition of Suttee throughout India by Lord William Bentinck, Governor-General.

1842. First war in Afghanistan. Disastrous retreat from Cabul.

1843. Conquest of Scinde.

1845. First Sikh war. Battle of Sobrahon.

1849. Second Sikh war. The Punjâb taken from the Máhárajah Dhuleep Singh.

1853. The second Burmese war.

1856. The kingdom of Oude annexed.

1857. Great Sepoy mutiny throughout Bengal.

A.D.

1858. Abolition of the East India Company, and transfer of its territories to the British crown.

1877. Queen Victoria proclaimed Empress of India by Act of Parliament.

1879. The second war in Afghanistan. Massacre of the British embassy at Cabul.

1880. Victory of Sir Fredrick Roberts at Baba Wali Khôtal.

CONTENTS.

CHAPTER VI.

CHAPTER VII.

CHAPTER VIII.

CHAPTER IX.

CHAPTER X.

CHAPTER XI.

CHAPTER XII.

CHAPTER XIII.

CHAPTER XIV.

CHAPTER XV.

CHAPTER XVI.

CHAPTER XVII.

CHAPTER XVIII.

CHAPTER XIX.

CHAPTER XX.

CHAPTER XXI.

CHAPTER XXII.

CHAPTER XXIII.

LIST OF ILLUSTRATIONS.

CHAPTER I.

THE EMPIRE OF THE GREAT MOGUL.

A.D. 1526—1857.

THERE has seldom appeared in the history of the world a succession of more splendid princes than the sovereigns of the Mogul dynasty during the sixteenth and seventeenth centuries; from the time when Babur effected the conquest of Hindostan down to the death of Aurungzebe in 1707. The deeds of the Emperor Babur are so full of romance, that they seem to warrant the trite saying of "truth being stranger than fiction." Sixth in descent from his lineal ancestor, Timour the Tartar, with a mother of the race of Ghengiz Khan, whose paternal inheritance was merely the city and district of Cabul, in Afghanistan, and who, shortly after his accession, was reduced to such straits of poverty, that even his servants abandoned him; Babur crossed the Indus, December 15th, 1525, at the head of only 10,000 picked horsemen, and after a series of brilliant victories captured Delhi, where he was proclaimed emperor, May 10th, 1526, and founded the Mogul dynasty, which gradually became possessed of so large a portion of Hindostan.

The extensive dominions possessed by the Mogul emperors in the time of Shah-Jehán and Aurungzebe

—which included the richest and most fertile portions of the earth, and in which they were not merely sovereigns, but possessors of so large a portion of the soil as to render unnecessary anything like the civil list of European monarchs in the present day—yielded them a revenue such as had never been known since the days of Solomon, when "silver and gold at Jerusalem were as plenteous as stones." Several of these Mogul princes were distinguished by a passion for architecture; and the unlimited means at their disposal enabled them to indulge their whims to the utmost extent. The very tombs which they raised over their deceased relations, such as Taj-Mahal at Agra, the most splendid mausoleum in the world, and the most touching tribute of affection ever paid by a Mohammedan prince to the memory of a beloved consort, would elsewhere have been deemed palaces for the living, save among the ancient Egyptians, who appear to have entertained similar feelings of regard for their cherished dead.

No single edifice, however stately, can give an adequate idea of the scale on which the architectural operations of the Mogul emperors, by means of their boundless wealth, were carried on. They had but to speak the word, and in a few years a range of rocky hills became the site of a new metropolis, fitted for the reception of half a million of subjects; and history records more than one instance in which a creation of this kind was commenced and completed by one prince, just as the magnificent palace at Westminster of the Houses of Parliament will be known to posterity as the production of a single reign. Notwithstanding this unlimited outlay in architecture, the Mogul emperors are thought to have been embarrassed by their wealth, and to have been scarcely able to find sufficient use for their hoards of gold, silver, and jewels, without employing them as materials for building and the adornment of their gorgeous palaces. To mention only a few instances of this sort, some of the halls in the Emperor's palace at Delhi had their floors and ceilings covered with silver, while the walls and columns of the finest white marble were inlaid with elegant flower-work composed of cornelians and other precious stones most delicately and tastefully executed. In that place there existed the celebrated gallery which it had been intended to cover with the foliage of a golden vine, bearing emeralds and rubies, fashioned so as to represent the fruit at different stages of ripeness; though only three stocks of this vine were ever completed, the materials required for the remainder having been expended on those far-famed thrones which outshone all the other wonders of the palace put together.

Taverner, a French merchant who visited India in the middle of the seventeenth century, enumerates no less than seven of these thrones. He describes five of them as being entirely covered with diamonds and pearls. The remaining one was the most celebrated of all, known as the *Tukt-Taous*, or "peacock throne," so called from the golden peacock with tail outspread, and consisting entirely of sapphires and other precious stones, which crowned the top of an overhanging canopy. The throne, somewhat like a camp bed in shape, was composed of solid gold, adorned with 108 pale rubies, weighing nearly 200 carats each; 130 emeralds; a lining of diamonds and pearls on the inner side of the canopy, and rows of fair pearls round the twelve pillars which supported it.

Such was the splendour and magnificence which surrounded the throne of the Mohammedan conquerors of Hindostan; whose monarchs, breathing only the atmosphere of boundless adulation during their lives, were naturally led to consider themselves as without rivals on earth; so that on their accession they were accustomed to discard the familiar names by which they had been known from their infancy, and to take instead some high-sounding title, such as "Lord of the Universe," or "Conqueror of the Earth," for their ordinary appellation. And theirs were not the only eyes which were dazzled by such worldly splendour; the fame of them had gone even to the ends of the earth, and the title of "Great Mogul," by which they were known in England and on the Continent, and which has become a proverb amongst us for the superlative degree of pomp and grandeur, remains to show with what wonder our ancestors, at no very distant period, listened to the tales they heard of the mysterious monarchs of the gorgeous East.

Yet the splendour of the Mogul emperors has long been a thing of the past; and though upwards of three centuries have elapsed between Babur's conquest of Hindostan and the final extinction of his unworthy descendant after the Sepoy mutiny of 1857, a certain degree of state was allowed to the king of Delhi, the pensioner of the British Government, up to the eve of the rebellion. What a contrast to the former splendour of the Mogul emperors is that presented in the scene which took place at Delhi in the early part of 1857. On January 27th, a military commission assembled in the palace of that city for the trial of Mohammed Bahádoor Shah, the last king of that once mighty race. After three weeks' judicial investigation the wretched monarch was found guilty of having ordered the murder of forty-nine Christians at Delhi, of waging war upon the British Government, and of exciting the people of India, by proclamations, to destroy the English. Sentence of death was recorded against him, which was eventually commuted into one of transportation, by the wise and noble clemency of Lord Canning, then Viceroy of India. His favourite wife, Zeenut Mahál, and his son, Jumma Bukht, decided to accompany him, and they were eventually exiled to Tounghoo, in Burmah. Thus perished for ever in ignominy and disgrace the unworthy descendant of a long line of illustrious princes, prominent among whom are to be found the renowned names of Babur, Shah Jehán, and Aurungzebe. And the vast appendage which once belonged to the Mogul monarchs has now passed into the hands of a race whose dominions at the time of the Mohammedan conquest in India were confined to two comparatively small islands in the Western Ocean, but which now, by the over-ruling hand of Providence, has obtained an empire on which it is said with truth, "The sun never sets;" and so far as British rule over India is concerned, this has been accomplished within the last hundred and twenty-five years, mainly through the skill and energy of three illustrious men, Clive, Warren Hastings, and Lord Lawrence.

CHAPTER II.

FROM THE FIRST EXPEDITION OF THE ENGLISH TO INDIA TO THE TREATY OF SURAT.

A.D. 1553—1613.

FEW great historic events have had a smaller beginning than that stupendous anomaly, the existence of the British Empire in India. That a little company of traders, subjects of a kingdom which then consisted of less than five millions, occupying two small isles in the Northern Ocean, should have succeeded in subjugating the whole of Hindostan, and of obtaining a greater empire than the Mohammedan conquerors ever possessed, is a phenomenon certainly unique in the history of mankind. And now that this company has been absorbed in the greater possessions of the British Empire, far exceeding that of Rome at the culminating point of her glory, we are enabled to realize what one of our own poets predicted a century since, when he sang in his *Ode to Boadicea,*—

> "Regions Cæsar never knew,
> Thy posterity shall sway,
> Where his eagles never flew;
> None invincible as they."

Towards the close of the reign of Henry VIII., one Robert Thorne, a London merchant, who had previously resided in Spain, addressed a memorial to the king, setting forth the benefit of a direct trade with China and the East. The text of the address discloses the ideas which our ancestors of that age entertained respecting travels by land and sea; for it was seriously proposed to reach India by the north-west passage, the route of so many subsequent attempts, and, as we are compelled to add, failures as well. Nevertheless this memorial laid the foundation of the later expeditions which were successively made in order to open a trade with the far distant East. In the year 1553, three ships, under the command of Sir Hugh Willoughby, with instructions from the highest authority of that day, Sebastian Cabot, sailed from Greenwich, May 10th, bearing letters from Edward VI., addressed to all the potentates of the earth, in furtherance of the design on hand. The little fleet became separated in the White Sea. Two of the ships were frozen in, and their crews perished, while one ship only returned to England to record the dreadful tale. Several other expeditions made similar attempts to reach India by the same route, until the last one, led by Henry Hudson, in 1579, served to satisfy the most sanguine that a north-west passage to the East was impracticable.

The supplies from the East had previously been obtained through the Mediterranean, by means of Genoa and Venice, then the leading naval powers of the world. A company chartered by Queen Elizabeth had commenced trading directly with Turkey and the Levant; but the supplies thus obtained were insufficient to meet the demand for

Eastern produce, now rapidly increasing in England. There had been a remonstrance from Spain against the successful attempt of Drake a few years before to sail through the Indian Ocean, which Elizabeth treated with characteristic contempt. She declared that the sea, like the air, was common to all who chose to make use of it, and that her subjects had as good a right as the Spaniards to sail where they pleased. An expedition direct to India was immediately set on foot. Four ships sailed May 1st, 1582; but the expedition proved a miserable failure, only reaching as far as the Brazils, and returning with but one ship out of the four. No further attempt to open a trade with India was made for several years; but after the destruction of the Spanish Armada in 1588, a body of London merchants obtained permission of the queen to despatch three ships to the East by way of the Cape of Good Hope, and these vessels sailed from Plymouth, April 10th, 1591. But this second attempt to reach India failed as completely as the first; and after a series of disasters, Captain Lancaster, who commanded the *Royal Edward*, was the sole survivor of the expedition, who succeeded in reaching England after an interval of three years, May 24th, 1594.

Following the example of the Portuguese, whose first attempt of trading with India had been as early as 1415, as well as that of the Dutch, who had succeeded in opening a trade with the East in 1596, a company was formed in London with a subscribed capital of £30,000, equivalent probably to about half a million stirling at the present time, setting forth in a petition to Queen Elizabeth the object in view, and embodying the results of the success effected by the Portuguese and the Dutch. The petition was favourably received by the queen, and in the year 1600 the company was finally embodied by charter under the title of *The Governor and Company of the Merchants of London trading to the East Indies.*

Five ships belonging to the new company sailed from England in the following year; and though they never appear to have reached India, they succeeded in capturing a Portuguese ship of nine hundred tons, with a rich cargo of Indian produce and manufactures, and established a factory at Bantam in the Isle of Java, where they traded very profitably, and returned to England after an absence of three years, one only of the five vessels composing the expedition having been abandoned at sea.

A third expedition, consisting of three small vessels, whose size may make us wonder how they could have escaped the perils of the stormy deep, sailed from England, March 12th, 1607. The *Hector*, under the command of Captain Hawkins, was the only one which succeeded in its object, and thus had the honour of being the first English ship which reached India by sailing into the harbour of Surat, north of Bombay, where the Portuguese had before established a factory. Captain Hawkins' subsequent adventures at the court of the emperor were of a romantic character in those early days of English intercourse with India. After remaining at Surat for some time, and finding it impossible to attempt any mercantile transactions with the natives without the emperor's permission, he bethought himself of King Edward's letter to the "Great Mogul," dated upwards of fifty years before, a copy of which he happened to have in his possession. So he determined, in the absence of any other diplomatic credentials, to proceed to Agra, where the Emperor Jehángeer, the father of the renowned Shah Jehán, was then residing. He was received honourably by the emperor, promised a handsome salary, and soon became a great personal favourite. By the emperor's desire he married an Armenian lady, who proved under trial a most faithful wife. But in the object of his mission he was most unsuccessful; the intrigues of the Portuguese Jesuits frustrated all his efforts to obtain the imperial permission to trade; his salary remained unpaid; he was in continual dread of being poisoned; and failing to receive any support from the emperor, he and his wife escaped with some difficulty to Surat, and were received by Sir Henry Middleton, who commanded another expedition under the provisions of a new charter granted by James I. in 1610.

It soon became evident that small enterprises in weakly armed vessels could have no chance of establishing a trade with India in face of the superior strength possessed by the Portuguese, and that it would be necessary to repel force by force. Accordingly four ships, fully armed, sailed from England, February 1st, 1612, under the command of Captain Best, and made direct for Surat, where they anchored early in September. Permission was obtained to trade with the natives, which was about to commence, when a Portuguese fleet of four galleons, convoying a number of trading vessels, entered the harbour. Captain Best at once decided on attacking this hostile squadron; all the Portuguese vessels were driven ashore, and the gallant Best remained victor in the fight. Hitherto the English had been regarded by the natives as mere traders, and looked down upon with a certain degree of contempt, which, artfully fomented by the Jesuit missionaries at Agra, had tended to Hawkins' discomfiture. But now the tables were turned; the Portuguese had been beaten on their own element; the English had established that reputation for valour, especially on the sea, which became proverbial in later years, finding expression in one of our most favourite national songs, "Britannia rules the waves," and its effect on the native mind was soon practically and beneficially apparent. The Emperor Jehángeer, as soon as Best's victory over the Portuguese became known, concluded a treaty, in which he promised his imperial protection to the English traders and settlers at Surat. An ambassador from England was permitted to reside at the court of the Great Mogul, and the custom dues were paid at the moderate amount of no more than 3½ per cent. This important treaty, which contained many other privileges in favour of the English, was received by Captain Best at Surat, February 6th, 1613, and may be regarded as the thin end of the wedge in respect to the progress of the British in India; for it was undoubtedly the first stone laid in that mighty superstructure, which has culminated in the overthrow of the Mogul dynasty, and our possession of the entire empire of Hindostan.

CHAPTER III.

FROM THE TREATY OF SURAT TO THE ESTABLISHMENT OF THE MADRAS PRESIDENCY.

A.D. 1613—1657.

THE permission given to Captain Best for the English to trade with the natives at Surat was followed up by the embassy which James I. sent to the Emperor Jehángeer. Sir Thomas Roe, the first ambassador sent to India to represent the British nation, sailed from England, January 24th, 1615, and arrived the following September at Surat, where he landed in great pomp, with eighty men-at-arms in his train. As the Mogul Emperor was then residing at Ajmere, Sir Thomas proceeded thither through the country of the Rajpoots, and was admitted to an audience in the early part of 1616. The Emperor Jehángeer received him with unusual honour, the Mogul courtiers informing him that no other ambassador, not even from their co-religionists the Mohammedans of Turkey and Persia, had ever obtained so flattering a reception. Many other interviews followed, which promised a successful termination to his mission, when the English ambassador found himself thwarted at every turn by the intrigues of the Portuguese Jesuits; until, after long perseverance and consummate address, he succeeded in procuring a confirmation of former grants of territory, as well as the privilege of having resident English agents at some of the principal towns in the empire.

The Portuguese, who had suffered a second defeat at the hands of Captain Best, shortly before the arrival of Sir Thomas Roe at Surat, were only prevented from continuing the war against the English settlement by the consciousness of their inferiority at sea. The Dutch, who were more equal to us in this respect, viewed with an equally jealous eye the success of the new company; and when the English attempted to obtain a share in the lucrative trade carried on by the Dutch with the Spice Islands, an event occurred, which, while it covered our fellow-Protestants with everlasting infamy, proved eventually of great benefit to the English, as it led to the settlement in Bengal, which eventuated in the establishment of the British Empire in India.

At the Isle of Amboyna, the largest of the Molucca group, and the richest in the produce of all Eastern spices, the Dutch had erected a strong castle, with a garrison of 200, as a protection for their growing trade. The English occupied at the same time a defenceless house in the town, guarded by only eighteen men; secure, as they vainly supposed, in its possession, by agreements and treaties with the Dutch. Yet these Dutch, pretending to suspect that this handful of Englishmen intended to deprive them of their strong castle, invited them one day to pay a friendly visit to the governor. On their arrival they were treacherously seized, and tortured on the rack until some of the weakest of them, under the agony of those infernal machines, confessed to certain words which their tormentors put into their mouths. No sooner were they released from the rack than they retracted the words which their agonies had forced from them. They were again racked by their merciless persecutors, and again repeated the confession which had been thus drawn from them. The end of this brutal specimen of Dutch justice was that Captain Towerson and nine other English were put to death, while the remaining eight were pardoned by the pretended magnanimity of their torturers. The Portuguese and nine natives of Japan were slaughtered at the same time as accomplices with the English, though all of them solemnly protested in their dying hour that they knew nothing whatever of the imputed plot.

After the occurrence of this frightful massacre at Amboyna in 1623, which excited as much horror as the tragedy of the Black Hole at Calcutta, which happened upwards of a century later, or the crimes connected with the Sepoy mutiny of 1857, the English abandoned the commerce of the Spice Islands to their unworthy rivals; and when, nearly two centuries later, they were captured by the gallantry of British sailors, during the French revolutionary war, it was one of the great errors of Lord Castlereagh and the British Government to consent to their restoration to the Dutch. Although the indignation with which the news of the massacre was received in England was immense, James I., with the characteristic indifference of his race to the sufferings of others, made no attempt to obtain redress or to punish these Dutch murderers;

and the trade of the East India Company with the Spice Islands came to an end.

In the meantime, however, the East India Company had obtained some important privileges from the Shah of Persia for commencing a trade at Gambroon, in the Persian Gulf; and two years later, in 1634, the Emperor Shah Jehán granted a firman, by which the trade of the whole of Bengal was opened to the English; and the origin of the famous city of Calcutta may be discovered in the humble factory then erected at Pepley, near the mouth of the river Hooghly. Charles I. had, however, some cause of dissatisfaction with the Company, on account of their attempt at independence from the royal control; though the only charge which he could bring against them was that in their trade they had never established permanent forts, and could not be depended on, as he said, for augmenting the glory of his kingdom. This shallow accusation only proved the insincerity of the king. Charles had got into trouble with his Parliament, and needed money; and so, in one of the many instances by which he endeavoured to enrich himself illegally at the expense of his plundered subjects, he granted a new charter to a new company, under the presidency of Sir Thomas Courten, who was rich enough to bribe high for what the king did not disdain to give. No time was lost by the new company, and before the factory at Surat could be informed of the transaction that had taken place in England, the Philistines were upon them, and they found their rivals at their doors.

About this period an interesting episode in the court of the Great Mogul led to the more secure establishment of the British trade on the eastern coast of India. A princess of the family of the Emperor Shah Jehán had been nearly burnt to death by her dress having accidentally caught fire, and her life being despaired of, an English physician was sent for from Surat, and Mr. Gabriel Boughton, the surgeon of an East Indiaman, was despatched to the emperor's court. His treatment of the princess was successful, and the emperor, in gratitude, desired him to name his reward; when, in the most disinterested and patriotic spirit, he declared he would accept nothing for himself, but instead requested an extension of privileges for his countrymen in the province of Bengal. "Let my nation trade with yours," was his generous reply; and having obtained this, he was sent across India, at the emperor's charge, to carry the compact out.* While thus engaged he visited Ráj-Mahal, where the emperor's son, Prince Shujah, had established his court; and was fortunate enough to render a second medical service of high value, for which he obtained permission to establish English factories at Balasore and Hooghly, and thus another step was acquired in the progress and growth of the British Empire in India.

* The late Sir Henry Halford, when President of the Royal College of Physicians, in an address delivered before the college on the "Results of the Successful Practice of Physic," mentioned this incident as "the circumstance most flattering to the medical profession in the establishment of the East India Company's power on the coast of Coromandel, for the efficient help of Dr. Gabriel Boughton in a case of great distress." And Sir Henry justly added, "This happy result of the successful interposition of one of our medical brethren suggests to my mind the question of the expediency of educating missionaries in the medical art."

MADRAS

Though the two East India Companies, the older one chartered by James I. and the new company by Charles I., continued to struggle from 1635 to 1646, the establishment of the former in Bengal gave it considerable advantages over its rival, and in the last-named year a new factory was established at *Chenna Putnum, i.e.*, "little city," where the modern Madras now stands, by permission of the Rajah of Chundergiri, who constructed a fortress which mounted twelve guns for the protection of the English traders, and which was named by them Fort St. George, after England's patron saint, the hero of the mediæval myth commonly known as St. George and the Dragon. Although at first the success of the new company was considerable, it was not continued. Its proceedings were more dilatory than the old, and by the establishment of a mint which issued a debased coinage, it obtained an evil reputation. The war which Charles was then waging against Parliament necessarily affected the prosperity of the two companies, when they both petitioned the Legislature to interfere—the old for the abolition of the new, the new for the freedom of trade; when the House of Commons resolved in the beginning of the year 1650 that one company only was to be permitted to carry on the trade; though, on the principle of what is everybody's business is nobody's business, the House abstained from deciding either how the two companies were to be united, or which was to be the rightful owner of the trade with India. The consequence of this parliamentary neglect was that for five years, from 1652 to 1657, the trade with India was thrown open to every English merchant who chose to embark in it. The master mind of Cromwell soon detected the impolicy of such a proceeding, so at the end of that period he performed a simple act of justice by renewing the privileges and confirming the charter of the old company which James I. had granted half a century before.

About this period we meet with the first mention in history of arbitration, or calling in a third party to settle national disputes in order to avoid the final issue of war, and which has been revived with some slight effect in our own day. It appears that the Dutch had obtained on one occasion some important advantages over the English traders to India. Three ships had been captured in the Persian Gulf, and the trade at Surat had been seriously checked. After the conclusion of the peace with Holland in 1654, the long-pending claims of the East India Company were submitted with those of the Dutch to the arbitration of the Swiss cantons. They decided in favour of the English; but of the large sum of £2,000,000 claimed, the final award only gave the moderate compensation of £88,600. After a friendly settlement of the accounts between the two companies, and Cromwell's renewal of James's charter to the old East India Company, Surat was maintained as a presidency with control over the Persian Gulf and the factories on the western coast of India, while on the eastern coast Madras became a second presidency, with authority over the factories at Peeply, Hooghly, and Balasore, which eventually belonged to the presidency of Bengal.

CHAPTER IV.

FROM THE ESTABLISHMENT OF THE PRESIDENCY OF MADRAS TO THE ERECTION OF THE CITY OF CALCUTTA.

A.D. 1657—1707.

THE year after the restoration of the Stuarts, the East India Company had little difficulty in obtaining from the needy Charles II. a confirmation of their charter, with many additional privileges. The Company was vested with the right of exercising civil jurisdiction and military authority, as well as the power of making peace and war with "the infidels of India," the State reserving to itself only such prerogatives with regard to any Christian or European governments. Under these provisions the East India Company became more respected in India, and their position was considerably improved. Two years later Charles obtained as a part of the dower of his Portuguese bride, Catherine of Braganza, the island of Bombay; but soon finding this dotation more expensive than profitable, he speedily ceded it for a consideration to the East India Company in the year 1668, when they transferred from Surat to Bombay the presidency over all their settlements on the western coast, and from that time the city began to spread on every side.

Trade was now carried on with the greatest part of Hindostan by means of the Company's factories and establishments on both sides of India, though they were frequently exposed to the hostilities of the natives, urged on by the jealousy of both the Portuguese and the Dutch. But the frequent wars among the natives encouraged the English to abandon the defensive and to adopt the offensive instead. As the Company had the power of making war and peace with "the infidels of India," they sent Captain Nicholson, with ten armed vessels and six companies of soldiers, to levy war against the Great Mogul and the Nabob of Bengal. The object of the expedition was to seize the city of Chittagong, a few miles east of Calcutta. After a variety of successes and defeats, during which the English burnt Balasore, together with forty sail of the Mogul fleet, in return for which the Nabob of Bengal plundered the English factories at Patna and Cossimbazar, the campaign ended in a way not very honourable to the British name. The Court of Directors ordered Sir John Child, the Governor of Bombay, to take the command, and to recover the factories which had been lost. While the Company's servants were carrying on pacific negotiations with the natives, Captain Heath arrived from England in a ship of war, and without troubling himself with the formality of declaring war, at once commenced hostilities. After plundering one or two native towns, he proceeded to Chittagong, where he suffered a defeat, as Nicholson had done before him. Heath then, taking with him all the Company's servants and goods, set sail for Madras; and Bengal, on which the English had already spent large sums, was for a time abandoned, and submitted again to the power of the Great Mogul.

At that period the throne was occupied by the Emperor Aurungzebe, the most powerful and illustrious sovereign of the Mogul dynasty. He had dethroned his father, Shah Jehán, under whose mild rule the empire seemed falling to pieces, and had triumphed over his brothers, who contested the throne with him. He had taken Hyderabad and other cities in the Deccan, and had extended his conquests to the limits of the Carnatic.

Aurungzebe, who had previously been well disposed towards the English, was indignant at their last proceedings against Chittagong without a formal declaration of war, so he issued orders for expelling them everywhere from his dominions. The factory at Surat was seized, the island of Bombay was surrounded by a fleet, and the English governor shut up in the castle. Another factory which the English possessed at Vizagapatam was taken, and there several of the Company's servants were put to death. But Aurungzebe soon felt the want of the copious streams which flowed into his treasury through the English factories; and so flattering himself into the belief that the East India Company would never be strong enough to be dangerous, he showed a readiiness to forget the past, while listening to proposals made by the English in a most humble and submissive way.

After some delay the East India Company, on the payment of £15,000, obtained the restoration of Bombay, and also the factory at Surat. But while this was taking place, the most powerful of all the enemies with whom England has had to contend obtained a footing in India. The French had formed an establishment in Pondicherry, and were now employed in fortifying the place, and in establishing a close connexion with those natives most hostile to the English. Such proceedings naturally quickened the desire of the Company to obtain an extension of territory, and a real dominion by treaty at all risks, by which they might become independent of the Great Mogul and all other powers in the world. "The truth is," says Sir John Malcolm, in his *Sketch of the Political History of India*, "that from the day on which the Company's troops marched one mile from their factories, the increase of their territories and their armies became a principle of self-preservation; and at the end of every one of those numerous contests in which they were involved by the jealousy, avarice, or ambition of their neighbours, or the rapacity or ambition of their own servants, they were forced to adopt measures for improving their strength, which soon appeared to be the only mode by which they could avert the occurrence of similar danger." So in 1689 the directors adopted the principle that independence was to be established and dominion to be acquired in India.

A few years later Aurungzebe had appointed his grandson Azim to be viceroy of Bengal: Moazzim, the viceroy's father, was in the meantime aspiring to his father's throne. To enable him to succeed, money and arms were required, and the Company, for valuable considerations, could promise both. For a large sum Azim sold to the Company the zemindarships of Chuttanuttee, Govindpore, and Calcutta. At the last-mentioned place the English commenced with great caution, in the year 1688, to erect Fort William. Nine years later, when the fort was strong, and a town had arisen under the shadow of its walls, the Company made Calcutta the seat of a presidency; and the place gradually began to rise to the dignity of capital of the British Empire in Hindostan.

CHAPTER V.

FROM THE ESTABLISHMENT OF THE PRESIDENCY OF CALCUTTA TO THE CAPTURE OF MADRAS BY THE FRENCH.

A.D. 1707—1746.

A NEW element of discord had been apparent for some time in the existence of a Scotch East India Company, which claimed to have been embodied by James I., and now issued its licences for free trade. The result of this over-trading between the rival companies was great; the English markets were glutted with Indian produce, while the English manufacturers, feeling the effects of the excessive importation of calicoes and silks, petitioned for their prohibition, and obtained some relief in the shape of increased duties on imported goods. These matters caused much alarm to the interlopers as well as to the English Company, until the year 1702 brought about the eventual amalgamation of all traders to India under the appellation of THE UNITED EAST INDIA COMPANY which was established under a charter granted by Queen Anne.

At this period the Company's possessions in India may be enumerated as follows: In western India, the factories of Surat, Baroche and others in the presidency of Bombay. In Persia they had factories at Ispahan, Shiraz, and Gambroon. On the eastern coast of India they possessed Fort St. George and the city of Madras, Fort St. David, with three square miles of territory, as well as factories at Cuddalore, Musilipatam, and other places. In Bengal, Fort William, with the rising city of Calcutta and its adjoining territory, with factories at Patna, Balasore, Raj-Mahal, and other places besides. Six years were allowed for the amalgamation of the two companies, when the final adjustment was made under an award by Earl Godolphin, then prime minister, dated September 29th, 1708.

The tranquillity and commercial prosperity which the peace of Utrecht in 1713, however discreditable to the Tory government of the day, brought to England and a great part of the Continent, contributed to raise the value of the British settlements in the East, and to encourage the Company to seek an extension of their dominion. The breaking up of the Mogul Empire, which commenced with the death of its greatest sovereign, Aurungzebe, in 1707, seemed to afford a good opening to their ambition. His four sons contended for the paternal dominion, as in the case of Herod the Great, and there was no dominant power then in India like that of Rome to apportion a tetrarchy apiece. During this unfraternal contest, the Mahratta chiefs, who had entered the service of the Emperor Shah Jehán, extended their conquests in the south, the Rajpoots virtually obtained their independence in the north, while the Sikhs, a remarkable sect who professed a pure theism, and attempted to reconcile the religion of the Hindus with that of Mohammed, ravaged the provinces of Delhi and Lahore.

Moazzim, the father of Azim, to whom Aurungzebe had entrusted the viceroyalty of Bengal, triumphed over his brothers, though only for a very brief period, as at the end of a few months he was dethroned by his nephew, Faroksheer, whose rule lasted for nearly seven years. Under his successor, Mohammed Shah, the Mogul Empire was wasted to a shadow, compared with its condition only a few years before, during the reign of the magnificent Aurungzebe. The Deccan was alienated under the rule of the Nizam-el-Moolk, in name a viceroy of the Mogul emperor, but in reality an independent prince. The Rohillas, who were descended from the former Afghan troops and settlers at Delhi, a fierce and warlike race, seized on the northern provinces; and in 1739 the Persians under Nadir Shah penetrated to Delhi, and slaughtered alike both Mussulmans and Hindus.

We have already had occasion to notice how the East India Company obtained their first footing in Bengal by Mr. Boughton's cure of the favourite daughter of the Emperor Shah Jehán; and eighty years later a similar piece of good fortune attended the Company from the same cause. In the year 1715, a Dr. Hamilton, who accompanied a commercial mission to Delhi, obtained on behalf of the Company a grant of three villages near Madras, with permission to purchase thirty-seven additional townships in Bengal, as a reward for curing the Emperor Faroksheer of a dangerous and painful illness, which was beyond the reach of the native physicians to cure. By the hostility of the Nizam, the Company were for a long time prevented from purchasing these townships, though permitted to obtain another privilege from the grateful emperor, viz., the right of conveying their goods from Calcutta through the province of Bengal, without duty or search. In a very short time the Company benefited by this grant to an enormous extent, though the French East India Company, who had made Pondicherry their stronghold, endeavoured to counteract their plans by every means in their power.

In the year 1742, when war between England and France seemed imminent, the French Company, then in its infancy, proposed to the English Company, that whatever might happen in Europe, there should be peace between them in India. The Court of Directors at first agreed to, and then rejected, this proposed neutrality; instructing their officers to watch, and, if possible, to circumvent every treaty which the French might endeavour to make with the natives on behalf of their own trade. Two years later the war which broke out between England and France in Europe and America rapidly spread to Hindostan. Labourdonnais, the governor of the Mauritius and the Isle of Bourbon, who had got together a warlike squadron by training the crews of all the French trading vessels which stopped at the Mauritius to the use of cannon, commenced his operations with an attack on Madras. The total number of his forces amounted to upwards of 3,600 men, a most motley crew, consisting of Frenchmen, Caffres, Negroes, and Sepoys, with upwards of 400 from Pondicherry.

The English in the colony of Madras did not exceed 300 men all told, of whom about 200 were soldiers, who occupied the Fort of St. George, then surrounded by a weak wall, and defended by four badly constructed batteries. About the middle of September, Labourdonnais appeared off the town, and immediately commenced a bombardment, which continued for five days, at the end of which the English garrison was compelled to capitulate. The French did not lose a single man, the English not above four or five; while, by the terms of the capitulation, Labourdonnais pledged himself to restore Madras to the English Company on payment of a fixed ransom.

In his instructions from the French Government, Labourdonnais was expressly prohibited from occupying any factory or establishment of the English, which seems to show that neither the home Government nor the French Company contemplated any idea of territorial conquest in India. M. Dupleix, however, as governor of Pondicherry, thought this a favourable opportunity for promoting the interest of his country, having previously formed in his own mind a plan of extensive conquest in India, his first object being to drive the English from the coast of Coromandel. Dupleix, who aspired to have the sole conduct of the war, regarded Labourdonnais as an intruder and rival. Now, however, he insisted that Labourdonnais should break the conditions of the capitulation, and keep possession of Madras. The brave sailor was determined to oppose such a proceeding, which would have been not only a breach of faith and honour, but also of the orders of the home Government; but a storm having arisen, which compelled him to put to sea, and caused the loss of two of his ships with their crews, Labourdonnais demanded that the treaty should be altered so as to allow an extension of time for the removal of the Company's goods; so the period of evacuation was consequently advanced from the 15th of October to the 15th of the following January. This was in accordance with the wishes of the crafty Dupleix, as he intended on his rival's departure to take possession of Madras, without paying any regard to the articles of capitulation.

Labourdonnais repaired to Pondicherry as soon as the weather permitted, and proposed several plans for the benefit of his countrymen, to none of which would Dupleix agree. After many quarrels he took his departure for France, to answer the accusations of his enemies, and to procure sufficient patronage at home, which might enable him to return with credit and power to India. On his voyage homewards, he was taken prisoner by a British man-of-war, which brought him to England, where he was hospitably received, and treated with distinction. On his subsequent arrival in France, he was imprisoned in the Bastile in 1748, where he remained more than two years without a trial; and when at length it took place, he was acquitted of all the charges made against him. But his sufferings had been great; he was reduced to poverty, and died soon after of a broken heart. Such is the reward often given by the government of an ungrateful country to the most deserving and distinguished of its citizens.

CHAPTER VI.

FROM THE CAPTURE OF MADRAS BY THE FRENCH TO THE CAPTURE OF DEVICOTTA BY THE ENGLISH.

A.D. 1746—1749.

THE unfortunate Labourdonnais had scarcely quitted Madras when the Nabob of Arcot, irritated by his attack on a settlement within his jurisdiction, sent his son, Mafooz Khan, at the head of 10,000 men, to drive the French from that place. The force which Labourdonnais had left behind him in Fort St. George exceeded 1,200 men, nearly all native French, under well-trained discipline. The natives were astonished and panic-stricken by the rapidity of their artillery; and after a brief struggle Mafooz Khan fled with all his host. Madras being now secure, Dupleix, the governor of Pondicherry, deliberately violated the convention made by Labourdonnais, ordering the officers to seize every article of property there, private or public, native or English, except clothes, furniture, and the jewels belonging to the women. After thus confiscating all their property, Dupleix offered the English residents the alternative of remaining as prisoners of war on parole, or being sent to Pondicherry. Some escaped to Fort St. David, but the governor and most of the inhabitants were taken to Pondicherry as prisoners, and publicly degraded by being marched through the streets.

Dupleix then turned his attention to Fort St. David, distant about twelve miles from Pondicherry. On the night of December 19th, 1746, he quitted Pondicherry with 1700 men, the greatest portion being French, arriving next morning before Fort St. David, which was occupied by about 200 English soldiers and 100 natives. The French had already begun to train the native Sepoys to European discipline, while the English delayed following so good an example. They had, however, hired about 2000 men, irregularly armed with swords and targets, bows and arrows, which were employed to defend the town of Cuddalore, in the immediate neighbourhood of the fort, and partly protected by walls. The French took up an advantageous position, making sure of the capture of both the fort and the town, when a large army appeared on their flank, and compelled them to make a disastrous retreat. This relieving army had been sent by the Nabob of Arcot, to avenge the defeat of his son at Madras, and captivated with the liberality of the English, who had promised a large sum of money if he would come to their help.

A second attempt was made on Fort St. David in the following month of January, 1747, when Dupleix embarked five hundred men in boats, in order to capture Cuddalore by surprise; but the wind and waves opposing, the detachment returned to Pondicherry without any result. Some ships of war arriving soon after, Dupleix skilfully represented that they were the advanced guard of a powerful fleet from France, and the Nabob began to waver in his alliance with the English. He saw that they were comparatively few in number, while the French were growing daily stronger. So he made peace with the French, recalled the army he had sent to the assistance of the English, and sent his son on a visit to Pondicherry, where Dupleix received him with great pomp. A third attempt on Fort St. David, in March of the same year, met with no better success; for the French had no sooner taken their position than an English squadron, under Admiral Griffin, was seen in the offing, which scared them back to Pondicherry; during which the admiral was enabled to throw in material succours to the fort, consisting of a hundred English soldiers and a force of seven hundred natives from Bombay and Tellicherry.

Early in the following January of 1748, Major Stringer Lawrence, an officer of distinguished merit, arrived at Fort St. David with a commission to command the whole of the Company's forces in India. He had not been there long ere Dupleix attempted a fresh night attack on Cuddalore. Lawrence allowed the French to approach the walls, and even to apply their scaling-ladders; and then poured forth such a destructive fire, that the French were driven back in great disorder. It should not be forgotten that although England had then upon her hands a war with Spain, France, and Holland combined, and had only recently recovered from the effects of the invasion of the Young Pretender in the affair of '45, she was enabled to despatch Admiral Boscawen with nine ships of the line to co-operate with eleven ships belonging to the Company in carrying on the war against the French in India. Boscawen arrived at Fort St. David in August, and joining his fleet with that of Admiral Griffin, found himself at the head of the largest force that any European power had as yet possessed in India. The land troops from England amounted to 1,400 men, and it was hoped that the loss of Madras would be speedily avenged by the capture of Pondicherry. The siege of the French capital, however, which lasted for thirty-one days, proved a miserable failure. The French were for a time regarded by the natives as the superior race; but before they could avail themselves of the prestige thus ingrained in the native mind, peace was concluded in Europe between England and France, and Madras was restored to the English.

It was now that the real ambition of Dupleix began to show itself. The war with the English had been confined to local affairs; but during its continuance he had already witnessed the ease with which a small force of Europeans had overthrown a host of native soldiers, and the anarchy which then ruled throughout the north of India, by the breaking up of the Mogul Empire, encouraged French and English alike to pursue their schemes, more or less avowed, of territorial aggrandizement. Sanhojee, a Hindoo prince, who, in the rapid revolutions of that country, had gained and lost the throne of Tanjore, repaired to Fort St. David, and entreated the assistance of the English in a war against his illegitimate brother, Pertaub Singh, who had dethroned him. As the price for such assistance, Sanhojee offered the fort and adjoining country of Devicotta, advantageously situated on the cost of Coromandel, about seventy miles south of Pondicherry.

In April, 1749, a force consisting of nearly 500 English with 1000 Sepoys marched from Fort St. David into Tanjore, and commenced operations by attacking the fortress which was to be ceded to the Company. But Devicotta proved stronger than was expected, and the English had to retreat after having failed in their attempt. Sanhojee's impatience, however, to recover his throne, and their own eager desire for territorial aggrandizement, soon induced the English to renew the attempt. A new expedition was fitted out at Fort St. David, under the command of Major Lawrence, the troops were landed, Devicotta was stormed, and after some hard fighting soon fell into the hands of the English. A truce was concluded with Pertaub Singh, the reigning sovereign of Tanjore, by his agreeing to yield the town and adjoining district, while the English, with a lamentable disregard of honour, agreed, not merely to desert Sanhojee, for whom and with whom they entered on the war, but also to secure his person, in order to prevent him from giving any further trouble to his illegitimate brother.

The siege and capture of Devicotta was rendered memorable from the fact of its being the second appearance of Clive, the real founder of the British Empire in India, on the scene of operations. He had attracted some attention in the previous year at the siege of Pondicherry, and was now regarded as the most promising of the young officers who were seeking to make their fortunes on the plains of

Hindostan. The possession of Devicotta, though it inflicted a stain on the English name, proved of immense importance to the East India Company in their subsequent proceedings, and thus concluded the first and comparatively insignificant attempt of English interference with the numberless quarrels and wars which were perpctually arising between the native princes and peoples of India.

CHAPTER VII.

DUPLEIX, GOVERNOR OF PONDICHERRY.

A.D. 1741—1754.

WHILE the events related in the last chapter were in progress, the French, under the guidance of Dupleix, were mixed up with the great revolution which had occurred in the Carnatic. In the year 1741, Chunda Sahib, on surrendering Trichinopoly to the Mahrattas, had been sent a prisoner to Sattara, while his wife and family had been committed to the care of Dupleix at Pondicherry, where his wife had been born and educated, and consequently spoke the native languages as her mother tongue. By this means she was enabled to conduct a secret correspondence with the native troops employed by the English at Fort St. David; but this treachery was discovered and punished. Madame Dupleix, however, succeeded in forming an intimacy with the wife of Chunda Sahib, and before long they arranged a plan for obtaining the latter's release; which was effected by a bribe of £70,000 given to the prime minister of Nizam-ool-Moolk, the nominal viceroy, but the real sovereign, of the Carnatic.

Early in 1748, Chunda left Sattara to join his wife and family; but being attacked by the Rajah of

Chittledroog, then at war with Bednore, he was again taken prisoner, and his arrival at Pondicherry was delayed. At this juncture the Nizam died, and a contest for the succession ensued between his second son, Nasir Jung, and his grandson, Mozuffer Jung. The latter was in no condition to enter on a contest with his uncle, until joined by Chunda Sahib, who had escaped from his second imprisonment, and who disclosed to him his connection with the French. They marched together towards the Carnatic, being joined on their way by 400 French soldiers and 2,000 disciplined Sepoys. The allies overthrew Anwur-wood-deen, the late Nizam's prime minister, at Ambor, without much difficulty, Anwur being killed in the battle. The conquerors entered Arcot with great pomp. Mozuffer Jung was proclaimed Soubahdar of the Deccan, and Chunda Sahib Nabob of the Carnatic. Thence the allies proceeded to Pondicherry, where Dupleix entertained his guests in royal state, receiving in return a grant of eighty-one villages near the town.

Dupleix now urged his allies to complete the conquest of the whole province; but Chunda thought he could do better for himself by attacking the Rajah of Tanjore, who only preserved himself by agreeing to pay Chunda the sum of £700,000. While the allies were thus engaged, Nasir Jung arrived from the Deccan with an immense army, drove them out of Arcot, and compelled them to retreat to Pondicherry.

During these operations the English Council at Madras were in doubts as to the best course to follow. Should they remain neutral? or which side should they support? This was in some measure decided by the act of Mohammed Ali, son of Anwur, who, after his father's death, fled to Trichinopoly to implore the aid of the English. After some delay, one hundred and twenty European soldiers were sent him; while, with great want of foresight, the Madras Council permitted Admiral Boscawen to sail with his fleet for England. As, however, they were committed to the side of Mohammed Ali, when Nosir Jung began to move his huge army of 300,000 men on Pondicherry, they sent to his camp a force of 600 men, under the command of Major, afterwards General, Lawrence, to which Ali himself added a contingent of 6,000 horse.

At the approach of this gigantic host, Chunda Sahib and his French allies retreated hastily to Pondicherry, where Dupleix had by great exertion succeeded in augmenting his forces to 2,000 Frenchmen, aided by a large and well-disciplined body of Sepoys. Some disputes about the booty having arisen between Dupleix and the French officers who commanded this force, numbers of them refused to fight, and M. d'Auteuil, their commander, seeing the defection becoming general, wisely retreated to Pondicherry. Chunda Sahib, whose own troops were beginning to desert him, thought he could do no better than follow the Frenchman's example, upon the well-known principle that—

> "He who fights, and runs away,
> May live to fight another day;"

which was exactly the case with Chunda Sahib; for while his colleague, Mozuffer Jung, surrendered himself like a coward to his uncle, Nasir Jung, Chunda gallantly fighting against his innumerable foes managed to escape from them all. Then Nasir Jung returned with his huge host to Arcot, while Major Lawrence, finding he could do nothing on behalf of British interests, marched his troops back to Madras.

It might be supposed that the French combination was now broken up; but no. Dupleix proved as active and intriguing as ever. He had many irons in the fire, and he now produced one which resulted in great and unlooked-for success. He discovered that there was a considerable amount of discontent in Nasir Jung's army, especially among the Patan chiefs, a set of ferocious and unprincipled mercenaries, ever ready to sell their sword to the highest bidder. Responding to the overtures of Dupleix, they at once engaged to perform various services, and, if necessary, to murder their present employer, Nasir Jung. M. d'Auteuil again took the field, and one of his officers, with only three hundred men, was allowed to penetrate by night into the very heart of the enemy's camp, and to kill upwards of a thousand, without losing more than two or three of his own men.

Moreover, Dupleix managed to send another expedition by sea, under the charge of General Bussy, to capture Musilipatam, a strong fortress about three hundred miles north of Madras; and this was carried by assault, after a night attack, in which the French experienced a very trifling loss. Mohammed Ali, who had with him a small English detachment under Captain Cope, all of a sudden declined to pay their expenses any longer, on which they were withdrawn to Madras. Chunda Sahib, with his French allies, at once attacked Ali, and routed his army with great slaughter. Continuing this career, Bussy captured by storm the hill fortress of Guijee, which had hitherto been deemed impregnable. This event had such a great effect, not only on the natives, but on the Europeans as well, that Nasir Jung renewed a correspondence which he had previously held with Dupleix. The wily Frenchman replied to his overtures in a friendly manner, and finding himself master of the situation, drew up a treaty of pacification, which he professed would satisfy himself and his allies. Mozuffer Jung was to be set at liberty, Musilipatam and its dependencies ceded to the French, and Chunda Sahib invested as Nabob of the Carnatic. These concessions he declared would restore the blessings of peace to the Carnatic, the unfortunate inhabitants of which had suffered the utmost extremity of misery from this and preceding wars.

Meanwhile the crafty Dupleix had arranged the revolt with the treacherous Patan chiefs, who formed an important portion of Nasir Jung's army. The doomed Soubahdar, after much hesitation, signed the treaty which the wily Frenchman had sent him, but the delay was the cause of his ruin. Dupleix, uncertain whether Nasir Jung would accept his terms, ordered his force, consisting of nearly 4,000 Frenchmen and Sepoys, to march from Guijee to attack an army supposed to be 300,000 strong. As they neared the camp, which extended for eighteen miles, they were led by a guide from their confederates to the division occupied by Nasir Jung, which they attacked at night. Early in the morning, Nasir Jung mounted his elephant to ascertain the progress of the fight, when he soon discovered that he was betrayed. Upbraiding the ferocious Patan chiefs for their treachery, the Nabob of Kurnool sent a ball through his heart, and he fell dead at the feet of the traitors, who at once cut off his head, stuck it upon a spear, exhibited it to the army, and the conflict came to an end.

Mozuffer Jung was immediately released, and proclaimed Soubahdar of the Deccan (although there were four brothers of the murdered Nasir) on the spot; and he who had so quickly passed from a prison to a throne hastened to Pondicherry to express his gratitude for the friendship, and admiration of the policy, of Dupleix. As a substantial proof of his thankfulness he lavished on his benefactor a great portion of Nasir Jung's treasures, naming him at the same time Governor of all the Mogul's dominions, from the river Kistnah, which flows into the Bay of Bengal, to Cape Comorin; and appointing his ally, Chunda Sahib, to be Dupleix's deputy in the government of Arcot.

Thus the result of the French policy proved for a time more successful than Dupleix in his most sanguine dreams could have supposed possible. He had obtained the government of a large portion of the Mogul's dominions, containing thirty millions of subjects. He had created a nabob of the Carnatic, and a soubahdar of the Deccan; Chunda was to be subject to him, the coinage was to be struck at Pondicherry, and Musilipatam, with its dependencies, yielding a revenue of £50,000 a year, was allotted to the French. For his own personal share of Nasir Jung's treasures, Dupleix was to receive £200,000 and the expense of the war; while gratuities to the French officers were provided for on equally liberal terms.

Mozuffer Jung had other claims to satisfy besides those of Dupleix and his companions. The traitor Patan chiefs demanded that the territories which they had usurped should be confirmed to them, with exemption from all tribute, and that half of Nasir Jung's treasure should be given to them. Mozuffer, as well he might be, was afraid of these turbulent feudatories, and would not trust himself among them without a French escort. Bussy therefore was despatched by Dupleix, in command of between two and three thousand Europeans and Sepoys, to the assistance of the Soubahdar of the Deccan, who marched for Hydrabad at the beginning of the year 1751. On entering the territory of the Nabob of Kurnool, an ambuscade was discovered, and Bussy gave orders for clearing the pass, which was quickly done by the French artillery. But in pursuing the fugitives Mozuffer received a Patan arrow in his brain, which proved as instantaneously fatal to him as the Patan bullet had in the heart of his predecessor, Nasir Jung. Instant action was necessary, as the native army would otherwise have disbanded themselves and returned to their homes; whereupon Bussy sent for Salabut Jung, the third son of Nizam-ool-Moolk, and caused him at once, with the consent of the army, to be proclaimed Soubahdar of the Deccan. By this measure tranquillity was at once restored, and General Bussy was deserving of the highest praise for the promptitude with which he acted, and for the success with which his conduct was rewarded. He might have exacted much more than he did from the Soubahdar, with many additional concessions to his own nation ; but he was satisfied in obtaining a confirmation of the grants made by his predecessor, Mozuffer Jung, and with this even the rapacious governor of Pondicherry was compelled to be satisfied.

Dupleix was now the greatest potentate in Hindostan. His countrymen boasted that his name was mentioned with awe and reverence in the palace of the Great Mogul at Delhi. The natives looked with amazement on the progress which, in the short space of four years, had enabled an European adventurer to make such rapid strides towards dominion in Asia. Nor was the vainglorious Frenchman content with the reality of power, as many of our wiser fellow-countrymen have been in the execution of their work, by which we have won the British Empire in India. Dupleix, with the characteristic love of a Frenchman's vanity, sought to display his assumed greatness before the eyes of his subjects and rivals. Near the spot where his policy had obtained its chief triumph by the fall of Nasir Jung and the substitution of his successor, he determined to erect a lofty column, on the four sides of which four pompous inscriptions, in four languages, should proclaim his glory throughout Hindostan. Medals stamped with emblems of his success were buried beneath the foundations of this stately pillar, while round it arose a town, bearing the haughty name of DUPLEIX FATI-HABAD, which is, being interpreted, "The City of the Victory of Dupleix."

This pillar, so characteristic a memorial of French

vanity, only remained long enough to show the evanescent nature of its power in India, which might have been compared to Jonah's gourd for growth, rather than to the slow but surer progress of the stately British oak; but if the philosophic historian seeks to inquire what has become of Dupleix's powcr, and where are the proofs of its continuance within half a century after he was gathered to his fathers,—where are they? echo is constraine d to reply, Where?

CHAPTER VIII.

THE RISE OF CLIVE—FROM THE CAPTURE OF ARCOT TO THAT OF CHINGLEPUT.

A.D. 1751—1752.

PROMINENT among the many great statesmen and warriors who have helped to win the British Empire in India, there stand out three great names, to whom under God the reward of success is more peculiarly due; who may be respectively characterized as Clive, "the founder," Warren Hastings, "the builder," and the late, as alas! we are now obliged to write the name, Lord Lawrence, "the preserver," when, under the throes of the mightiest mutiny which ever shook an empire to its base, he retained the Punjaub in its allegiance by his judicious action, and was thus enabled to send the much-needed help to the British army in its life and death struggle with the traitors who had seized Delhi, the former capital of the ancient Mogul Empire, when it ruled as late as the beginning of the last century throughout the whole of Hindostan.

With the death of Aurungzebe in 1707, as we have already seen, the Mogul Empire fell fast into decay. A line of feudal princes soon raised themselves to independence in Rajpootana. The lieutenants of the Emperor founded separate sovereignties at Lucknow and Hyderabad. The plain of the Upper Indus was occupied by a race of religious fanatics called the SIKHS. Persian and Afghan invaders crossed the Indus, and succeeded in sacking Delhi, the capital of the Moguls. Plundering hordes known under the name of the MAHRATTAS, the natives of India, whom the Mohammedan conquerors had long held in subjection, poured down from the highlands along the western coast, ravaged the country as far as Calcutta and Tanjore, and finally set up independent states at Poonah in the west, and Gwalior in the north of India.

We have seen how skilfully Dupleix availed himself of the disorder around him; how he had succeeded in appointing the virtual sovereigns of the Deccan and the Carnatic, under the respective titles of Soubahdar and the Nabob; while for himself, as representing the French Government, he had obtained a kingdom superior in population to the greatest European monarchies of that age, embracing a population of thirty millions of subjects. The time was now come to decide whether they should belong to France or England, as successors to the Mogul inheritance, the magnificent empire of Hindostan.

A curious embroglio ensued at the time when the French had proclaimed Salabut Jung soubahdar of the Deccan on the death of Mozuffer Jung. The English and French in the Carnatic, though their respective nations were at peace in Europe, had taken different sides in the politics of India, and the eventual superiority was about to be fought out under cover of them. The English would probably have acknowledged Chunda Sahib as the nabob, if they could secure Trichinopoly, a place then of vital importance to their ally, Mohammed Ali; but to this Dupleix would not consent; and Chunda Sahib's first act, after taking possession of Arcot in 1751, was to lay siege to Trichinopoly with his own army, assisted by a contingent of eight hundred French. For the English to raise the siege would seem impossible. The small force then at Madras was without a commander. Major Lawrence had returned to England, and not a single officer of reputation remained in the settlement. After this small force had been placed under the command of a Captain Cope, who proved his incapacity as much as his more noted namesake, Sir John Cope, had done a few years before at Prestonpans, the command was given to a Captain Gingen, who appears to have been as weak and undecided as his predecessor; for as Gingen, whose force consisted of five hundred English, one hundred Caffres, and one thousand Sepoys, was marching to the relief of Trichinopoly, he was met by Chunda Sahib, who, after leaving the chief portion of his army for the siege of Trichinopoly, hurriedly marched to oppose him. The armies met near the fort of Volconda, where the English behaved in such a way as British troops have rarely done; they fled at the first shot, leaving the Caffres and Sepoys to bear the brunt of the fight alone. Gingen, however, contrived eventually to reach Trichinopoly, and to throw himself with his much reduced force within its walls, quickly followed by Chunda Sahib, who made sure of soon having the place in his possession.

At this moment, "big with the fate of Cato and of Rome," the star of young Clive rose on the horizon. He had been employed in the commissariat department to the force which Gingen commanded; had witnessed the ill behaviour of the English at Volconda, and had now returned to Fort St. David to expose the incompetency of the commander, and to seek employment in another direction. In a fortunate hour the Council promoted Clive to the rank of captain, and adopted the plan which his daring genius had formed, and which was nothing else than to relieve Trichinopoly by making a sudden attack upon Arcot, the capital of the Carnatic, representing to his superiors that, unless some vigorous efforts were made, Trichinopoly would fall, Mohammed Ali would perish, and the French would become masters of the whole of India. Without loss of time Fort St. David and Madras were emptied of their troops, which amounted, when all told, to only two hundred English and three hundred Sepoys, with three small pieces of cannon. His staff of officers counted only eight, six of whom had never been in action, and four of the six were merely clerks in the mercantile service of the Company, who, inflamed by Clive's example, had given up the pen for the sword, in order to follow him.

On the 26th of August, 1751, Clive set forth from Madras on his memorable expedition, with that confidence in his success which genius of the highest order alone can inspire. In three days he reached a pagoda about forty miles inland, where he learnt that the fort of Arcot had not been drained of its troops for the siege of Trichinopoly, but still had a

LORD CLIVE.

garrison of eleven hundred men. Nothing daunted, the brave Englishman wrote to Madras for two eighteen-pounders to be sent after him without delay, and continued his march until he arrived within ten miles of Arcot. The scouts employed by the enemy reported they had seen the English marching unconcernedly through a terrible storm of thunder, lightning, and rain. The native garrison, considering this a bad omen, instantly abandoned the fort; while in a few hours after their departure Clive entered the city in the midst of thousands of timid spectators, and took possession of the deserted fort, where he found eight pieces of cannon, besides a large quantity of powder and shot.

Clive suspected that he should not be suffered to retain so important a conquest undisturbed. He instantly made preparations for sustaining a siege. The garrison which had fled had recovered from its dismay, and having been reinforced by 3,000 men, returned and encamped close to the town. In the dead of night Clive marched out of the fort, attacked the enemy by surprise, and after slaying great numbers, dispersed the rest, and returned to his quarters without losing a single man.

Chunda Sahib, on hearing of Clive's marvellous success, at once despatched his son, Rajah Ṡahib, with 10,000 men to invest Arcot, which seemed quite incapable of sustaining a siege. The walls were in ruins, the ditches dry, the battlements too low to protect the soldiers. The little garrison had been greatly reduced in numbers; only 120 English remained, together with 200 Sepoys; the provisions ran short; and the commander who had to conduct the defence under such discouraging circumstances was a young man not twenty-five years of age, whose military experience had been almost limited to that of an officer of the Commissariat department, and who had been in his earlier days book-keeper in the office of the East India Company!

During fifty days the siege went on; and though all hope of relief from Madras had failed him, Clive maintained the siege with a vigilance and ability which would have done credit to the oldest general in Europe. The breach, however, increased day by day, and the garrison began to feel the pressure of hunger. Under such circumstances any troops so scantily provided with officers, for the whole number had been reduced to four, might have been expected to show signs of insubordination; and the danger was doubly great in a force composed of men differing widely from each other in religion, manners, tongue, and colour. But the devotion of that noble little band to its chief surpassed anything recorded in history during a similar time of trial. *The Sepoys came to Clive, not to complain of their scanty fare, but to propose that all the grain should be given to the English soldiers, who required more nourishment than the natives of India; while the thin gruel, they said, which was strained away from the rice, would suffice for themselves.* We may search the annals of the world before we meet with so touching an instance of military fidelity, or the influence of so commanding a mind.

An attempt at relief by the Government at Madras had failed, when hope dawned upon them from another quarter. A body of 6,000 Mahrattas under the command of Moorary Ráe had been engaged to assist Mohammed Ali; but thinking the French power irresistible, they had hitherto remained inactive on the frontiers of the Carnatic. The fame of the defence of Arcot roused them from their torpor. Moorary Ráe declared that he had never before believed that Englishmen could fight, but that now he was willing to help them, seeing that they had learnt to help themselves. Rajah Sahib, who commanded Chunda's army, heard that the Mahrattas were in motion, and that there was no time to lose. He first endeavoured to bribe Clive, who rejected his offers with becoming scorn. He then vowed that he would storm the fort and put every man to the sword. Clive replied that his father was an usurper, that his army was a mere rabble, and that he had better not send such a set of poltroons into a breach defended by British soldiers.

Rajah Sahib, stung to the quick by such a reply to his overtures, determined to make the attempt, and selected a great Mohammedan festival as the day well suited for a bold military enterprise. As was the case nearly a century later, when the Russians issued forth from Sebastopol on that dark November morn* to attack the British at Inkermann, stimulating drugs were employed to aid the effect of religious zeal; and the besiegers, drunk alike with enthusiasm and bang, rushed furiously to the breach. Clive, who had received secret intelligence of the design, had made all his arrangements, and, exhausted with fatigue, had thrown himself on his bed. He

* The Mohammedans stormed Arcot Nov. 14th, 1751; the Russians stormed the heights of Inkermann Nov. 5th, 1854.

was awakened by the alarm, and was instantly at his post. The enemy came on, driving before them elephants whose foreheads were armed with plates of steel, expecting that the gates would yield at once to these living battering-rams. But the elephants, notwithstanding their pachyderm hides, no sooner felt the force of the English bullets than they turned round on their friends, and rushed furiously away. A raft was launched by the besiegers on the water which filled the moat on one side of the fort. Clive, perceiving that his raw artillerymen did not thoroughly understand their business, like Napoleon on a similar occasion, took the management of his guns himself, and cleared the raft in a few minutes. The besiegers had succeeded in effecting two breaches in the walls, which they thrice attempted to storm; but they were received with so well-directed a fire, that it soon quelled the courage even of fanaticism and intoxication. The attack lasted for more than an hour, during which upwards of 400 of the enemy had fallen. The little garrison, which at the commencement only numbered eighty English with 200 Sepoys, passed an anxious night, expecting a renewal of the attack in the morning. But when the day broke, the enemy, like the Assyrian host of old, whose defeat has been so graphically described by one of our own poets, had entirely disappeared, and were no more to be seen. Thus ended a siege which had lasted nearly two months, and had raised the reputation of the British arms in India from the lowest to the highest pitch.

Being reinforced that same evening by a detachment which the Government of Madras had at length sent him, Clive, after leaving a small garrison in the fort, set off from Arcot, November 19th, with two hundred English and seven hundred Sepoys, in pursuit of Rajah Sahib. Having been joined by a small body of Mahratta horse, he gave the enemy battle at a place called Arull, and completely routed a combined force of French and Sepoys, in number between two and three thousand. The valour of the Mahrattas was encouraged by the booty they made; for they captured four hundred horses, as well as Chunda Sahib's military chest containing one hundred thousand rupees. Six hundred Sepoys employed by the French immediately changed sides, and joined Clive; while the Governor of Arull abandoned the cause of Chunda Sahib and the French for that of Mohammed Ali and the English. Following up his advantage, Clive inflicted another defeat on the enemy at a place named Caveryhark, where he captured twelve pieces of artillery, with sixty Frenchmen, while fifty of that nation and three hundred Sepoys were found dead on the battlefield. Clive now returned to Fort St. David, where the Madras Government received him with transports of joy, deeming him to be equal to any future command.

Encouraged by the brilliant success which had attended Clive in his various defeats of the French and their native allies, and which, considering the disparity of the means at his disposal, may be justly compared to the most brilliant of Napoleon's campaigns, viz., his first and greatest one of Italy in 1797, the Government of Madras determined to send him a detachment to reinforce the garrison of Trichinopoly. But just at this juncture Major Lawrence arrived from England, and assumed the chief command. From Clive's wayward character in early life, and the brilliant achievements which he had recently performed, it might have been expected that he would not have acted with similar zeal in a subordinate capacity. But as in the case of those distinguished seamen, Nelson and Collingwood, half a century later, there was happily no professional jealousy between them. Lawrence had early treated him with kindness, and Clive in return cheerfully placed himself under his orders, and exerted himself as strenuously in the second post as he would have done in the first. Lawrence well knew the value of such assistance; and though, like most military men who make the profession a study, he was disposed to look with contempt on all interlopers, he confessed that Clive was an instance of the well-known proverb, that "there is no rule without an exception;" and with laudable candour he thus expressed himself on his young friend's merit: "Some people," he wrote, "are pleased to term Captain Clive fortunate and lucky; but in my opinion he deserved and might expect from his conduct everything as it fell out—a man of undaunted resolution, of a cool temper, and of a presence of mind which never left him in the greatest danger—born a soldier; for, without a military education of any sort, or much conversing with any of the profession, from his judgment and good sense he led on an army like an experienced officer and a brave soldier, with a prudence that certainly warranted success."

The French had no commander to oppose the two

friends. Labourdonnais had left India, and had died in France of a broken heart. Bussy had marched northwards with the Nizam, and was fully employed in looking after his own interests and those of his country, at the court of that prince. Dupleix, though equal in intrigue to every European who had borne a part in any of the numerous revolutions in India, was quite incapable of conducting military operations. He was accused by his enemies of personal cowardice, and he defended himself in a way which proved there was some justice in the charge; for he said that he thought it right to keep himself out of the neighbourhood of powder and shot, as noise was unsuited to his genius, and he found it difficult to pursue his meditations amid the din of arms.

Hence, as might have been expected, the English triumphed everywhere. After a series of brilliant operations, the French and Chunda Sahib were shut up in the fort of Seringham, on an island in the river Cavery, opposite to Trichinopoly. Here they were summoned to surrender at discretion; when M. Law, the French commander, accepted the proffered terms, and six hundred Europeans besides Sepoys became prisoners of war, while thirty pieces of cannon rewarded the skill of the victors. Chunda Sahib, who had been recently lord of the Carnatic, finding himself deserted by his troops, fled to the camp of his enemies, and surrendered to Monajee, general of the Rajah of Tanjore, a wily Hindu, who promised him his protection, and then proved it by placing him in irons. A violent dispute now arose between Mohammed Ali, the Mahratta chiefs, and Monajee, who one and all claimed the person of the prisoner. To put an end to the quarrel, Major Lawrence proposed that the fallen potentate should for the present be delivered up to the English; but the disputants separated without coming to any agreement, and before the discussion could be renewed Monajee settled the question by cutting off the head of Chunda Sahib, and sent it to his now fortunate rival, Mohammed Ali, who exhibited it in triumph throughout his army.

The English were now eager to attack the fortress of Gingee, the only strong place in the Carnatic which remained in possession of their foes; but inasmuch as their Indian auxiliaries had all retired to their homes, and the English had only their own Sepoys to assist them, their numbers were too few to warrant success, and the first attempt failed. This gave encouragement to Dupleix to renew the intrigues by means of his wife, and to inflame the dissensions which were then beginning to break out between Mohammed Ali and the Regent of Mysore. By this means Dupleix managed to form another considerable army; and the Madras Government decided on sending Lawrence, with a force of four hundred English, with six thousand Sepoys and troops in the pay of Mohammed Ali, to encounter him. Lawrence met the French on the plains of Bahoor, only two miles from Fort St. David, and obtained a decisive victory, which would have been more complete if his native auxiliaries had been less anxious to plunder than to fight.

The English general was now enabled to dispatch Clive to take Covelong, an important fort about twenty miles south of Madras, which was garrisoned by fifty French and three hundred Sepoys. The only force which could be spared to Clive consisted of two hundred recruits just arrived from England (said to have been the very refuse of the London jails), and also of five hundred newly raised Sepoy troops, and four pieces of cannon. With these raw recruits, which no officer but Clive would risk his reputation by commanding, Clive ventured on the hazardous feat of attacking Covelong, garrisoned by Europeans, and defended by thirty pieces of cannon. A shot from the fort killed one of these London jail-birds, on which the rest flew away with all imaginable speed, and it was with the utmost difficulty that Clive could succeed in rallying them. On another occasion the noise of a gun terrified these British recruits so much, that one of them was found some hours later at the bottom of a well, which he philosophically considered the safest place from the fire of the merciless foe. Clive, by accustoming them to danger, and by exposing himself wherever the fire was hottest, gradually shamed them into courage; and by the time the siege was over, the recruits had become heroes; and Covelong surrendered to this gallant army, which must be ranked as one of the most marvellous exploits in Clive's wonderful and romantic career. Nor did it end here; for the very morning after the surrender of Covelong, a large body of the enemy's troops were seen advancing with the evident intention of relieving the fort. Clive instantly took measures to prevent the enemy from learning that they were too late; laid an ambuscade for them on the road; killed one hundred of them at the first fire; took three hundred prisoners; drove off the enemy; pursued them to the gates of another fort named Chingleput, about twenty miles distant; laid siege to that fort, reputed one of the strongest in India; made a breach, and was on the point of storming, when the French commander capitulated, and was allowed to retire with his men. Thus ended the campaign of 1752, after the most brilliant and rapid series of victories on the part of Clive, who soon after sailed for England to recover his strength and health, which he had so nobly expended on behalf of his country in laying the foundation of the British Empire in India.

CHAPTER IX.

FROM THE TREATY OF PONDICHERRY TO THE BLACK HOLE OF CALCUTTA.

A.D. 1754—1756.

THE operations begun under Clive were continued under Lawrence; for although there was peace in Europe between the French and English from the treaty of Aix-la-Chapelle in 1748 to the beginning of the "Seven Years' War" in 1756, it was not so in the Carnatic, where these two nations, by their representatives, were still in arms against each other, and virtually contending for the possession of Hindostan. Clive had scarcely left for England, when Dupleix's intrigues obtained for a time the most signal triumphs. The Regent of Mysore abruptly broke off his alliance, and joined the French; while his example was followed by the Mahratta chief, Moorary Ráo, who considered that he had not obtained a fair share of the booty.

After a series of operations with varied success, which we have not time to detail, the English army under Lawrence met the allied forces at a place called "the Golden Rock," and a spirited action took place between them, in which the Mysoreans and the Mahrattas took a less prominent part. The latter occasionally made a charge, and did some mischief; while the former, like a certain Belgian regiment at Waterloo, kept at a respectful distance, and watched the fight from afar; so that the contest was in reality confined to the English and the French. Soon the superiority of the British bayonet was evident; the French fled from the field, leaving some cannon behind them; while Lawrence returned in triumph to Trichinopoly, though at the same time he was constrained to confess, like Pyrrhus in his contests with the Romans, that one or two more such victories would have completely undone him, and proved as fatal as a defeat.

The war in the Carnatic lingered on until October, 1754, when Dupleix found himself superseded by M. Godehen, who had been specially sent from France to put an end to the war. A suspension of hostilities was soon agreed upon between the French commissioner and Mr. Saunders, the Governor of Madras. A more formal treaty was drawn up two months later, the first article of which specifies that the companies should renounce all "Moorish dignities," and refrain from further interference with the native powers. The possessions of each were to be equalised, and the treaty was to continue in force pending the confirmation or otherwise of the respective authorities in Europe.

Although the treaty of Pondicherry put an end to the war in the Carnatic between the French and English, it did not prevent the repetition of the contests and quarrels which were perpetually arising between the native powers. Nunjeraj, the Regent of Mysore, demanded the cession of Trichinopoly, which the Nabob, Mohammed Ali, declined to yield.

The French complained that the English continued to keep their troops with Mohammed, in order to enable him to collect his revenue and reduce his refractory subjects in the Carnatic, while the English justified their action by showing that the French under Bussy continued the same services, and on a more extensive scale, to Salabat Jung, the Soubahdar of the Deccan. It soon became evident that the peace of Pondicherry would not be of long duration. Clive, when in England, afforded much information to the Court of Directors and the home Government respecting the effects of the treaty of Pondicherry, and the real strength of the French under so good a commander as Bussy in the Deccan ; and had convinced them, as he said, that "so long as there was a single Frenchman in arms in the Deccan, or in India, there could be no peace For his part, he desired nothing better than to dispute the mastery of the Deccan with M. Bussy." It was then doubtless as clear to Clive's enterprising and sagacious mind, as he publicly avowed in after years, that the conqueror of the Deccan would be the ruler of Hindostan. Such was one of the early steps in Clive's marvellous career by which the British Empire was won in India.

Many signs indicating that the war between England and France would again break out, the directors of the East India Company thought it advisable to send an able commander to the Company's settlements in the East. They therefore appointed Clive governor of Fort St. David ; the king gave him the commission of a lieutenant-colonel in the British army, and early in 1755 he again sailed for India.

The first service on which Clive was employed after his return to the East was the reduction of a nest of pirates on the western coast of India. The chief of these corsairs were a race of Mahrattas, who bore the name of Angria, and who nominally acknowledged the Péshwah, or supreme head of the Mahrattas, much in the same way as the Algerines, before Lord Exmouth's brilliant action at Algiers, professed allegiance to the Ottoman Porte. But these pirates, who had committed great depredations in various parts of the country, and who then held possession of a large portion of the coast south of Bombay, had recently defied the Péshwah's authority, who was induced in consequence to seek the assistance of the English, who had likewise suffered from these lawless sea rovers. In March, 1755, the Péshwah prepared to co-operate with the English for the reduction of the piratical forts, and Commodore Jones, with a vessel of forty-four guns, and with the aid of the Mahratta fleet, attacked and captured the fortress of Severn-droog, which was made over to the Péshwah, according to agreement, the English receiving in return the city and district of Bancote, the first territorial possession obtained by them on the western coast, after Bombay. The season was then too far advanced for further operations; but early in the following year the British fleet under the command of Admiral Watson, consisting of fourteen vessels, of which three were ships of the line, and carrying nearly two thousand troops of English and Sepoys, under the command of Colonel Clive, who had recently arrived in India, on his way to Fort St. David, proceeded to attack the fort of Gheriah, the chief stronghold of the Angrian pirates. Admiral Watson speedily destroyed the whole of the piratical fleet, while Clive attacked the fortress by land. The place soon fell, and a booty of £150,000 was divided among the conquerors. Clive then proceeded to the government of Fort St. David; but before he had been there two months he received intelligence which called forth all the energy of his bold and active mind.

Of all the provinces of Hindostan which had been subject to the sovereigns of the Mogul dynasty, unquestionably the most wealthy was that of Bengal. No part of India possessed such natural advantages both for agriculture and for commerce. The great commercial companies of Europe had long possessed factories in the rich plains formed from the alluvial soil of the river Ganges, as it winds its course through the province of Bengal. The French were settled on the Hooghly branch of it, at the city of Chandernagore. Higher up the stream the Dutch traders held Chinsweah; while nearer the sea the English carried on their trade at a place subsequently celebrated as the capital, Calcutta, under the protection of the guns of Fort William, named after England's great deliverer, the Prince of Orange, and one of the greatest sovereigns that ever ruled the British Empire.

The great province of Bengal had long been under the government of Averdy Khan, an Afghan officer, who had commanded the troops of Shujah-ood-Deen, the Emperor's viceroy, and had finally succeeded in obtaining the post for himself, and who, like other viceroys of the Great Mogul, had become virtually independent. He died at an advanced age in 1756, alike regretted by the natives and European settlers, and the sovereignty descended to his grandson, a youth under twenty years of age, who bore the name of Suráj-ood-Dowlah. No opposition was made at first to his succession, though later his uncle, who had been charged with the government of Purneah, had left a son named Shoukut Jung, who, having inherited his father's property, was intriguing at Delhi to obtain the viceroyalty of Bengal in place of his cousin. Suráj-ood-Dowlah at once marched against him; but before he could reach Purneah he received intelligence that one Kishen Das, the son of Rajah Bullub, the late governor of Decca, who had inherited his father's great wealth, had proceeded to Calcutta with a letter of introduction to Mr. Drake, the governor, and had carried all his wealth with him. To get possession of this wealth had been Dowlah's desire for some time past, and the manner in which Kishen Das had evaded him, and sought the protection of the English instead, excited him to a furious degree. He wrote to Mr. Drake, demanding that the fugitive should be given up, with all his property, and that Calcutta should be dismantled of the fortifications which had recently been erected. It was in vain that the English governor assured him that the fortifications had only been partially repaired in case they should be attacked by the French. Suráj-ood-Dowlah refused to listen to these excuses, and in the month of June, 1756, marched with his army, fifty thousand strong, to attack Calcutta.

Unhappily at this time the government of Calcutta

was as unfitted to deal with such a foe as Dowlah, as the fortifications, which had been partially repaired by Col. Scott the year before, were insufficient to resist him. The servants of the East India Company at Madras had been forced by Dupleix to become statesmen and soldiers; while those at Calcutta were mere traders, and were now completely bewildered at the approaching danger. Mr. Drake, the governor, who had heard much of Dowlah's cruelty, was so frightened that he hastily took refuge in the nearest ship; while Captain Murchin, the military commandant of the factory, thought that he could not do better than follow so bad an example. Happily all the English women, save one, who were in Calcutta, with their children, were safely embarked on board the vessels lying opposite Fort William, when the ships' commanders, alarmed by a sudden discharge of fire arrows from Dowlah's army, weighed anchor, and dropped two miles down the river.

Mr. Holwell, the second member of council, was not dismayed by the desertion of the governor and the commander of the garrison, and made the best preparations he could for the defence. It must ever remain the source of deepest regret to know, in reference to the awful occurrence which subsequently took place, that if the English ships which were so close at hand, or even a portion of the crews, had returned, the fort could have been successfully defended; for there were many on board the fleet who would cheerfully have borne a part in the defence; and it reflects no little disgrace on the commander of the fleet, that to the last the signals of distress from the fort, though perfectly visible in the ships, were left unanswered, when the enemy, on the 21st of June, seeing the defenceless nature of the place, made their assault with much vigour. Mr. Holwell, finding further resistance hopeless, admitted a flag of truce sent by the Nabob. Taking advantage of the momentary suspension, a rush was made by the enemy; the officers, with their men, many of whom were intoxicated, were disarmed, and great numbers of the English fell into the hands of the victors. Suráj-ood-Dowlah visited the fort in state, seated himself with regal pomp in the large hall of the factory, and ordered Mr. Holwell to be brought before him. He talked about the insolence of the English, and grumbled at not finding more than £50,000 in the treasury; but promised to spare the lives of his prisoners, and retired to rest.

Then was committed that great crime, ever memorable for its singular atrocity, and no less memorable for the tremendous retribution which overtook the guilty tyrant. The English captives were left to the mercy of the guards, who determined to secure them for the night in the common prison of the garrison, known then and ever after, from the horrible celebrity of that night, by the ominous name of THE BLACK HOLE OF CALCUTTA. Even for a single European, that dungeon would have been distressingly close. The space was only twenty feet square; the air holes were small; and it was the summer solstice. The number of the prisoners was 146. When they were ordered to enter the cell, they imagined that the soldiers were joking, and being in high spirits at the Nabob having promised to spare their lives, they laughed at the absurdity of the notion. But they were quickly undeceived. The guards threatened to cut down all who refused to move. The captives were driven into the cell at the point of the sword, and the door was instantly shut and locked upon them.

Nothing in history or in fiction approaches the horrors which were recounted by the few survivors of that terrible night. It will be best to draw a veil over its terrors. Suffice it to say when day broke, and the Nabob gave permission for the door to be opened, it was some time before the soldiers could make a lane for the survivors by piling on each side the numerous corpses, on which the burning climate had already begun to do its loathsome work. When at length a passage was made, twenty-three ghastly figures staggered out one by one from that hideous grave. A pit was instantly dug; the dead bodies, one hundred and twenty-three in number, were flung promiscuously in, and covered up.

But these things, which cannot be told or read after a lapse of more than a hundred and twenty years without feelings of indignation and horror, awakened not an atom of remorse in the breast of the savage Dowlah. He inflicted no punishment on the murderers, nor displayed any feeling for the survivors. Mr. Holwell,* unable to walk, was carried before the tyrant, who reproached him, threatened him, and sent him to Moorshedabad, confined in irons, together with some of his companions, who were thought to know more than they chose to tell about the treasures of the Company.

* Mr. Holwell survived the horrors of that night upwards of forty years, dying at the advanced age of eighty-seven, in the year 1798.

Suráj-ood-Dowlah in the meantime sent letters to the Great Mogul at Delhi, describing in glowing terms his conquests over the English at Calcutta. He placed a garrison in Fort William, forbade any Englishman to dwell within the neighbourhood, and commanded that the city should henceforth bear the high-sounding name of ALINAGORE, *i.e.*, "The Gate of God." Before the end of June the British had not a single possession in Bengal which they could call their own. The ships dropped down to Fuldah, a town near the mouth of the river Hooghly; while the commander, sending news of the terrible catastrophe to Madras, patiently awaited the result.

CHAPTER X.

FROM THE BLACK HOLE OF CALCUTTA TO THE BATTLE OF PLASSEY.

A.D. 1756—1757.

IT took nearly a month before the news of the fall of Calcutta reached Madras, upwards of four hundred miles distant, the time which it takes for a traveller from India to reach London in the present day. The cry of the whole settlement was for instant vengeance. Within two days after the arrival of the intelligence, it was determined that an expedition should be sent to the Hooghly, and that Clive, who had recently arrived from England, should command it. Of the two thousand English soldiers then at Madras, nine hundred, with fifteen hundred Sepoys, were considered sufficient to punish Suráj-ood-Dowlah, who ruled over a larger number of subjects than the king of France. Some time was lost by unseemly discussions in the Council, but at length five ships of the Royal Navy, under the command of Admiral Watson, with five of the Company's fleet, sailed from Madras on October 16th, and after a long passage reached the mouth of the Hooghly in the middle of December. As the ships, carrying nearly four hundred guns, ascended the river with something like a triumphant procession, it excited the utmost consternation amongst the natives, who had never seen such an armament in their waters before.

Dowlah was revelling in fancied security at Moorshedabad, so profoundly ignorant of the state of foreign countries, that he was wont to say there were only ten thousand men in all Europe, and it never occurred to him that the English would dare to invade his dominions, when he received the news of the English armament having appeared off the Hooghly. He instantly ordered all his troops to assemble at Moorshedabad, and marched towards Calcutta.

Clive had commenced operations with his usual vigour. He attacked the fort of Buj-Buj, narrowly escaping with his life from over-confidence; but broadsides from the fleet destroyed the fortifications, and a large force under the native Governor of Calcutta fled in dismay. He then stormed the garrison of Fort William, recovered Calcutta, and replaced the surviving members of the Council in their posts, which they had with such cowardice abandoned. Suráj-ood-Dowlah, already disposed to make some concessions to the English, was confirmed in his pacific disposition by these evident proofs of their power. He accordingly made overtures to the chiefs of the invading armament, and offered to restore the factory, and to give compensation to those whom he had despoiled.

Clive's profession was war, and he felt there was something vastly discreditable in making any terms or having any intercourse with such a monster of wickedness as he who had been guilty of the crime

MOORSHEDABAD.

committed in the Black Hole of Calcutta. But his power was limited. The timid civilians, who had fled so ingloriously from their posts, had the principal direction of affairs, and these were only too eager to be compensated for their losses. Between them and Clive serious dissensions had already arisen: they protested against his independent exercise of power, and he flatly refused to obey them; while the Government of Madras, having learnt that war had broken out in Europe between England and France, were anxious for the return of the army which they had sent to Calcutta. The promises of Dowlah were large, the chances of a contest with the Nabob, on account of his enormous superiority in numbers, were doubtful; and as Clive was reminded by the Madras Government that he must return by the time allotted to him, viz., the month of April, he at length consented, though with great reluctance, to treat with his cruel and unworthy foe.

With this negotiation commences a new chapter in the life of the founder of the British Empire in India. Hitherto he had been a soldier, carrying into effect with eminent ability and valour the plans of others; and though his crowning victory of Plassey was yet in the future, henceforth he is to be regarded rather as a statesman than a general, whose military movements are to be considered as subordinate to his political designs.

The negotiations between the English and the Nabob Suráj-ood-Dowlah were carried on by two agents, Mr. Watts, a civilian in the service of the Company, and a native Bengalee of the name of Omichund, one of the wealthiest merchants residing at Calcutta, who had suffered great losses by Dowlah's expedition against that place. The Nabob behaved with all the faithlessness of an Indian statesman and all the levity of a youth whose mind had been enfeebled by the exercise of uncontrolled power. He promised, retracted, hesitated, evaded. At one time he advanced his army on Calcutta; but no sooner did he see how well the English were prepared to resist him, than he fell back in alarm, and consented to make peace with them on their own terms; but no sooner was the treaty concluded, than he formed new plans for counteracting its effects.

Dowlah commenced his intrigues with the French authorities at Chándernagore, and invited Bussy, the commander of the French forces in India, to march from the Deccan to the Hooghly, and co-operate with him in driving the English out of Bengal. In the beginning of February he made a second attempt on Calcutta, the outposts of his army being quartered within the Mahratta ditch. Clive determined to attack his camp in the morning, but a thick fog intervening prevented the success which he anticipated. Nevertheless he inflicted sufficient injury on the enemy to compel the Nabob to withdraw his army to a distance of three miles, and he again opened negotiations with the English. The result was a treaty highly favourable to the Company; all their possessions were to be restored, all their previous privileges confirmed, and they were to be allowed to fortify Calcutta as much as they pleased. Many, however, thought, as Admiral Watson with a sailor's frankness expressed it, that "until the Nabob was well thrashed he could not be depended on," and the result proved he was more than right.

At this juncture Clive was most anxious to prevent the Nabob from making any coalition with the French, which, indeed, the treaty clearly prevented him from attempting; but as the untrustworthy nature of Dowlah was well known to Clive, he determined to strike a decisive blow against the French before they could be strengthened by new arrivals from South India or Europe. Clive crossed the river on February 18th, at the head of his troops, with the intention of marching on Chándernagore. No sooner did his design become evident to the French, than they claimed the Nabob's protection. For some time he hesitated between the two. On the one hand were the English flushed with victory, but, as he considered, in no great strength; on the other, the French at Chándernagore appeared to be strong enough to hold the place until reinforced by Bussy, who was then at the head of a powerful army in the Northern Circars. He therefore sent them money, forbade the English to advance, and prepared to send a large body of troops to defend Chándernagore.

This caused some delay, and negotiations were carried on with the French by means of Omichund, the wealthy merchant; but the French commissioners admitting that they had no power to override the decision of the chief authorities at Pondicherry, the negotiations broke down. Clive and Watson, being fully aware of the possible junction of Bussy's forces with those of the Nabob, determined to make the attack at all risks, though Admiral Watson wrote to

Dowlah in plain terms that the capture of Chándernagore was the only course left for them to pursue, unless he adhered firmly to the English, adding in reply to an evasive letter which the Nabob had sent him, that "such a war would be kindled in his country as all the waters of the Ganges would not be able to extinguish."

The garrison at Chándernagore had not meanwhile been idle. The defences had been strengthened, and some vessels had been sunk in the channel of the river which flowed past the town, though with less effect than a similar deed of the Russians a century later, when they barred the entrance of the British fleet into the harbour of Sebastopol; for when, on the 14th of March, Clive invested the fort of Chándernagore by land, and the siege operations were carried on for the next ten days, Admiral Watson's fleet was enabled to move up by means of a new channel shown to him by a deserter from the enemy. After two hours' bombardment the garrison held out a flag of truce, and by the afternoon of the same day the terms of capitulation were finally settled. The fort, the garrison, consisting of nearly five hundred European troops, together with all the military stores, fell into the hands of the English, and their triumph was complete.

Dowlah had hated the English while he was still able to oppose to them their French rivals. The French were now vanquished, and he began to hate the English more fiercely than ever. His unprincipled mind oscillated between servility and insolence. One day he sent money to Calcutta as compensation for the horrible crime he had committed; the next day he sent a present of jewels to Bussy to induce that officer to come to his help against Clive, "the daring in war,"* as the Nabob termed him, adding, "on whom may all bad fortune attend." He ordered his army to march against the English; then he countermanded his orders. He tore up Clive's letters one moment; the next he addressed him in language of Oriental servility. He ordered Watts, the English Commissioner, then at Moorshedabad, out of his presence, and threatened to impale him alive; he again sent for Watts, and begged pardon for the insult.

The infatuated Nabob was perpetrating such acts of cruelty amongst his own subjects, that at length a conspiracy was formed against him, in which Roydullub, his chancellor of the exchequer, Meer Jaffier, the commander of his troops, and Jugget Seit, the richest banker in India, were implicated, to drive the monster off his throne. The plot was confided to the English, and a communication was opened between the conspirators at Moorshedabad and the committee at Calcutta. In the committee there was at first much hesitation, until Clive gave his voice in favour of the plot; and his firmness bore down all opposition. It was determined that the English should lend their powerful assistance to depose Suráj-ood-Dowlah, and to place Meer Jaffier in his stead on the throne of Bengal. That the English were fully justified in so acting, when we remember the past actions of Dowlah, and regard the insecurity of the English in the future, there cannot be two opinions, though the dissimulation

* The name of Sabut-Jung, or "The Daring in War," was the one by which the brave Clive was best known to the natives of India.

practised by Clive is considered by some to have cast a stain on his moral character.

It should not, however, be forgotten the character of the men with whom Clive had to deal. He knew that the standard of morality among the natives of India differed widely from that established in England. He knew he had to deal with men destitute of every idea of what is honourable and right and fair; with men who would give any promise without hesitation, and break it without shame; with men who would unscrupulously employ corruption, perjury, and forgery without stint, in order to accomplish their ends. His letters show that the great difference between Asiatic and European morality was ever in his thoughts. And Clive was no sooner matched against an Indian intriguer, than he determined to beat him with his own weapons, and descended without scruple to words and deeds which his nature would otherwise have led him to scorn.

Hence, while giving his sanction to the conspiracy which was to dethrone the Nabob, he thought it necessary to write a "soothing letter" to him, in order to disarm all suspicion, while his messenger at the same time carried a letter to Mr. Watts, the Commissioner at Moorshedabad, with these words, "Tell Meer Jaffier to fear nothing. I will join him with five thousand men who have never turned their backs to the foe. I will march day and night to his assistance, and stand by him as long as I have a man left."

The treaty with Meer Jaffier having been signed, and all being now ready for action, Mr. Watts fled secretly from Moorshedabad, and Clive at once began to put his troops in motion, while he addressed a letter to the Nabob, of a very different character from that of his previous communications. He set forth all the intolerable wrongs which the English had suffered, offered to submit the points in dispute to the arbitration of Meer Jaffier, and concluded by announcing that, as the rains were about to set in, he and his army would take the earliest opportunity of waiting on the Nabob for an answer.

Clive summoned the troops he had dispatched to Calcutta, and set out from Chándernagore at the head of three thousand men, one thousand of whom were British, conspicuous among whom were the men of the 39th regiment of foot, which still bears on its colours, amidst many honourable additions won under Wellington, the name of PLASSEY, as well as the proud motto, *Primus in India.* Clive might have called the Mahrattas to his aid, for the Péshwah offered him higher terms of compensation than the treaty with Meer Jaffier contained ; but he well knew that the price of such aid meant the plunder of Bengal, and nobly declined it. What was to be done must be by British troops and Sepoys commanded by British officers, or not at all.

Suráj-ood-Dowlah instantly assembled his army, and marched to encounter the English. It had been agreed that Meer Jaffier should separate himself from the Nabob, and carry over a part of the army on which he could depend to Clive. But as the decisive moment approached, the fears of the conspirator overpowered his ambition, and he remained like Stanley at Bosworth Field, three centuries before, to see who would win the day. Clive had advanced to

Catwah, where he halted; the Nabob lay with a mighty host a few miles off at Plassey: but still Meer Jaffier delayed to fulfil his engagements, and returned evasive answers to the earnest remonstrances of the English general.

Clive was then in a most distressing situation; he had no faith in the sincerity of his confederate; and whatever confidence he might place in his own military talents or the valour and discipline of the British troops, it was no light thing to engage an army twenty times as numerous as his own, and on which the future of the British Empire in India might be said with truth to have then rested. On this occasion, for the first and last time in his career, he called a council of war. The majority pronounced against fighting, and Clive declared his concurrence with the majority. In after years he said *he never called but one council of war, and that if he had followed its advice the British would never have been masters of Hindostan.* The meeting had no sooner broken up, than he retired alone, under the shade of some trees, and passed an hour in deep and anxious thought. Before long his mind recovered its wonted firmness, and he came back determined to risk everything, and gave instant orders for passing the river at early dawn.

In many wonderful scenes have British troops been engaged during the last two centuries in every part of the known world, but it may be doubted, considering the daring nature of the service, the contrast in point of numbers between the two armies, its importance, both in the history of the world and that of the British Empire in India, whether anything equals (not even Wellington's crossing the Douro near Oporto) the crossing of the Ganges by Clive's gallant little army on the memorable morn of June 22nd, 1757. The same evening that small force, dragging its eight pieces of cannon by hand, had reached a grove of mango trees near Plassey, within a mile of the foe. Clive was unable to sleep; he heard throughout the night the clang of the cymbals and the beating of drums from the Nabob's numerous host. It is not strange that Clive's stout heart should have sunk within him when he reflected against what odds, and for what a prize, he was in a few hours to contend.

The day broke, that memorable day which was to decide the fate of the British in India. At sunrise Suráj-ood-Dowlah's vast army—consisting of forty thousand infantry, with nearly twenty thousand cavalry, infinitely superior to those drawn from the effeminate population of Bengal, and accompanied by fifty pieces of cannon of the largest size, together with some smaller guns under the direction of a few French auxiliaries—began to move towards the grove wherein the English army lay. The battle commenced with a cannonade, in which Dowlah's artillery did scarcely any execution, while the answer from the small field-pieces of the British produced a great effect. Several of the Nabob's chief officers fell. Disorder began to spread through his ranks. His own terror increased every moment. One of the conspirators recommended a retreat. Such insidious advice was only too readily received. He ordered his army to fall back, and this order decided his fate. Clive snatched the decisive moment, like Wellington at Salamanca in after years, and ordered his troops to advance. No mob attacked by regular soldiers was ever more completely routed. The little band of French auxiliaries, who alone endeavoured to make a stand, were swept down the stream of fugitives. In one hour Suráj-ood-Dowlah's vast host was dispersed to the winds, though only five hundred of the vanquished were slain. Everything in the camp had fallen into Clive's hands, their guns and their baggage, with numberless head of cattle, remained in the power of the conquerors. With the loss of twenty-two killed and fifty wounded, Clive had scattered an army of nigh sixty thousand men, and subdued an empire larger and more populous than the United Kingdom itself; and Clive's own modest and graphic account of the battle, which is fully given in Sir John Malcolm's "Memoirs," possesses even more interest now that the results of the great victory can be fully estimated, than it did when it first excited the wonder and admiration of the people of England. Thus was laid, as it was commonly said, and subsequent events proved the truth of the saying, the foundation of the British Empire in Hindostan.

CHAPTER XI.

THE RESULTS OF THE VICTORY AT PLASSEY.

A.D. 1757-8.

THE victors pursued Dowlah's scattered hosts for about six miles, and then halted for the night at Daudpore, where Clive received a letter of congratulation on his success from Meer Jaffier, who came with his division, and encamped hard by during the night. The following morning he repaired to the English quarters, not a little uneasy at the reception which awaited him, as he was conscious that his conduct during the battle must have appeared to his English allies most strange. He gave evident signs of alarm when he found the troops drawn out to receive him with the military honours due to his rank, thinking they intended to kill him or take him prisoner. But his apprehensions were speedily removed; Clive came forward to meet him, embraced him, and saluted him as Nabob of the three great provinces of Bengal, Bahar, and Orissa. His fears were then sufficiently removed to allow of an hour's consultation with the British nabob-maker. Clive listened graciously to his apologies, and advised him to march without delay on Moorshedabad, in order to secure the palace and the treasury of the fugitive tyrant.

Suráj-ood-Dowlah fled from the battle-field with all the speed which a fleet camel could carry him, and arrived at his capital in a little more than twenty-four hours, quickly followed by Meer Jaffier, who reached Moorshedabad the same evening. Before his arrival, however, Dowlah, after consultation with his chief officers, and rejecting their advice to place himself in the hands of the English, as his conscience must have told him that the tragedy of the "Black Hole" could never be forgotten or forgiven, and pretending to agree with those who advised him to try again the fate of arms, he gave orders for the assembling of his forces. Hearing, however, of the arrival of his commander-in-chief, Meer Jaffier, like James II. under similar circumstances, when William of Orange was approaching Whitehall, he decided on instant and secret flight. Disguised in a mean dress, with a casket of jewels in his hand, he let himself down at night from a window of his palace, accompanied by his favourite wife and a single attendant, threw himself into a boat, and ascended the river towards Patna, where he hoped to find Mr. Law with the French forces under his command.

No sooner was his flight discovered, a few hours later, than Meer Jaffier despatched parties of horsemen in various directions to scour the country in pursuit. The tyrant in the meanwhile had reached within twenty miles of the place where the French lay on their march to meet him; but having landed in order to have a meal cooked, in a lonely fakeer's hut by the river-side, he suddenly found himself confronted by a man whose ears he had caused to be cut off only a year before. Escape was impossible, for his flight was known, and the pursuit was close; so he was speedily conducted back to his capital, amid the execration of his subjects. On the very night of his arrival he was put to death in his prison by Meerun, the eldest son of Meer Jaffier, while his body, after having been exhibited in public, was buried in the tomb of his grandfather, Alverdy Khan, the gallant defender of Bengal against the plundering Mahrattas. Clive has been blamed for not having saved the life of the tyrant, but he had not been informed of his capture; he had scarcely arrived in Moorshedabad at the time, and it seems as unjust to accuse Clive for not having made an effort to save the life of the tyrant who was morally guilty of the death of 123 Englishmen, murdered in the Black Hole of Calcutta, as was the accusation brought sixty years later against the Duke of Wellington, under somewhat similar circumstances, for not having endeavoured to save the life of Marshal Ney after the victory at Waterloo.

Two days after Plassey, Clive, with his army, arrived at Mandipoor, and sent Mr. Watts, with an escort of Sepoys, to pay a congratulatory visit to Meer Jaffier, and to look after the English share of the treasure. Watts, who was intimately acquainted, from long residence at Moorshedabad, with the intrigues of the unprincipled politicians in high places there, was secretly informed that Meerun, the son of Meer Jaffier, and Hassein Khan, an officer of distinction, were engaged in a plot to assassinate Clive, who therefore deemed it prudent to postpone his entrance into the capital until four days later, when he entered surrounded by two hundred English soldiers and three hundred Sepoys, all of whom were accommodated in the spacious palace allotted to Clive.

Shortly after his arrival he was waited on by the crafty Meerun, with all the cringing flattery and adulation of the East; and Clive, accompanied by Meerun, paid the return visit to his father, Meer Jaffier, whom he found installed in the grand hall where Suráj-ood-Dowlah was wont to give audience. The *musnud*, or throne, was at the top of the hall, and Clive, perceiving that Jaffier kept at a distance from the regal seat, took him by the hand, and led him with the same dignity which we may suppose belonged to the renowned king-maker, the famous Earl of Warwick, four centuries before, and seated him on the throne of Bengal. When Jaffier was thus enthroned, Clive presented to him, after the immemorial custom of the East, an offering of gold, and then, turning to the crowd of natives who filled the hall, congratulated them on the good fortune which had freed them from a tyrant.

The new sovereign was now called upon to fulfil the engagements into which he had entered with his English ally. A conference was held at the house of Jugget Seit, the great banker, for the purpose of making the necessary arrangements. The result of the conference was that a shower of wealth fell copiously on Clive, the army, the Company, and its leading servants. In addition to the sums specified in the treaty, Meer Jaffier made a present of half a million sterling to the army and navy, to each member of the Committee of Calcutta the sum of £24,000, while to Clive individually there was allotted, as a first instalment, the sum of £160,000. The sum of

£800,000, in coined silver, was sent down the river from Moorshedabad to Fort William, for the use of the Company. The fleet, consisting of more than one hundred boats, conveying this treasure, performed its triumphant voyage with flags flying and music playing. Calcutta, which a few months before had been desolate, was now more prosperous than ever. Trade revived, and the signs of abounding affluence soon appeared in every English house of the new capital of the British Empire in India. So profuse was the wealth which had been showered down on the founder, that Clive is said to have walked between heaps of gold and silver, crowned with rubies and diamonds, from which he was at liberty to help himself; but so cautious and just was his conduct on the occasion, compared with his services, that when, in after years, he was subjected by a committee of the House of Commons to a most severe examination for the way in which he effected the revolution that overthrew Suráj-ood-Dowlah, and which eventually established the British Empire, he defended himself with such marked success, though he subsequently complained of the injustice of treating the Baron of Plassey as a sheep-stealer, that he was acquitted of all the charges brought against him. He admitted that he had received immense sums from Meer Jaffier, but he denied in so doing that he had violated any obligation of honour or morality. He laid claim, on the contrary, to the praise of eminent disinterestedness. He described, in forcible language, his situation after his victory at Plassey—how sovereigns were dependent on his pleasure; an opulent city afraid of being given up to plunder;

wealthy bankers and trembling princes were bidding against each other for his smiles; vaults piled with gold and silver, diamonds and jewels, thrown open to him alone—until at length he wound up his peroration with an oath: "Mr. Chairman, at this moment I stand astonished at my own moderation."

It soon became evident, after Clive had raised Meer Jaffier to the throne of Bengal, that he could only remain as long as he was upheld by the strong hand which placed him there. He had none of the talents or virtues which his post required; and his son and heir was just such another as Surâj-ood-Dowlah. Many chiefs were in open insurrection against the new sovereign. The Viceroy of Oude, who was in truth an independent sovereign, menaced Bengal with invasion; and nothing but the firm hand and authority of Clive could support him, and this he was now in a better position to do than he had ever been before; for on the news of the battle of Plassey reaching England, the directors of the East India Company instantly appointed Clive governor of their possessions in Bengal, with the highest marks of gratitude and esteem.

Clive's power was now boundless, and far surpassed even that of Dupleix in the South of India. Meer Jaffier regarded him with slavish awe. On one occasion a native chief, whose followers had been engaged in a brawl with some of the Company's Sepoys, was reproved by the Nabob in the following terms:—"Have you yet to learn who this Col. Clive is, and in what station God has placed him?" The chief, who, as an old friend of Meer Jaffier, could venture upon liberties, replied, "Affront the Colonel!

I, who never get up in the morning without making three profound *salaams* to his jackass!" This was scarcely an exaggeration. Europeans and natives alike bent before that great mind. The English regarded him as the only person in India who could keep Meer Jaffier to his engagements; Meer Jaffier regarded him as the only man who could protect the new dynasty against turbulent subjects and neighbours who coveted the possessions of the Nabob of Bengal.

Clive used his power ably and vigorously for the advantage of his country. He sent an expedition against the eastern coast of South India, termed "the Northern Circars," wherein the French still retained the ascendancy; and entrusted the enterprise to a young officer of great promise, named Forde; who was then little known, but in whom Clive had detected military talents of a high order. Forde, with five hundred British troops and over two thousand Sepoys, proceeded by sea to Vizagapatam, a strong fortress in the Bay of Bengal, midway between Calcutta and Madras. Here he was joined by Anundráj, the Rajah of the place, who had recently succeeded in ousting the French garrison, but was unable to prosecute this advantage, being fearful of French reinforcements arriving, who would be able to recover the fort. Anundráj had previously applied to Clive for assistance, in the hope that the English would secure to him certain territorial claims, and eventually appoint him sovereign of the Deccan. Before setting forth, a treaty was made between Col. Forde and the Rajah of Vizagapatam, by which the latter undertook to supply £5,000 a month for the expense of the English army.

The allied forces set forth in November, 1758, and advanced as far as Peddajoar, where they encountered M. Conflans, who had been left by Bussy in command of a force of exactly the same number as that which Forde commanded, viz., five hundred French soldiers and two thousand Sepoys. After a smart action the French were thoroughly defeated by the English and the Sepoys in their employ alone. Conflans had the forethought to send off his military treasure on fleet camels; but the spoils were considerable: thirty pieces of cannon, fifty ammunition tumbrils, seven large mortars, with a large provision of shells, a thousand draught bullocks, and all the tents of the French army, graced the victor's spoils. When the rout of the French began, Forde, thinking that the cavalry of his ally might be of some use, called upon the Rajah to order them to charge; but he might as well have attempted to call spirits from the "vasty deep;" for these Indian cavaliers, and all their infantry besides, with their noble commander in the midst of them, had conveniently taken up their quarters in the bed of a river, then completely dry, where they remained in perfect shelter during the action, and from which they refused to move so long as fighting was going on. Moreover, the Rajah would no more pay than fight; so that Forde, who had spent all the little money he had brought with him, for several weeks was utterly unable to move. In the beginning of March, 1759, Forde, after having obtained a small sum from the niggardly Rajah, marched upon Musilipatam, the strongest fortress

which the French possessed on that coast, and after a brilliant siege of twelve days' duration, assaulted it at three points, when Conflans surrendered at discretion.

In the meanwhile, Meer Jaffier, in his sovereignty of Bengal, fulfilled to the letter the saying of our great dramatist—

> "Uneasy sits the head that wears a crown;"

for not only had many native chiefs, far and near, rebelled against him, but he was surrounded by foes, all eager for his throne, or for a slice of his rich territory. Several Rajahs had united with Shujah-ood-Dowlah, the Nabob of Oude, against Meer Jaffier, and their cause was subsequently aided by Shah Zada, the eldest son of the Great Mogul, who had established himself in Rohilcund, and had a considerable army of Rohillas, half soldiers, half robbers by profession, but a braver race than any in the lower parts of Hindostan. Before long Shah Zada commenced his march against the Nabob of Bengal with a mixed army of 50,000 Rohillas, Mahrattas, and Afghans. Meer Jaffier felt that he had no hope but in Clive; so he daily besieged with urgent entreaties the new English president at Moorshedabad, whom Clive had sent there as the Company's representative, and who proved to be none other than the future Governor-General of India, the illustrious WARREN HASTINGS. He had before called Clive's attention to the incessant intrigues and broils which were daily taking place at the court, and predicted that, unless Clive interfered, the whole fabric of government would fall to pieces, and that the provinces of Orissa and Bahar would be severed from Bengal even before the arrival of Shah Zada and his army. Although Clive at the time could only count upon having 400 British soldiers and 2,500 Sepoys, in consequence of the expedition under Col. Forde, and by having sent out other detachments to Madras, he nevertheless resolved to meet the mighty confederacy which threatened Meer Jaffier; but he ordered Forde to continue his conquests in the Northern Circars, and to proceed, if his assistance was needed, to Madras. Clive began his march late in February, and in a few days reached Moorshedabad, writing to the secret committee at Calcutta that he hoped soon to give a good account of Shah Zada, who was then shortly expected to besiege Patna, the capital of Bahar, where it was reported that Ramnarain, the Governor, had betrayed his trust, and gone over to the foe. This happily proved false; but not to trust too much to Hindoo valour, Clive hurried forward a detachment of Sepoys under the command of Ensign Mathews, to assist in the defence. But this was unnecessary: the dread of Clive's name was sufficient to disperse the invading army; and on the 5th of April, the day before Mathews could reach Patna, Shah Zada, then heir-apparent to the Great Mogul, at the head of an army of 50,000 men, raised the siege, and retreated before an ensign's detachment of British soldiers, marching under the prestige of Clive's great fame and name! Nothing probably equal to this can be found in the annals of the history of the world.

The "Daring in War" and "Protector of the Great," as Clive was justly termed by the natives, entered Patna without any parade or triumph; and it was acknowledged by all who saw him there, that he was in reality lord of all that part of India.

Meanwhile the Shah Zada continued his hurried flight by crossing the river Caramnassa into Oude, where he expected to obtain assistance from his ally; but the Nabob, with the usual Indian faithlessness, declared himself the enemy of the fugitive prince, who, now deserted by all, knew not whom to trust or where to flee. Considering that Clive had more generosity as well as power than all his false friends put together, he threw himself on the mercy of this English foe. Nor was he mistaken. Clive supplied him with money to enable him to escape to some safer country. He then directed his arms against some of the Rajpoot chiefs of Bahar, who had assisted Shah Zada ; and having reduced them to submission by policy, rather than by fighting, having tranquilized the whole country by processes which appeared to the native mind to partake of the nature of magic, Clive returned quietly to Calcutta, and resumed his post as Governor of the East India Company's enlarged possessions in the province of Bengal.

CHAPTER XII.

CLIVE'S FIRST GOVERNMENT OF BENGAL.

A.D. 1757—1760.

GREAT were the services which Clive had rendered to his ally, Meer Jaffier, as well as to this poor phantom of a power now rapidly passing away, the Great Mogul, whose firmans still retained their prestige with myriads of the natives of Hindostan who saw in him the descendant of the once mighty Aurungzebe. The Emperor's vizier informed Clive, as one mark of special favour, that the English were at liberty to erect a factory at the imperial city of Delhi, little anticipating that in that very place a century later the last representative of the Great Mogul would be condemned to death, and most deservedly so, for crimes committed against that very power which was then beginning, through the valour and skill of Clive, to undermine and eventually to supplant his own.

The joy of Meer Jaffier was as unbounded as his fears had been great, and they led him to bestow on his preserver a princely token of gratitude. He obtained for Clive a patent of nobility from the Emperor, who conferred on him the title of "Shoukut Jung," together with a jahgeer or estate of the value of three lacs or £30,000 a year, from the quitrent which the East India Company were bound to pay to the Nabob for the extensive lands held by them to the south of Calcutta, and which in addition to his previous gains enabled Clive to vie in amount of fortune with the richest members of the British peerage.

But the gratitude of Meer Jaffier did not last long. He began gradually to suspect that the power which had set him up might pull him down; hence he commenced seeking support against the formidable strength by which he himself had hitherto been upheld. He well knew how impossible it would be to find an army in India which could withstand the English, small though their numbers were, when commanded by such a general as Clive had proved himself to be. The power of the French had been completely destroyed in Bengal; but the fame of the Dutch had once been great in the Eastern seas, and it was not known in India how greatly their power had declined in Europe. Secret communications passed between Meer Jaffier and the Dutch at Chinsurah, and urgent letters were sent exhorting the Batavian Government to fit out an expedition which might balance the power of the English in Bengal. The Dutch authorities were naturally eager to extend their authority, and to share with the English some of the gorgeous spoils of the East.

At this moment there was no war in Europe between England and Holland; but the governors of the various European settlements in India frequently acted upon the principle of the old buccaneers in America—that treaties binding on European nations did not extend to the regions in which they were living, and that there was no peace beyond the equinoctial line. The Batavian Government were as ready to send an expedition as the Dutch traders at Chinsurah were to request it; and before long news reached Calcutta that a great armament, like the Spanish Armada of two centuries before, was preparing to contest the prize of Bengal with the hitherto triumphant English.

Meer Jaffier played his part well. When Clive sent him notice of the approaching invasion, he pretended to be greatly alarmed, and expressed his hope that the English, in virtue of the existing treaty, would oppose it with all their might. In August, 1759, a single Dutch ship of war arrived in the Hooghly, with European troops on board. Clive reported its arrival to the Nabob, who sent a pretended threatening letter to the Dutch, while he ordered his troops at the town of Hooghly to join the English. The Dutch solemnly protested that this ship had been driven in by stress of weather, and would retire as soon as water and provisions were obtained. The vessel, however, continued to lie where she was, and attempts were secretly made to forward the troops to Chinsurah by concealing them in the bottom of native boats; but this failed, by Clive giving orders that every native boat should be stopped and searched. The Dutch remonstrated against such proceedings; but Clive, thoroughly aroused to the coming danger, continued to stop the soldiers, and to send them back to their vessel, blandly informing the Dutch authorities at Chinsurah that he was in Bengal in a double capacity; first, as an English officer, whose country being at war with France, he was justified in searching all vessels, to see that no French troops were introduced into the country; and second, as an auxiliary to the Great Mogul he was bound by treaty to oppose the introduction of any European or foreign troops whatever into the province of Bengal.

Two months later Meer Jaffier arrived in person at Calcutta, under the pretence of honouring Clive with a visit. The day after his arrival Clive received intelligence that six more Dutch ships of war had arrived at the mouth of the Hooghly, crammed with soldiers, partly Europeans and partly Malays, from Batavia and other settlements of the Dutch. "Now," wrote Clive, "the Dutch mask fell off, and the Nabob, conscious of his own unfaithful dealings with us, was greatly disconcerted and confused." He, however, sought to make light of it; told Clive he was going to reside at Hooghly for a few days, from whence he would chastise the insolence of the Dutch, and drive them speedily from the river, where they had no business to be.

On quitting Calcutta a few days later, in place of going to Hooghly as he pretended, the Nabob took up his abode at a place about half-way between the fort and Chinsurah, where he received the Dutch authorities, who came to visit him in the most gracious and friendly manner, writing at the same time to Clive to inform him that he had thought proper to grant some slight indulgence to the Dutch, whose ships would quit the river as soon as the season would permit. But Clive was too experienced to be so easily deceived, especially as at that very time the season would have permitted the departure of the vessels with the greatest safety. Hence Clive was convinced that the Dutch had no intention of departing, but that Meer Jaffier had done even more than given them permission to remain. A few days later he learnt that the Dutch fleet was moving up the river, while the Dutch agents were enlisting troops of every denomination at Chinsurah, Cossimbazar, and even as far north as Patna, and this evidently with the connivance of Meer Jaffier, and the more open support of his son Meerun. Clive saw the peril at a glance; for the junction of the army in the fleet with the large amount of troops already collected at Chinsurah would be followed by a declaration of the Nabob in favour of the Dutch, and an immediate attack upon the English settlements in Bengal.

No time was to be lost; and though Clive's force of English soldiers was inferior in point of numbers to the Europeans on board the Dutch fleet, without counting those in garrison at Chinsurah, he determined to act without a moment's delay. At the critical moment some members of the Calcutta Council hesitated at commencing a war between England and Holland on their own responsibility. Clive himself felt that the home Government could not wish to see such a war added to that in which England was already engaged with France. Moreover he had recently remitted to England a great part of his fortune by means of the Dutch East India Company, and he therefore had the strongest interest in avoiding a quarrel. But patriotism of the highest order outweighed all such feelings; he was satisfied that if he suffered the Dutch fleet to pass up the river, and to join the garrison at Chinsurah, Meer

Jaffier would throw himself into the arms of these new allies, and the English power in Bengal would be exposed to the most serious danger. Clive truly said that "A public man may sometimes be called upon to act with a halter round his neck;" but Clive, on this, as on every previous occasion, proved himself equal to the crisis.

Clive took his resolution with his accustomed boldness, ably seconded by Colonel Forde, who had recently arrived at Calcutta from his career of conquest in the Northern Circars and the Deccan. On the 19th of November, Forde moved from Calcutta with the small body of troops under his command, speedily captured the Dutch settlement at Barnagore, crossed the river the next day with four pieces of artillery, and marched upon Chándernagore, in order to strike terror into the factory at Chinsurah, and to be ready to intercept the Dutch troops in case of their landing. The rest of the English troops in Bengal, and as it happened the largest proportion, Clive sent down to the forts on the river under the command of Captain Knox. Mr. Holwell, who had survived the tragedy of the Black Hole, as well as the subsequent barbarous treatment of Suráj-ood-Dowlah, took charge of Fort William, garrisoned by about 250 English militiamen, while Clive remained at Calcutta, dividing his time between the fleet and the two divisions of the army, on whom so much at that time depended—even the continuance of the British power in the province of Bengal. Three ships of war belonging to the East India Company had followed the Dutch fleet into the Hooghly, and were lying in the lower part of the river, between that squadron and the sea. As soon as the Dutch ships began to ascend the river in order to reach Chinsurah, Clive ordered the three English vessels to pass them, and station themselves above the batteries of Fort William. The Dutch commander, on seeing the English vessels advancing, sent to tell Commodore Wilson that if he attempted to pass he would fire into him. On the 21st of November, the Dutch landed an army of 1,500, which was intended for the defence of Chinsurah, and by means of their fleet seized some of the Company's vessels, and burnt their storehouses at Fulda. These hostile deeds freed Clive from all embarrassment, and decided him to act with vigour. After having landed their troops, the Dutch fleet dropped down the river to a place appropriately named, in anticipation of their subsequent defeat, "Melancholy Point," where the three English ships were lying ready for action. No sooner were the Dutch troops landed, than Clive sent Captain Knox across the river to reinforce Forde, and ordered Commodore Wilson to demand instant restitution of everything which the Dutchmen had seized belonging to the East India Company; and in the event of refusal, to "fight, sink, burn, and destroy the whole of the Dutch fleet." The next day the demand was made and refused, when the brave English commodore, without hesitating an instant on account of the great disparity of strength and numbers, three against seven, and without being able to derive any assistance from the land batteries, which were too far off, proceeded at once to the attack, and with such spirit that in the course of two hours he inflicted upon the Dutch a most signal defeat. Six of the ships struck their flags, while the seventh was captured in endeavouring to escape.

The day following, the army of fifteen hundred Dutch and Malay soldiers, alarmed at the destruction of their fleet, halted and wavered on their march to Chinsurah ; before many hours they had blundered into a defile, where retreat was difficult, and further advance almost impossible. Forde, with the quick eye of a soldier, saw the error, and was anxious to take advantage of it without delay, but hesitated to attack the troops of an European nation previous to a regular declaration of war. So he sent a hasty message across the river to Clive, to tell him that "if he had the order of Council, he could attack the Dutch with a fair prospect of destroying them." Clive, who was engaged in playing a game of cards when the note reached him, took out his pencil, and wrote on the back of it, "Dear Forde, fight them immediately. I will send you the order of Council to-morrow."

This brief despatch decided the question. Though Forde had only three hundred English and eight hundred Sepoys, he proceeded to attack the far stronger army of the Dutch without delay. The engagement, which took place in the valley of Bedarra, about four miles from Chinsurah, was short, but decisive. Notwithstanding that the Dutch had been reinforced by part of the garrison of Chinsurah, Forde in less than half an hour inflicted on them a total defeat, the fugitives leaving on the field between three and four hundred killed, and double that number being taken prisoners. Thus within a few hours the English defeated the Dutch both by land and sea, reminding the historical student of a similar event twenty-two centuries before, when the Greeks under Pausanias won the famous victory of Platæa, while their fleet on the same day inflicted as disastrous a defeat on the Persians off Mycale, the year after the celebrated battle of Thermopylæ.

From the field of battle Forde marched on Chinsurah, which he could easily have taken by a *coup de main*, but he abstained, writing to Clive for further orders. The Dutch in abject submission implored a cessation of hostilities. Deputies were appointed on both sides; the Dutch disavowed the proceedings of their fleet, acknowledged themselves the aggressors, and agreed to pay all the costs and repair all the damages caused by this brief war, which for rapidity can only be compared to the war between Prussia and Austria, a hundred and ten years later, and which culminated in the defeat of the latter on the plains of Sadowa.

Three days after the battle of Bedarra, Meer Jaffier's son Meerun, whom Clive is said to have rarely mentioned without the significant prefix of "scoundrel," encamped within two miles of Chinsurah, at the head of seven thousand horse. Had the Dutch proved victorious, he would have joined them in destroying the English; but now that the English had triumphed, he hoped to be allowed to share with them the spoils of the beaten foe. The terrified Dutch instantly applied to Clive for protection, entreating him to save them from the violence of the Mussulmans, forgetful of the fact that only two years before, when Suráj-ood-Dowlah was marching on Calcutta, and the horrors of the Black Hole were looming in the distance, and the English sought the aid of their European and Protestant brethren, the Dutch then turned a deaf ear to the appeal. Clive, however, in the spirit of Christian philanthropy and British magnanimity, forgot the past, and hastened to their assistance. Notwithstanding that Meerun's cavalry outnumbered the British and Sepoy infantry seven times over, such was the terror of Clive's name that Meerun under his dictation agreed to a treaty with the Dutch, and then withdrew his army from the scene of expected plunder.

The few remaining months of Clive's first government of Bengal were devoted to tranquilizing the country, and securing as far as human wisdom could do the splendid prize which he had obtained in thus laying the foundation of the British Empire in India. When his departure for England was announced, it filled the mind of Warren Hastings, who was then beginning to display those talents which marked him as the future successor of Clive in India, as well as of others, with doubt and alarm; for it was universally felt by the English in Bengal, that Clive was the only Atlas which could support the ponderous machine, which had already grown to such a portentous size. But Clive, on the other hand, had great objects in view. He knew that peace with France was in contemplation, which was effected three years later, and earnestly desired to communicate with the home Government personally before such a peace was concluded. He had already written his views at length to Mr. Pitt the elder, afterwards the first Earl of Chatham, then one of the principal Secretaries of State, and one of Clive's warmest admirers. Pitt, who was one of the few men in authority capable of appreciating the genius of Clive, or his design of founding the British Empire in India, had called him in the House of Commons "a heaven-born general," and declared that though "bred to the desk, he had displayed a military genius which might well excite the admiration of Frederick the Great." Clive laid before him in a lengthy despatch the enormous advantages and the gorgeous empire which England would assuredly obtain in Hindostan, if the Government would only send a force of between one and two thousand troops to effect so beneficial a conquest. Having made all necessary arrangements, and having paid a farewell visit to the Nabob of Bengal at Moorshedabad, Clive sailed for England in February, 1760. He had provided for the future as far as his means and information enabled him to attempt it, and he left behind him brave and experienced Englishmen, all more or less trained by himself, to carry on the work, and to build on the foundation which he had so securely laid. Clive's prediction respecting the war in the Carnatic was fully justified by the result; and the capture of Pondicherry by the English within a year after his departure foreshadowed the complete destruction of all Dupleix's grand designs for attempting to create a French empire within the limits of Hindostan.

CHAPTER XIII.

CLIVE'S SECOND GOVERNMENT OF BENGAL.

A.D. 1765—1767.

THE same year which saw Clive's departure from India, witnessed the virtual extinction of the empire of the Great Mogul, though it may faintly be discoverable in the kings of Delhi as late as the year 1857. But with the murder of the Emperor Alumgeer II. by his vizier, Shaháb-ood-deen, the last of the old Mogul emperors in reality ceased to exist. The Vizier made a son of Prince Kámbuksh the nominal sovereign of Delhi, but he was never acknowledged by any one ; and when subsequently Alumgeer's son, the Imperial Prince Ally Johur, a fugitive in Bengal at the time of his father's death, ascended the throne under the proud title of SHAH ALLAM, "the King of the World," it was found that the once grand empire of the Moguls was reduced to a few small patches of territory around the capital of Delhi.

The result of the great battle of Paniput, in October, 1760, between the Mohammedans and the Mahrattas, in which the latter received such a disastrous defeat, was to give the Punjaub and all the north-west provinces of India, with the exception of Scinde, into the hands of the conqueror of the Mussulman, Prince Ahmed Shah Abdally, who became a powerful and popular sovereign in that part of Hindostan. But there was arising at the same time a power founded by the genius of one man, of a race occupying the far distant isles of the northern seas, which eventually, like the iron monarchy of the Jewish prophet Daniel, was destined to absorb one kingdom after another, until the whole of that mighty empire, from the Himalayas in the north to Cape Comorin in the south, found rest and protection under the ægis of the British Empire.

After Clive's departure, Mr. Holwell assumed the presidency of Bengal, pending the arrival of Mr. Vansittart, a Madras civilian, who had been selected by Clive, and had received his nomination from England. But no sooner was the commanding genius of Clive withdrawn, than blunder after blunder was committed by the Council at Calcutta, until it appeared probable that the power which he had so rapidly acquired for his country would be as suddenly overthrown and lost. During the five years which followed the departure of Clive from Bengal, the misgovernment of the province, through the insatiable desire of the members of the Council to grow rich, had reached such a point that it seemed hardly possible it could go further. What could be expected from a body of public servants exposed to such temptations that, as Clive once said, flesh and blood could not bear it, armed with irresistible power over millions of the trampled-down race of Hindus, responsible only to a company of traders, situated so many thousands of miles distant, that the average interval between sending a despatch and receiving the answer was between one and two years? Cruelty, so abhorrent to an Englishman's nature, was not among the vices of the Company's servants. But the cruelty of a Roman pro-consul, who in the days of the Empire managed to squeeze out of a province, in the course of a single year, the means of raising marble palaces on the shores of Italy, could scarcely have produced greater evils than sprang from the unprincipled eagerness of the governing body at Calcutta to grow suddenly rich. They pulled down their creature, Meer Jaffier, who had become imbecile, and set up in his place his own son-in-law, Meer Cassim, who deliberately proposed to the English Council at Calcutta to have his father-in-law put to death, after the usual fashion of revolutions in India. Finding that Meer Cassim was unwilling to allow any one else but himself to grind his subjects to the dust by oppressions which yielded him no profit, the Council pulled down Meer Cassim, and set up Meer Jaffier, notwithstanding the latter's incurable leprosy. Having thus proclaimed him sovereign of Bengal, and obtained from him some fresh grants of territory for the benefit of the Company, the English placed him again on the throne at Moorshedabad, and both parties prepared for war.

Before long, Meer Cassim proceeded with a considerable force to meet the English. His troops had been disciplined by a Swiss of the name of Sumroo, a serjeant of the French army in India, and his artillery was excellent. In July, 1763, the English army, which consisted of 650 Europeans, with 1,200 Sepoys, defeated Meer Cassim at Cutwah, and again at Gheriak in the following month. This double defeat so enraged Meer Cassim, that he gave full vent to his passion and ferocity. On arriving at Patna, he ordered several of his principal subjects, who were known to be friendly to the English, to be thrown into the Ganges, while he directed that all the English then in the city should be put to death, which bloody work was done by Sumroo, who fired volleys into their prisons until upwards of two hundred were killed,—a deed which rivals in atrocity, though not in prolonged agony, the tragedy of the Black Hole at Calcutta, only seven years before.

After a third defeat, Meer Cassim fled to the Vizier of Oude, and formed a league with him. These allies, who had been joined by Shah Allum, the pretended "King of the World," marched upon Patna, which was then defended by the English, but were beaten back, and retreated on the plains of Buxar, where they were thoroughly defeated by Major Hector Munro, with seven thousand troops under his command, the largest force as yet assembled in India under the British flag.

The victory of Buxar virtually placed the province of Bengal in the hands of the conquerors. Shah Allum voluntarily gave himself up to them. The kingdom of Oude was declared to have been forfeited, and Meer Cassim managed to escape by flight the punishment he so richly deserved. But the treasure, which amounted to no less a sum than £3,000,000, was entirely lost to the English through the accidental breaking down of a bridge, the consequence of which was that the Council of Calcutta had no means of recruiting the public finances or of satisfying their own private desires. They applied to their puppet, Meer Jaffier, for assistance, who, now worn out by age and care, died at Moorshedabad in

January, 1765, though not before he had disbursed the large sum of £530,000 among the private claimants of the Council.

Meer Jaffier's death rendered a new appointment necessary, and Nujm-ood-Dowlah, his second son, was elected to succeed him. This event was too tempting to be resisted; and in these days of order and propriety we read with as much amazement as indignation the sums which were demanded as of right, and received without the slightest compunction, by the senior officers of the Calcutta Council. According to the high authority of Mill's History of India, the total sum disbursed among the English at Calcutta from the Moorshedabad treasury amounted to no less than £2,169,655, while the payments on account of "restitutions" reached £3,770,883, making a sum total of nearly £6,000,000 sterling. Enormous fortunes were thus rapidly accumulated at Calcutta; while 30,000,000 of human beings were reduced to the lowest extremity of want. They had been accustomed to live under tyranny, but never before under such tyranny as this. Under their old masters, the natives had one resource which was wanting now. When the evil became insupportable, the people rose and pulled down the Government; but the English Government was not to be so shaken off. Oppressive as the most oppressive form of heathen despotism, it was strong with all the strength of civilization. The natives never attempted resistance. Sometimes they submitted in patient misery, at other times they fled from the white man as their fathers had fled from the Mahrattas, who robbed them under another form. It is recorded that the palanquin of the English traveller was often carried through silent villages and towns, which the report of his approach had rendered desolate.

But, as well as being often objects of fear to the plundered natives, the English were objects of hatred to the neighbouring states, to all of which they invariably presented a dauntless front. A succession of able commanders formed by Clive upheld their country's fame; and the account by a Mussulman historian of that period is a striking testimony to British power. "It must be acknowledged," he says, "that this nation's presence of mind, firmness of temper, and undaunted bravery, are past all question. They join the most resolute courage to the most cautious prudence; and if to so many military qualifications they knew how to join the arts of government; if they exerted as much ingenuity and solicitude in relieving the people of God, as they do in whatever concerns their military affairs, no nation in the world would be preferable to them, or more worthy of command. But the people under their dominion groan everywhere, and are reduced to poverty and distress. O God! come to the assistance of Thine afflicted servants, and deliver them from the oppressions which they suffer."

The state of affairs at Calcutta at length began to create uneasiness at home. Every fleet brought back successful adventurers from India, known by the name of "Nabobs," who were able to purchase rich manors in England, and to build stately mansions; but they also brought back alarming accounts of the financial prospects of the East India Company, both at home and abroad. The universal cry from friends and foes alike was that Clive, and Clive alone, could save the empire which he had founded in the East.

Clive was in consequence nominated Governor and Commander-in-Chief of the British possessions in Bengal, and sailed for the third and last time to India, reaching Calcutta in May, 1765. There he found the whole system of government more fearfully disorganised than he had anticipated. Meer Jaffier, whose eldest son, the "scoundrel" Meerun, had predeceased him, died while Clive was on his voyage out. The Company's servants at Calcutta had received stringent orders from home not to accept presents from the native princes; but over-eager for gain and the spoils of the East, like the Prætorian guards of old, they again set up the throne of Bengal to the highest bidder. The sum of £140,000 was distributed among the leading men of the Calcutta Council; and in consideration of this bribe an infant son of the deceased Nabob was placed on the throne of his father.

The news of this ignominious bargain met Clive on his arrival; and his resolute determination to cleanse the Augean stable is thus pathetically alluded to in a private letter to a friend: "Alas!" he writes, "how is the English name sunk! I could not avoid paying the tribute of a few tears to the departed and lost fame of the British nation. However, I do declare, by that great Being who is the searcher of all hearts, and to whom we must be accountable if there be a hereafter, that I am come out with a mind superior to all corruption, and that I am determined to destroy those great and growing evils, or perish in the attempt."

At the first meeting of the Council after his landing, Clive announced his determination to make a thorough reform. Johnstone, one of the most unscrupulous of the pilferers, attempted an opposition. Clive interrupted him, and haughtily demanded whether he meant to question the power of the new Government. Johnstone was instantly cowed, and disclaimed any such intention. All the faces in the assembly grew long and pale, and not another whisper of dissent was heard. Clive nobly redeemed his pledge. During the remainder of his stay in India, which was limited to less than two years, it is not too much to say that he effected one of the most extensive, difficult, and salutary reforms that was ever accomplished by any statesman, considering the limited means at his disposal, and the distance of the superior Government at home, whose faithful servant he proved himself to be.

Clive then had it in his power to triple his already splendid fortune; to connive at abuses while pretending to remove them; to conciliate the good will of all the English in Bengal, by giving up to their covetousness a helpless and timid race, who knew not the country whence their oppressors came, and whose complaints had little chance of being heard by the Company in England, at a distance of fifteen thousand miles of sea. He knew that if he applied himself in earnest to the work of reformation, he should raise every bad passion in arms against him. He knew how implacable would be the hatred of those ravenous adventurers, who, confident of being able under the previous system to accumulate enormous fortunes in the course of two or three years, now found all their hopes blown to the winds. But Clive was the right man in the right place; and having determined on the course of high-minded justice to all, English and natives alike, he nerved himself for a contest far harder to fight and to win than the great victory of Plassey. At first success seemed hopeless; but soon all obstacles bent before that iron will. The receiving of presents from the natives was rigidly prohibited. The private trade of the servants of the Company, which was injurious to the Company itself in the greatest degree, was put down. The whole settlement seemed to be set as one man against these necessary measures; but Clive declared that if he could not find sufficient support at Calcutta, he would send for assistance to Madras to enable him to carry on the administration. The most factious of his opponents he turned out of office, while the rest submitted to the inexorable will of the Governor-General; and in a short space of time all resistance had ceased and come to an end.

Clive had thus succeeded in putting down all opposition of the civil service; but that of the army was still more difficult to meet. Some of the retrenchments ordered by the directors at home affected the interests of military service; and a storm arose which neither Cæsar nor Napoleon would willingly have faced. It was no light matter to meet the opposition of those who held the power of the sword in a country governed solely by the sword. Two hundred British officers engaged in a conspiracy against the Government, and determined to resign their commissions on the same day, expecting that Clive would grant any terms rather than see the army, on which alone our empire in India rested, left without commanders. They little knew the resolute and unconquerable spirit with whom they had to deal, and which so closely resembled the iron will of the great Protector, Oliver Cromwell. Clive had a few officers around him on whom he could rely. He sent to Madras for a fresh supply, and gave commissions even to mercantile agents of his own original profession, who were prepared to support him at this crisis, and he sent orders that every officer who resigned should be instantly brought up to Calcutta. The conspirators soon discovered their grand mistake. The Governor was inexorable. The troops, especially the Sepoys,* over whom Clive had always possessed extraordinary influence, stood by him with unshaken fidelity. The leaders in the plot, of whom Sir Robert Fletcher was the chief instigator, were arrested, tried, and cashiered. The rest begged to be allowed to withdraw their resignations, and those Clive treated with great lenity. To the ring-leaders he was inflexibly severe. While he sternly upheld the power of the Governor-General, he passed by all personal insults with magnanimous disdain. One of the conspirators was accused of having planned the assassination of the Governor; but Clive would not listen to the charge, declaring with the spirit of

* It is a remarkable fact that when the English soldiers assembled in arms at Mongheer in support of their mutinous leaders, they were overawed by the Sepoy regiments commanded by British officers. Happily there was no actual outbreak, either at Mongheer or in the camp at Serajpoor, but the sudden arrival of a regiment of Sepoys, who had marched 104 miles in fifty-four hours, probably prevented what was in contemplation.

a noble-minded Briton, "The officers are Englishmen, not assassins."

Having thus succeeded in reforming the civil branch of the service, and in quelling the most dangerous conspiracy ever attempted by British officers in any part of the world, Clive was enabled to turn his attention to the foreign policy of the Government in Bengal, and in this he was as successful as he was eleven years before, after his crowning victory at Plassey. The very day of his arrival, May 3rd, 1765, the Vizier of Oude, with his Mahratta and Rohilla allies, had been defeated by the British under General Carnac, which decided him to throw himself on the generosity of the English, as the Emperor Shah Allum had virtually done the same after the battle of Buxar, fought eight months before. And it must have been a strange sight for the natives of Hindostan to have witnessed the descendant and heir of the Great Mogul, who bore the proud title of "the King of the World," as well as his most powerful subject, the Vizier of Oude, bidding for the support of a small company of traders from the far West, whose existence in Bengal not many years before was confined to the twenty-three unhappy Englishmen who had come out alive from the Black Hole of Calcutta.

It was a situation of no little difficulty, and which required for its solution the presence of a master mind. Clive proved himself equal to the occasion. After settling the difficulties respecting the army at the Council Board of Calcutta, the affairs of the Vizier of Oude were finally decided. His dominions, which he had forfeited by an unprovoked war, were

8

restored to him, except two districts, viz., Corah and Allahabad, which were reserved for the Emperor. He had to pay half a million sterling for the expenses of the war, and the Rajah Bulwunt Singh, who had rendered material assistance to the English, was confirmed in his possession of Benares and Ghazipoor. The Emperor Shah Allum was permitted to retain £260,000 of the annual revenue of Bengal, Behar, and Orissa, but he was required to relinquish his claim to the arrears which had accumulated. He had already twice offered "the dewany," as it was termed, *i.e.*, the revenue management of Bengal, to the English, once to Clive and subsequently to General Carnac. On Clive again proposing this arrangement for the benefit of the East India Company and the natives alike, the Emperor readily accepted the proffered terms. On August the 12th, 1765, Shah Allum, the representative of the Great Mogul dynasty, took his seat on a throne hastily constructed of the dining tables and an armchair in Lord Clive's tent, somewhat different from the splendid scene which was witnessed a hundred and twenty years later, when our gracious Sovereign was proclaimed Queen-Empress of India; and delivered into the hands of Clive an imperial firman, conferring in perpetuity to the English nation the three great provinces of Bengal, Orissa, and Behar, which possessed a population of 25,000,000, considerably greater than that of the United Kingdom in the middle of the eighteenth century, and a revenue of £4,000,000 sterling, which was larger than the annual revenue of England not many years before.

It would have been easy for Clive during the brief

period of his second administration in Bengal to have accumulated wealth such as no subject in Europe then possessed. Without subjecting the rich inhabitants of the province to any pressure beyond that to which their mildest rulers had accustomed them, he might have received presents which would have raised his private income to £300,000 a year. The neighbouring princes would have gladly paid any price for his favour. But he conscientiously adhered to the rules which he had laid down for the guidance of others. The Rajah of Benares offered him diamonds of great value. The Vizier of Oude pressed him to accept a large sum of money, together with a casket of costly jewels. Clive courteously refused them; and it should not be forgotten that he made no boast or merit of his refusal, as these facts did not come to light until after his death.

One large sum, indeed, he thought fit to accept. Meer Jaffier had left him by will the sum of £60,000 sterling; and as the rules which he had laid down for the benefit of the Company only extended to presents from the living, it could not of course include legacies from the dead. So Clive accepted the gift, but not for himself. He made the whole of it over to the East India Company, in trust for officers and soldiers invalided in their service; and that which still bears the honoured name of "The Clive Fund" owes its origin to this princely donation.

With this noble proof of Clive's disinterested liberality we may draw to a close our sketch of the share which he had in founding the British Empire in India. His second administration, which only lasted rather less than two years, was crowded with events which added greater and more lasting lustre to his reputation than his first. He had effected a most necessary reform in preventing any further plundering of the mild and inoffensive Bengalese by the officials of the East India Company, which the character of the one and the rapacity of the other made so easy, and which had heretofore been recognized by both parties as almost akin to prescriptive right.

He had put down the most dangerous mutiny that had ever disgraced an army of English soldiers, without having recourse to the desperate measure which his great prototype, Cromwell, on a like occasion, was once compelled to take. The objects which he had most at heart in laying the foundation of the British Empire in India, viz., the possession of the three great provinces of Bengal, had been secured with marvellous ease, and with the voluntary consent of the sovereign representative of the Great Mogul dynasty, which for so long a period had held sway over the millions of Hindostan; and one of his last acts before leaving Calcutta was to put on record a minute of his opinion, but which time and the fate of empires has flatly contradicted, and which makes us wonder at finding such to be the mature judgment of so great a man, that "*any further extension of territory in India, on the part of England, would be a scheme so extravagantly ambitious, that no government in its senses would ever dream of it.*" The state of Clive's health made it necessary for him to return to Europe. At the close of January, 1767, he quitted for the third and last time the country to which he had come twenty-three years before a friendless and penniless lad, and on whose destinies he had exercised so mighty an influence through the possession of a genius which has rarely been equalled, and in its own peculiar line probably never been surpassed.

If we were to draw a comparison between Clive and those to whom history, whether ancient or modern, has conceded the name of "great," there is scarcely one which must not pale before the merits of the founder of the British Empire in India. From his first entrance on the scene of his subsequent fame dates the renown of the English arms in the East. Till he appeared, his countrymen were despised as a lot of mere trading pedlars, while the French were regarded as the only people from the West capable of war, and formed to command Clive's courage and genius, together with his ability to carry out the principles, so tersely expressed by the Roman poet of *Carpe Diem*, dissolved the charm which had beguiled the native mind. With the brilliant defence of Arcot commences his long series of triumphs, which closes with the crowning victory of Plassey. Nor must we forget the enormous disadvantages under which he won his great military triumphs; compared with those whom the world considers heroes, whether it be an Alexander or a Napoleon, as tried by this test, their star appears to pale before him. What shall we say of the former? He ascended the throne at the age of twenty, crossed the Hellespont at twenty-two, at the head of an army of 35,000 men, of the famous Macedonian phalanx, the finest troops which the world had then seen, surrounded by a staff of most able generals, and trained in the science of war from his cradle. He won his crowning victory of Arbela at twenty-five, reached the limit of his conquests by the invasion of the Punjaub, and his triumph over Porus (scarcely a thousand miles distant, by the way, from the battle-field of Plassey), and after being guilty of the most atrocious acts of refined cruelty, which place him on a par with the greatest monsters of ancient or modern times, and which, consequently, make the lines more applicable to him than to the conqueror for whom they were intended :—

> "He left a name at which the world grew pale,
> To point a moral or adorn a tale."

Alexander, miscalled "the Great," ended his worthless life as a drunken sot at the early age of thirty-three.

Clive, on the other hand, began life as a clerk to a company of traders, without having the slightest knowledge of the rudiments of war ; and it was not until the age of twenty-one that he adopted the military profession, and received an ensign's commission in the service of the East India Company, whose army had previously consisted of some native soldiers, armed with bows and arrows, to defend the three or four ill-constructed forts which they then owned on the eastern coast of Hindostan. At twenty-six, Clive was simply a lieutenant, in charge of the commissariat department, during the campaign of Captain Gingen, which ended in such a disastrous fiasco for the commander of a set of poltroons. A few months later he obtained his first command, at an earlier age than that of Napoleon Buonaparte, when he commenced his astonishing career in Italy, and proved, by his brilliant defence of the city and fortress of

Arcot, that he was indeed, as the great Lord Chatham had called him, "a heaven-born general;" and the skilful defence of which became the first step in his grand career, that eventually made him the founder of the British Empire in India.

How justly has Macaulay said, in the admirable portrait he has drawn of Clive's character, "The fame of those who subdued Antiochus and Tigranes grows dim when compared with the splendour of the exploits which the young English adventurer achieved at the head of an army not equal in numbers to one half of a Roman legion. . . . Clive's name stands high on the roll of conquerors; but it is found in a better list, in the list of those who have done and suffered much for the happiness of mankind. To the warrior, history will assign a place in the same rank with Lucullus and Trajan. Nor will she deny to the reformer a share of that veneration with which France cherishes the memory of Turgot, and with which the latest generations of Hindus will contemplate the statue of Lord William Bentinck."

CHAPTER XIV.

RISE OF WARREN HASTINGS. FROM HIS APPOINTMENT AS A WRITER TO HIS RETURN TO ENGLAND AS MEMBER OF COUNCIL AT CALCUTTA.

A.D. 1750—1764.

THERE is a remarkable similarity in many points between the two great men, Clive and Warren Hastings, to whom we are indebted more than to any one else for the foundation and consolidation of the British Empire in India. Lord Macaulay, in his account of the duel between the Governor-General of Bengal and that hostile member of his council, Sir Philip Francis, remarks, "In a very short time it was made signally manifest to how great a danger the Governor-General had on this occasion exposed his country. A crisis had arrived, in which he, and he alone, was competent to deal. It is not too much to say that if he had been taken from the head of affairs, the years 1780 and 1781 would have been as fatal to our power in Asia as to our power in America."

And of Clive's power to preserve our colonies in America to the mother-country, the same great historian gives it as his opinion, when the disputes with the colonists had become so serious that war was inevitable, and ministers were anxious to avail themselves of Clive's services, that "had Clive still been what he was when he raised the siege of Patna, and annihilated the Dutch army and navy at the mouth of the Ganges, it is not improbable that the resistance of the colonies would have been put down, and that the inevitable separation would have been deferred for a few years."

Seven years after Clive's birth, Warren Hastings first saw the light, December 6, 1782; and the same number of years, wanting one, intervened after Clive had quitted India for the third and last time, when Warren Hastings succeeded him in the important position of Governor-General of Bengal.

Both were sprung from good old families in reduced circumstances; both alike landed in India friendless and almost penniless; both may be said to have changed their professions, which were originally the same as commercial agents in a trading company; the one becoming the greatest soldier and the other the greatest statesman of the period in which they lived; while both achieved greatness at an age when the character of most men is only beginning to be formed.

Warren Hastings, however, had this advantage over Clive in boyhood; at ten years of age he was sent to Westminster School, where for the next seven years he gradually learnt both to obey and to command; and as Wellington used to say that his dandy officers proved the best soldiers in the Peninsular war, so it may be said that at Westminster Hastings learnt something which was of use to him in the stormy struggles of his after life. At the proper age he got into college, head of the election;* and such was his capacity for learning, and so evident were his talents, that when by the death of his uncle and guardian he was bequeathed to the care of a distant relative, who was only too glad to get rid of the unwelcome burden by shipping him off to India, Dr. Nichols, the head master of Westminster, offered to defray his expenses at the university, in order to save his favourite pupil from banishment to the other end of the world.

In October, 1750, Warren Hastings reached Bengal, and was immediately placed at a desk in the secretary's office at Calcutta, then a purely commercial settlement. After having passed two years in keeping accounts, Hastings was sent up the country to Cossimbazar, on the Hooghly, and which may be regarded as a sort of suburb to Moorshedabad, the then capital of the great province of Bengal. Here, for several years, Hastings was employed in making bargains for silks and stuffs with the native brokers. While thus engaged, Suráj-ood-Dowlah succeeded to the government, and, as we have before noticed, began his reign by declaring war on the English. The defenceless settlement of Cossimbazar, lying close to the capital, was instantly seized, and Hastings was sent a prisoner to Moorshedabad, and by this means was preserved from the tragedy of the Black Hole of Calcutta.

In this sad event, however, the greatness of Warren Hastings may be said to have originated; for when Mr. Drake, the Governor of Fort William, and his companions so unworthily deserted their post, they took refuge on the dreary Isle of Fulda, near the

* See Appendix.

mouth of the river Hooghly; and being anxious to obtain information respecting the proceedings of the Nabob, no person seemed so likely to furnish it as Hastings, then a prisoner at large in the neighbourhood of the court. He thus unexpectedly became a diplomatic agent, and soon established a high character for ability and resolution. The conspiracy which eventually succeeded in replacing Surâj-ood-Dowlah by Meer Jaffier was then in progress; and Hastings was admitted into the secret. It was necessary to postpone the execution of the design, on account of the rumours which had already reached the ears of Dowlah, and which were sufficient to arouse his suspicions. It appears that when the plot was nearly ripe for execution, Clive learnt that Omichund, the wealthy banker of Moorshedabad, and confidential agent of the Nabob, was likely to play false. The artful Bengalee had been promised a liberal compensation for all that he had lost when Dowlah's troops plundered Calcutta. But this would not satisfy him; and as he held the threads of the whole conspiracy, and the lives of Mr. Watts, the chief commissioner, Meer Jaffier, Hastings, and others, were at his mercy, he determined to take advantage of the situation, and to make his own terms, by demanding the large sum of £300,000 as the price of his secrecy and assistance. The Council at Calcutta, incensed by the treachery, and appalled by the danger, knew not what course to take, until Clive proved himself more than Omichund's match in Omichund's own arts; and the wily Bengalee was caught in his own trap.

When the plot, which has already been noticed in

a previous chapter, was ripe for execution, Warren Hastings, with Mr. Watts and others, secretly left Moorshedabad, and fled to Fulda. Clive put his troops in motion, and the victory of Plassey terminated the campaign. Hastings, young and ardent, and excited by Clive's example, who, from having been, like himself, a mercantile agent of the Company, had now become one of the most distinguished generals of the age, offered to serve as a volunteer in the ranks, and for some time he carried a musket, fighting with the accustomed energy of a Westminster schoolboy* at the battle of Plassey. But the quick eye of Clive soon perceived that the head of the young volunteer would be more useful than his arm; and so, when the overthrow of the tyrant Suráj-ood-Dowlah was accomplished, and Meer Jaffier proclaimed Nabob of Bengal, Hastings was appointed by Clive to reside at the court of the new prince, as agent or representative—the same, in fact, as ambassador—of the East India Company, being the first to hold such an office with any of the native sovereigns in India.

Warren Hastings remained at Moorshedabad until 1761, when he was appointed member of the Council at Calcutta, and was obliged to reside there during the interval between Clive's first and second adminis-

* The author's first battle at Westminster, A.D. 1828, was fought with a boy of the name of Milman, who shortly after left the school, and of him he heard nothing more until nearly fifty years later he discovered that his former schoolfellow and boyish foe was the deservedly lamented Robert Milman, Bishop of Calcutta, who died in 1876; and whose episcopal jurisdiction, curious enough to say, extended over the same places which are so frequently mentioned in this sketch, viz., Bengal, Oude, the Punjaub, etc., etc.

tration—an interval which left on the fame of the East India Company a stain, scarcely effaced by many subsequent years of just and humane government. Mr. Vansittart, the Governor, whose venality, together with that of the Council, has been mentioned in a preceding chapter, was at the head of a new and anomalous empire. On one side was a band of English functionaries, daring and intelligent, but only too eager to enrich themselves with the spoils of the East. On the other side was a great native population, helpless, timid, and accustomed to crouch under oppression. To keep the stronger race from preying on the weaker was an undertaking, as we have already seen, which subsequently tasked to the uttermost the talents and energy of the noble-minded and illustrious Clive. A war of the natives of the effeminate East against the power and commercial instincts of the Anglo-Saxon race was like a war of sheep against wolves. The only protection which the conquered could hope for was in the moderation, the clemency, and the enlarged policy of the conquerors. That protection at a later period they found; but when at first the English power came amongst them, it was unaccompanied by Protestant morality.

There was an interval, after the battle of Plassey, when Clive, having returned to England, had ceased to direct the Council at Calcutta, between the time at which the natives of Bengal became our subjects, and the time when Clive returned to undertake the government of Bengal for the second time, and to enforce upon the Council the obligation of discharging towards them the moral obligation of rulers,

When Clive left India in the early part of 1760, Mr. Holwell presided until the arrival of Mr. Vansittart from Madras, and it was he who planned the scheme, which he persuaded the new Governor and the Council to adopt, of virtually offering the vice-royality of Bengal for sale. This was done, as we have before mentioned, by putting down Meer Jaffier and appointing his son-in-law, Meer Cassim, in his place. Of the £200,000 which Meer Cassim paid for this ignoble transaction, upwards of £58,000 fell to the Governor's share, and £30,000 to that of Mr. Holwell, the rest being divided amongst the other members of the Council.

Of the conduct of Hastings at this time little is known, and all that is known redounds to his honour; his name does not appear in the list of the presents acknowledged to have been received from Meer Cassim, nor does he appear to have had anything to do with another episode in the history of Mr. Vansittart's government which has brought such indellible disgrace on his name, and which necessitated the reappointment of Clive to the presidency of Bengal. When the Council of Calcutta, by the abuse which they made of the *dustuks* or "permits" for exempting goods from the payment of duty, thus benefiting themselves at the expense of the public, they stopped an important service of the revenue, and Meer Cassim speedily found himself as poor as his predecessor. Looking around him for some great prey, his greedy eye fell upon Ramnarain, the Governor of Patna, whose treasury and life had been sought by Meer Jaffier, but preserved and declared sacred by Clive.

When Mr. Vansittart, the Governor, first learnt the nature of Meer Cassim's designs, he ordered Major Carnac, the distinguished commander of the British troops in Bengal, to afford every protection to Ramnarain, who had recently rendered the English much valuable assistance in repelling the attacks of the Emperor Shah Allum. But, alas! soon the temptation became too strong to be resisted; the Governor, weak and unstable as water, listened to the perfidious suggestions and promises of Meer Cassim; and pretending to be offended at the free language of Major Carnac, who sought to keep him in the path of honour, sent Colonel (afterwards Sir Eyre) Coote, who had recently returned to Bengal from his great victory over the French at Pondicherry, to supersede Major Carnac at Patna. But Coote had as high a sense of honour as Carnac; and on discovering what was expected from him, he refused to be either an active agent in, or a passive spectator of, the betrayal and ruin of the Hindu Governor of Patna. Vansittart then recalled Coote, and Ramnarain was left to the tender mercies of the new Nabob. He was thrown into prison, his house was plundered, and his servants tortured to make them confess where their master's hidden treasures lay, but which eventually proved to be more like a molehill than a mountain. The disappointed tyrant, Meer Cassim, whose character partook of a mixture between the hyæna and the tiger, as shown in his slaughter of two hundred English prisoners, fearing the indignation of their countrymen, did not put Ramnarain to death at once; but two years later, when he had drawn his sword against those who had made him viceroy of Bengal, he murdered his prisoner in cold blood, together with several other chiefs, both Mussulmans and Hindus.

Other acts of venality and rapacity were perpetrated by the Governor Vansittart and his Council before Hastings came amongst them, and from which, as his subsequent conduct proved, he was entirely exempt. When Hastings took his seat as member of the Council at Calcutta, and saw what was going on, as well as discovered his inability to repress the evil, all that he could do was to abstain personally from plundering and oppressing the natives as his colleagues considered it their prescriptive right to do. It is certain that Hastings at this time was poor, and it is no less certain that by cruelty and dishonesty he might easily have become rich. He was never charged with having borne any share in any of those abuses which then prevailed, which inflicted such a stain on the English name; and we may feel assured that if he had any hand in those abuses, the unscrupulous foes, who afterwards persecuted him with such unrelenting severity, would not have failed to discover and to proclaim his guilt. The scrutiny to which his whole life was afterwards subjected, mainly by the blinded passion of Sir Philip Francis, a scrutiny which Macaulay has justly pronounced to be "unparalleled in the history of mankind," proved advantageous to the illustrious accused. It may be that certain blemishes were brought to light, but it is equally certain that Hastings' great services, his honourable poverty, and the success with which his government was crowned, far outweighed the accusations brought against him. And it may be justly

WARREN HASTINGS.

said with regard to those insignificant persons who formed the governing body at Calcutta, from Plassey to the end of Hastings' rule, his hands and those of Clive were the least stained of any.

After three years in office, Hastings returned to England in 1764, a few months before Clive left for India, with a very moderate fortune, which was soon reduced to nothing by his praiseworthy liberality to poor relations and the rascality of his agents in Bengal, in whose hands he had placed the greatest part of his savings.

CHAPTER XV.

THE GOVERNMENT AT MADRAS DURING THE WARS WITH HYDER ALY.

A.D. 1759—1772.

HASTINGS remained nearly five years in England without employment, when he began to look again towards India. He had little to attach him to England, and his pecuniary embarrassments were considerable. He solicited employment from his former masters, the directors of the East India Company, and they gladly accepted his services, with high compliments both to his abilities and integrity, while appointing him at once to the office of Member of Council at Madras. It is recorded to his honour, that though forced to borrow money for his outfit, he refrained from withdrawing any portion of the sum which he had appropriated to the relief of those relatives who were poorer than himself. In the spring of 1769 he sailed for India, and for the next eighteen years was exclusively engaged in consolidating that wondrous superstructure whose foundation was laid by the mighty genius of Clive—the British Empire in India, and which, under the fostering care of the Anglo-Saxon race, has now become, during the reign of her gracious Majesty the Queen-Empress Victoria, the greatest power the world has ever seen.

Before, however, entering upon the subject of Hastings' rule at Madras, it may be well to give a brief sketch of the political events which had occurred in that presidency previous to his becoming a member of the Council, and which resulted in the expulsion of the French from every part of India, and the complete supremacy of the English over their European rivals.

The Seven Years' War between England and France, which commenced in 1756, was carried on as vigorously in India as in Europe. A few months before Clive quitted Calcutta, the English fleet under Admiral Pococke had two indecisive actions with the French off the coast of Coromandel, though the effect of the last was to compel the French fleet to take refuge first at Pondicherry, and then to retreat to the Mauritius, notwithstanding General Lally's urgent entreaty with the French Admiral to the contrary. By this Lally's position was materially weakened; and in order to do something for the honour of France, he calculated upon being able to make a successful attempt on the English settlement at Madras. His own officers were, however, in despair, chiefly on account of there being no funds for carrying on the campaign. Having at length collected about £10,000, of which the greater portion came from Lally himself, the French commander seriously set himself to the task of capturing the city and the fort, one of his officers, the Count d'Estaign, wisely remarking that "it was better to die by a musket-shot under the walls of Madras, than to starve at Pondicherry."

Lally laid siege to Madras, and after nine weeks'

continuance, with considerable loss to both sides, and a breach in the walls having been effected, he was about to storm the fort on February 16th, 1759, when an English fleet, with a reinforcement of six hundred king's troops, arrived in the roads, and the opportunity of capturing Madras was lost to the French for ever and a day. Lally retreated to Arcot, and his troops having been for some time without pay, and running short of provisions as well as of powder and shot, thought they could better themselves by breaking out into open mutiny. Having succeeded in quelling the mutiny, and having obtained sufficient funds to set his troops in motion, Lally encountered the English under Colonel (afterwards Sir Eyre) Coote, who had recently arrived at Madras, on the plains of Wandiwash. The forces were pretty nearly equal in point of numbers, the English having a larger number of Sepoy troops, while the French had more Europeans ; and the result was a complete overthrow of the French, who lost upwards of six hundred Europeans, independent of the loss amongst the Sepoys ; and if the English native cavalry had only done their duty, the French army might have been entirely destroyed during their enforced retreat.

The condition of the French in the Carnatic during the spring of 1760 was now rendered desperate, as all their previous conquests had passed away, save the city of Pondicherry, which the English army under Coote were prepared to invest before the close of the year. The city was sorely straitened for provisions ; and Lally, the French commander, at length adopted the dreadful expedient of expelling between one and two thousand natives, of all sexes and ages, without provisions, who wandered for seven days between the city walls and the British army, subsisting upon roots of grass, or whatever they could find in the earth. Coote's desire was to compel them to return to the city, until, finding that they were mercilessly fired upon by their French protectors, Coote, with the generosity of an Englishman, allowed them to pass through his lines into the open country. On the 15th of January, 1761, when there were only two days' provision remaining, Lally surrendered the city and fortress to the British. The troops taken captive amounted to upwards of two thousand, and the cannon to five hundred; while one hundred mortars, together with immense stores of powder and shot, attested the value of the conquest.

Thus the capture of Madras by Labourdonnais, in 1746, was more than revenged by Coote's capture of Pondicherry in 1761; for the French power in India, after a vast expenditure of lives and money, was now completely overthrown, as three places alone remained to them when Pondicherry fell,—Tiagar and Ginjee in the Carnatic, which were reduced a few months later, and Matré on the western coast, which capitulated in the following year to Monson; so that in 1762 the French attempt to rival the British power in India came to an end. It is true that by the peace between England and France in 1763, Pondicherry was restored to the French, who retained possession of it until the breaking out of the French revolutionary war in 1793, when it was captured by an English force under Colonel Braithwaite, and India knew the French no more.

The treatment which Lally received from his

Government on returning to France has left a deep stain on the Bourbon dynasty, in the person of that contemptible monarch, Louis XV. His enemies had exaggerated his losses, blackened his character, and attributed all the odium of defeat to him alone. On his arrival in France, Lally was subjected to worse treatment than either Labourdonnais or Dupleix had received at the hands of that light and volatile nation. He was cast into prison, where he remained for a year and a half, when he was subjected to a most unfair trial, and hastily condemned to death. The day the sentence was promulgated he was put to death, being dragged to the scaffold with a large gag in his mouth, in order to prevent him from addressing the people. Thus perished the last of the three victims to French policy in India; while the fortifications of Pondicherry, which had been erected at an enormous cost, were afterwards razed to the ground by the Madras Government, and thus the humiliation of the French in India was complete.

The capture of Pondicherry in 1761 had raised the English power in the Carnatic to a great height, and the Government at Madras were placed by this success in as advantageous a position as the Calcutta Council had been four years before by the battle of Plassey. The Northern Circars, a large district on the Coromandel coast, had been bestowed in 1765 upon the English, by the Emperor Shah Allum, in free gift, as the imperial deed expressed it: "To their heirs and descendants, for ever and ever; free, exempt, and safe from all removal and from all demands of the Dewany Office, or the Imperial Court, etc., etc." Clive, who was then head of the Calcutta

Council, had urged upon the Madras Government the necessity for their taking possession at once; but Mr. (afterwards Sir Robert) Palk, the President of Madras, and his Council, hesitated, and the opportunity was allowed to pass without anything being done. When in the following year the Madras Government attempted to give effect to the Emperor's deed of gift, the Nizam resisted, and having obtained the assistance of Hyder Aly, war was declared by the English against the allies.

After two defeats inflicted on the allied armies, Hyder's son, Tippo Sahib, was obliged to withdraw from Madras, which he was on the verge of attacking; and the Nizam, finding that Hyder was sending back his guns and stores to his capital, quietly threw him overboard, and commenced negotiations for an alliance with the English. To this he was driven by a very serious danger; for the Bengal Government had already despatched a force under Colonel Peach to the Northern Circars, which advanced without difficulty to within eighty miles of Hyderabad, and took possession of the whole country. At this juncture, if the Madras Council had only possessed ordinary firmness and ability, they might have considered the former treaty annulled, and while dictating their own terms as to the Carnatic and expenses of the war, have occupied the Northern Circars in virtue of the Emperor's free gift. But they did neither; and the treaty of Madras, between the Nizam and the Council, signed February 28th, 1768, contained conditions so impracticable, that it met with the stern reproof of the directors at home, as well as producing a war with Hyder Aly, then at the zenith of his power.

The Madras Government not only denounced Hyder as an usurper and freebooter, but they also agreed to take the tableland of Mysore from him, and hand it over to the Nizam, as well as paying the Nizam a large annual sum for that and the Northern Circars, to which they already had a legal claim by the Emperor's free gift, if Mysore should be conquered. This was a feeble imitation of Clive's action respecting the Dewany or double government in Bengal; but the only effect in Madras was to make a bitter enemy of Hyder Aly for the rest of his life. The directors commented most severely on the treaty, and anticipating the possible consequences which might ensue respecting their possessions in India, they observe: "The protection of these is easily within reach of our power, and may mutually support each other, without any country alliance whatever. If we pass these bounds, we shall find no security but in the subjection of the whole, which, by dividing our force, would lose us the whole, and end in our extirpation from Hindostan." In a subsequent despatch they add, "Instead of pursuing pacific measures with Hyder Aly, as we think you ought to have done, knowing as you did our sentiments with respect to extending our territories, you have brought us into such a labyrinth of difficulties, that we do not know how we shall be extricated from them."

The directors then go on to recommend that "if Hyder Aly be extirpated," the rajahs and others whom he had dispossessed should be restored. So far, however, from Hyder having been "extirpated," he appeared in May, 1768, with his army before Ban-

HYDER ALI

galore, which the English commander precipitately abandoned, leaving even his sick and wounded and artillery behind him. Freed thus from the presence of the English, Hyder held all the native princes to ransom, and by these means obtained funds for the prosecution of the war against Madras. If the Council had only attended to the advice of the directors, they would have met Hyder half-way, and a treaty for the mutual advantage of both might have been concluded without war.

After various incidents which took place during the second war with Hyder, amongst them being the remarkable march of Hyder at the head of 6,000 chosen cavalry, advancing 130 miles in three days and a half, and bringing him within five miles of Madras, the Council were obliged to treat with the sovereign of Mysore, and in April, 1769, peace was concluded between them. By this treaty mutual conquests were to be restored; an offensive and defensive alliance between Hyder and the English was agreed upon; and worse than all, the English were saddled with the whole expenses of the war. The best excuse which can be made for this hasty treaty was given by the Council of Madras, who, in their defence, declared that they had made peace because they had no more money to make war.

Towards the close of the year 1769, after the treaty with Hyder Aly had been made, Warren Hastings arrived at Madras, and took his seat as member of the Council. At that period, owing to the war and the incompetency of the Government, the trade of the Company was in a very disorganized state. Hastings' natural tastes would have led him rather to political than to commercial pursuits, as the experience which he had acquired under Clive in Bengal proved his competency as a diplomatic agent. But Hastings likewise knew that the favour of his employers depended chiefly on their dividends, and that their dividends depended chiefly on judicious investments. He therefore wisely determined to apply his vigorous mind for a time to this department of business, which had been much neglected since the Madras Council had ceased to be clerks, and had become negotiators and conductors of war instead.

In the course of his two years' residency at Madras, Hastings effected, as Clive had done at Calcutta five years before, some important reforms. The directors of the East India Company notified their high appreciation of his services, and were so much pleased with his conduct at Madras, that they considered him the most efficient person to place at the head of the new Government in Bengal, for which place he sailed in the early part of the year 1772.

CHAPTER XVI.

WARREN HASTINGS' GOVERNMENT OF BENGAL, TO THE END OF THE ROHILLA WAR.

A.D. 1772—1774.

WARREN HASTINGS arrived at Calcutta in February, 1772, but did not take his seat as President of the Council until the April following, devoting the interval to a close study of the machine which he was expected to regulate, and which he found to be cumbersome and ill-adapted to the work which it was expected to perform. Bengal was still governed according to the system which Clive had devised fifteen years before, which, though skilfully contrived for the purpose of facilitating and concealing the great revolution which transferred all real power from the native princes to a company of English traders fifteen thousand miles distant, when that revolution was complete, could produce nothing but inconvenience. Thus there were two governments at the same time, the real and the ostensible. The supreme power belonged to the East India Company, and was in truth a most despotic power, the only restraint being the justice and humanity of the English conquerors. But though thus absolute, in reality the English had not yet assumed the style and title of sovereignty; they held their territories in

Bengal as vassals of the Great Mogul; they raised their revenues as collectors appointed by the Emperor of Delhi; their public seal was inscribed with the imperial titles; and their sole currency was that of the imperial coin.

But the great change which had taken place in the political situation of the presidency of Bengal had been met by no adequate change in the condition or powers of its government. This was still the same both in construction and name that it used to be before the battle of Plassey, when the settlement was purely commercial; while the orders from the directors were all framed so as to check every attempt to become lords of the soil of Hindostan. Forgetting that they had already acquired absolute dominion over an extensive district, with a population exceeding the then population of the United Kingdom, the directors were continually reminding their servants that they were the agents, not of a military, but of a trading body; and that every step taken with a view to change the system would be regarded by the directors with extreme displeasure.

For years after Plassey the internal government of Bengal was delegated by the Calcutta Council to a native minister stationed at Moorshedabad, where the Nabob still kept his court. All military and foreign affairs were alike withdrawn from his control; but the other departments of administration were confided to him alone. His own salary amounted to £100,000 per annum, while the allowance of £320,000 a year, guaranteed by treaty to the Nabob, passed through the minister's hands, and was, to a great extent, at his disposal. The collection of revenue, the administration of justice, the maintenance of order, were left to this high functionary; and for the exercise of his immense power he was responsible to the Council at Calcutta alone.

So splendid an appointment was naturally an object of ambition to the most powerful natives. Clive, who, as president, had to make the first appointment, found it difficult to decide between rival candidates. Two, however, stood out prominently from the rest, each of them the representative of a race and of a religion. One of these was Mohammed Reza Khan, a Mussulman of Persian extraction, who, if tried by the standard of Indian morality, might be pronounced a man of integrity and honour. His competitor was a Hindoo Brahmin of the name of Nund Comar, one of the basest scoundrels that ever existed in a land where smooth excuses, elaborate falsehoods, chicanery, perjury, and forgery are the weapons, which are the notorious characteristics of the Bengalese. In Nund Comar these national signs were strongly developed. The servants of the Company had repeatedly detected him in the most criminal intrigues. On one occasion he brought a false charge against one of his co-religionists, and tried to substantiate it by forged documents. At another time it was discovered that while professing the strongest attachment to the English, he was engaged in several conspiracies against them, and in particular, that he was the medium of a correspondence between the court of Delhi and the French authorities at Pondicherry. For these and many other criminal practices he had been long detained in confinement. But his talents for intrigue, together with some influence in certain quarters, had procured his liberation, and he was again at liberty to carry out the designs against the interests of the British in India which the most crafty of the subtle Bengalese could devise.

Clive was unwilling to place a Mussulman at the head of the administration in Bengal; yet he felt it absolutely impossible to confer such immense power upon his Hindu rival, to whom every species of villainy had been repeatedly brought home. Therefore, though the Nabob used his interest in favour of the latter, Clive, after some hesitation, decided wisely in favour of Mohammed Reza Khan. When Hastings became president of the Council at Calcutta, Mohammed had held power seven years. An infant son of Meer Jaffier had become Nabob by his father's death, and the guardianship of the young prince's person had been confided to the minister.

Shortly after Hastings had reached Calcutta he received a letter, addressed by the Court of Directors, not to the Council generally, but to himself in particular, ordering him to arrest Mohammed Reza Khan, together with all his family and partisans, and to institute a strict enquiry into his seven years' administration of the province of Bengal. The dispatch further added that Hastings would do well to avail himself of the assistance of Nund Comar in the investigation. His vices were readily acknowledged; but even from his vices, the dispatch argued, much advantage might be derived, especially if he was properly encouraged by hopes of future reward. Such was the morality which prevailed with the directors of the East India Company in that venal age, when, as Walpole observed of the previous generation, every man had his price. The wily Bengalee had his agents in London, and there is no doubt but that some of the authorities at the East India House were influenced by the solid reasons which those agents skilfully employed.

Hastings bore no good will to Nund Comar. Many years before, a quarrel had arisen between them at Moorshedabad, which all the authority of their respective superiors could hardly compose. To Mohammed, on the contrary, Hastings had no feelings of hostility; nevertheless he proceeded to obey the instructions of the directors with that ready obedience which was a marked feature in his character. He had determined to get rid of the double government in Bengal. The orders of the directors furnished him with the means of effecting his purpose, and dispensed him from the necessity of discussing the matter with his council. He took his measures with his usual skill and vigour. At midnight the house of Mohammed Reza Khan, at Moorshedabad, was surrounded by a battalion of Sepoys. The minister was aroused from his slumbers, and informed that he was a prisoner. With the creed of a devout Mussulman, he bowed his head and submitted himself to the will of God.

Thus the revolution of transferring the internal administration from Moorshedabad to Calcutta, from native to English hands, was effected without difficulty or danger by the vigorous action of Hastings. A system of civil and criminal justice, under English superintendence, was established. The Nabob was no longer to be permitted to have an ostensible share in the government. As the present one was a minor, it was necessary to provide guardians for his person and property. His person was entrusted to a lady of his father's harem, known by the name of the Munny Begum. The office of treasurer of his household was bestowed on a son of Nund Comar; Hastings considering that as the father's crimes were too notorious to allow of his being employed, it was a master stroke of policy to reward the unprincipled parent by promoting the inoffensive son.

As soon as the old system of double government was dissolved, and the East India Company installed in the full sovereignty of Bengal, Hastings had no motive to treat Mohammed Reza Khan with severity. His trial had been postponed from time to time, on various pleas, till the organization was completed, when he was brought before a committee, over which Hastings, as governor, presided in person. After a long hearing, in which Nund Comar appeared as the accuser, and displayed the inveterate rancour of his base and infamous character to its fullest extent, Hastings pronounced that the charge had not been made out, and ordered the fallen minister to be set at liberty.

Nund Comar had designed not only the complete ruin of his rival, but also to obtain the appointment for himself; but his malevolence as well as his cupidity had been bitterly disappointed. Hastings had made him a tool, and the rival, so long envied and so implacably persecuted, had been dismissed unhurt. The situation so long and ardently desired had been abolished. It was very natural, therefore, that Hastings should from that time be the object of the most intense hatred to the crafty Brahmin; and the time was not far distant when, through the influence of an Englishman in authority, of a character nearly as base as Nund Comar's own, that hatred would exhibit itself in the vilest form, and the desperate and deadly struggle would terminate in the penal death of Hastings' vindictive foe.

In the meanwhile Hastings was compelled to turn his attention to the finances of the East India Company, which, at the time of his becoming president of Calcutta, were in a most embarrassed state, amounting in the year 1772 to nearly £2,000,000 sterling. Among the current expenses to which the presidency was subject, the payments to the Emperor of Delhi, and his nominal viceroy, the Nabob of Bengal, were not the least burdensome; and now that the English had taken on themselves the whole expense of government, Hastings considered that the income of these two decaying potentates might justly bear a reduction. The allowance of the Nabob of Bengal was reduced from the annual payment of £320,000 to half that amount, and which, be it remembered, was still four times as much as the British Government allows at this moment to another dispossessed prince on the other side of India. That of the Emperor of Delhi was withdrawn altogether, on the plea that the representative of the Great Mogul was no longer independent; and inasmuch as he was no longer able to defend the cities of Allahabad and Corah, which the English had ceded to him after the battle of Buxar, in 1764, Hastings thought fit, on the conqueror's principle, to resume possession of them. The situation of these two places was such that there would be little advantage and great expense in retaining them; so Hastings, who wanted a revenue for the Company, which they eagerly sought, and not territory, which they as earnestly declined, determined to sell them. A purchaser was easily found in the then ruler of Oude. This rich province had, in the breaking up of the Mogul Empire fallen to the share of a great Mussulman house, which, in the year 1820, was permitted by the British Government to assume the title of "king," but which was forfeited in less than forty years later, at the time of the great mutiny, when the kingdom of Oude became a part of the British Empire in India.

At this time the ruler of Oude, though he held the power, did not venture to use the style of sovereignty. To the appellation of nabob, or viceroy, he added that of "Vizier of the Monarchy of Hindostan." Shujah-ood-Dowlah, the then ruler of Oude, was on excellent terms with the English, and he was in possession of a full treasury. Allahabad and Corah were so situated that they might be of great use to him, as they could be of none to the Company. So the buyer and seller speedily came to an understanding, and the provinces which had been taken from the rapidly decaying Mogul Empire were made over to the Government of Oude for the sum of half a million sterling.

There was another matter of still greater importance to be settled between the President of Calcutta and the Vizier of the monarchy of Hindostan, which an eminent historian considers, though this is strenuously denied by his biographer, has left "a stain on the fame of Hastings and of England." Among the military adventurers who were allured to the Mogul standards from the neighbourhood of Cabul and Candahar, places which have a fresh interest for us in this year of grace 1881, were several gallant bands known by the name of the Rohillas. Their services had been rewarded with large tracts of land east of Delhi, known as Rohilcund, with the city of Bareilly as its capital. In the general confusion after the death of Aurungzebe, the Rohillas became virtually independent. They were honourably distinguished by courage in war, and by skill in the arts of peace. While anarchy raged from Lahore to Cape Comorin, their little territory enjoyed the blessings of repose. Agriculture and commerce flourished among them; nor were they negligent of the charms of poetry and song. Many persons who have not long passed away could remember having heard aged men talk with regret of the golden days when the Afghan princes ruled in the vale of Rohilcund.

Shujah-ood-Dowlah had set his heart on adding this rich district to his own territory, and he offered the East India Company forty lacs of rupees, or £400,000, the amount of the bond which he had been promised by Hafiz Rehmut Khan, one of the Rohilla chiefs, if he were placed in possession of the province, besides paying the costs of any troops employed in his service. The Rohillas had been unceasingly at war with one or two of the three parties, the Mahrattas, the Emperor of Delhi, and the Vizier of Oude, by whom their district was surrounded, and at different times they had succeeded in playing off one against the other. Hence Hafiz's bond to the Vizier, which, when called upon, he was either unable or unwilling to meet. The Rohillas were no sooner freed from their strongest and most dangerous foes, the Mahrattas, than they forgot the serious obligations under which they had come. They resisted all Dowlah's applications for the forty lacs, and made preparations to overrun and seize a country known as "the Dooab," not for him, but for themselves.

The Vizier was greatly irritated at their fickle and dishonest conduct, and proposed to Hastings that they should be signally punished, hinting at the same time the propriety of displacing these turbulent Afghans, and annexing their territory to that of Oude. And inasmuch as they held the native population in subjection by the right of conquest, just as the English did themselves, and were becoming too weak to maintain themselves in that right, the Vizier could scarcely be expected to put his own power in jeopardy in order to maintain theirs. The question for him to decide was whether he would submit to the occupation of their country by the Mahrattas, or himself take possession, and convert what had hitherto been a source of weakness to one of strength to himself and to the English as well.

It has been well observed that the first duty of those in authority, when making treaties with foreign states, is to try and secure some solid advantage for their own. Hastings, like the rest of the English community in India, felt the force of Dowlah's arguments; he saw at that moment the growing power of the Mahrattas with alarm, and was not less willing than the Vizier himself to impose some check upon it. Mindful of the directors' positive instructions not to grasp at additional territory, he resolved that the Vizier should pay in money for the assistance he craved. Hastings therefore, with the consent of his Council, proceeded to Benares, where a treaty was concluded between the East India Company and the Vizier of the monarchy of Hindostan, which said treaty was confirmed by the Court of Directors at home, as in their despatch of March 3rd, 1775, they say, "*We, upon the maturest deliberation, confirm the treaty of Benares.*" Nevertheless there is no act in Warren Hastings' brilliant career which has brought down upon his head more hostile criticism and animadversion. Macaulay, in the graphic portrait which he has drawn of this wonderful man in his account of the grounds on which the House of Commons might, as he thought, have impeached Hastings, says, "With great diffidence we give it as our opinion that the most correct course on the whole would have been to impeach on the Rohilla charge, and to acquit on the Benares charge. Had the Benares charge appeared to us in the same light which it appeared to Mr. Pitt (who voted for the impeachment upon that ground alone), we should without hesitation have voted for acquittal on that charge. The one course which it is inconceivable that any man of a tenth part of Mr. Pitt's abilities can have honestly taken was the course which he took. He acquitted Hastings on the Rohilla charge. He softened down the Benares charge till it became no charge at all, and then he pronounced that it contained matter for impeachment."

While, therefore, we are decidedly unable to assent to the extremely severe reflections which Macaulay has passed upon Hastings' conduct in the treaty of Benares, which resulted in the Rohilla war, and which met, let it not be forgotten, with the entire approval of the directors at home, so neither can we accept the acquittal which his ardent biographer is ready to bestow on everything said or done by the inculpated Governor-General. The truth lies between the two. It seems inexcusable that any English ruler should have assented to the deliberate hiring of English troops to aid the Vizier of Oude in an act of spoliation. Moreover it was something akin to treachery, because the Rohillas had already professed their attachment to the English, and high trust in their good faith. On the other hand, there was the possibility, and if so, the very grave danger, of the Rohillas coalescing with the Mahrattas and the Emperor against Oude, as well as the necessity of supporting the Vizier of Oude against all possible foes. Consequently, when the Vizier appealed to Hastings to furnish troops for service in Rohilcund, the treaty of Benares left him no option; he was compelled to obey; so in January, 1774, the necessary orders were issued, Colonel Champion assumed the command, and the campaign began.

The Rohillas fought with their accustomed bravery, but the presence of British troops brought the war to a speedy conclusion. On the 23rd April they attacked the Rohillas in position, and defeated them with the loss of two thousand men and their brave leader, Hafez Rehmut Khan, together with one of his sons. Colonel Champion extolled their bravery highly, while he did not spare the severest reproaches upon his ally, the dastardly Vizier of Oude, who fled from the battle-field, leaving the English troops entirely unsupported. And it was not until the most distinguished chiefs had fallen, fighting bravely, that the Rohilla ranks gave way. Then the Vizier and his rabble followers returned to plunder the camp of their valiant enemies, whom they never had dared to look in the face. The English soldiers kept unbroken order while the tents were pillaged by these worthless allies; and many voices were heard to exclaim with bitter sarcasm, "We have had all the fighting, and these rogues are to have all the profit." The Rohillas quickly rallied, however, under a new leader named Fyzoolla Khan, and would inevitably have defeated the Vizier, as soon as the British troops had been withdrawn, but he had skilfully opened negotiations with the new leader, and on Fyzoolla's agreeing to receive a jahgeer, or estate, yielding £150,000 a year, the Rohilla war came to an end.

Whatever blame may be attached to Hastings for consenting to a treaty which required the employment of British troops for such a purpose as we have seen, there can be no question as to the results of his financial policy from the moment he became president of the Council of Calcutta; and it was with lawful pride that he records in his memoirs the following notice: "In less than two years I saw the debt (of £2,000,000) completely discharged, and a sum in ready cash of the same amount actually accumulated in store in the public treasury." Hastings had likewise relieved the finances of Bengal from military expenditure amounting to a quarter of a million per annum, and thrown that charge on the Vizier of Oude. It may with truth be said of Hastings' financial policy, as soon as he became Governor of Bengal, that it was as successful in India as that of another great finance minister's (the late Sir Robert Peel) was seventy years later, by his introduction of free trade in England.

CHAPTER XVII.

THE NEW GOVERNMENT AT CALCUTTA, TO THE DEATH OF NUND COMAR.

A.D. 1774-5.

BEFORE continuing the history of Warren Hastings' rule in Bengal, it may be well to take a survey of the causes which led to the change in the administration of the presidency, and which resulted in the introduction of his unwearied foes into the Supreme Council of Calcutta, where for four years their conduct was such as to render it almost impossible for Hastings to continue in the presidential chair.

At the opening of the session of Parliament in 1772, when Hastings had been appointed to the presidency, the speech from the throne had recommended that some notice should be taken of Indian affairs. About two months later, Clive's old antagonist, Mr. Sullivan, then chairman of the Court of Directors, moved in the House of Commons for leave to bring in a bill "for the better regulation of the affairs of the East India Company and of their servants in India, and for the due administration of justice in Bengal." Sullivan's principal object was to shift all blame from the Court of Directors, and to throw it wholly and solely upon the servants of the

Company. With the unforgiving rancour of little minds, he could not forget the stigma with which Clive had marked his conduct as chairman (then an annual office) seven years before. It will be remembered that some years after Clive had quitted India on his first government of Bengal, the affairs of the Company had fallen into such confusion, through the incompetency of his successors in office, that, notwithstanding the iniquitous behaviour of the directors in endeavouring to rob Clive of the property which he had so fairly won by his brilliant services in India, and which compelled Clive to bring an action against the directors in order to recover his rights, they were forced to seek his aid as the only person competent to deal with the matter and to preserve the empire which he had so gloriously won to the British nation.

Clive, with the nobleness of his nature, at once acceded to their urgent request, generously offered to give up the estate of £30,000 per annum to the Company after a prescribed term of years, while at the same time he stated his resolute determination not to return to India so long as his enemy Sullivan held the office of chairman of the Company. Sullivan was infuriated at this open rebuke, and endeavoured to resist; but though he had a large party of adherents amongst the proprietors of Indian stock, not one could be found to back him in his insane project. Consequently Sullivan had to retire; Clive sailed for Calcutta, and our Indian Empire was saved. The time had now arrived when Sullivan hoped to obtain his revenge; and after using every means in his power to blacken Clive's reputation, Sullivan publicly declared in the House of Commons that he was the fountain-head of all the mischief. Clive, who was then a member of the House, rose to speak in his own defence, and his speech astonished every one by its strong sense and high spirit. He had rarely addressed the House before, and then only in a negligent and off-hand manner. But now that his honour and property were aimed at, the victor of Plassey convinced the most distinguished speakers in that illustrious assembly that one who had become so great in arms was no less great in the art of oratory. The elder William Pitt, then Earl of Chatham, was that night under the gallery of the House of Commons, and he expressed his opinion of the speech by declaring that it was "one of the most finished pieces of eloquence he had ever heard."

Although Clive was subjected by a Committee of the House of Commons to the most unsparing scrutiny of all the acts and motives by which he had effected the great revolution in Bengal, and thus laid the foundation of the British Empire in India, his foes were not permitted to triumph over him. The proceedings of the British House of Commons afforded an admirable foil to the wretched government of Louis XV., which, as Macaulay truly remarks, "had murdered directly or indirectly almost every Frenchman who had served his country with distinction in the East;" as when it was moved that Lord Clive had abused his powers and set an evil example to the servants of the public, the previous question was put and carried; while the motion that Lord Clive had rendered great and meritorious services to his country was carried without opposition. And thus the malignant attack of Sullivan and his adherents completely broke down.

The embarrassments of the East India Company, through the desire of the directors to pay much higher dividends than they were fairly earning, just as certain bank directors have of late been endeavouring to do in this speculative age, and which has brought such distress and ruin on so many innocent families and individuals, had increased exceedingly after failing to obtain assistance from the Bank of England, as heretofore. Mr. Sullivan, as chairman of the Company, was compelled to announce to Lord North, then Prime Minister, that the insolvency and the ruin of the Company was inevitable if they were not allowed to borrow a million more from the confiding public. Thus it happened to the East India Company, as it has happened to others, both before and since, when reduced to the condition of borrowers, those from whom they asked money thought proper to give advice and to interfere in their affairs. Lord North received the application with cold reserve, and referred the directors to Parliament for the aid and assistance which they wanted.

After reducing their dividend from 12½ to 6 per cent., the directors were compelled most unwillingly to apply to Parliament, which resulted in the Government agreeing to lend the Company £1,400,000 on the most severely just conditions, one of them being that the Company should never pay a dividend higher than 6 per cent. until the whole of the debt was discharged. Nor did Lord North cease his interference here. Clive and others had represented both to King George III. and the Government that the Court of Proprietors who formed the East India Company was then a complete bear-garden, full of anarchy, confusion, and the most selfish intrigues, and that the direct influence and intimidation which the proprietors exercised over the directors must for ever prove a bar to all good government. And as if to prepare his way by an act of kindness to the tottering East India Company, Lord North took the fatal step of granting them leave to export tea to America duty free, a bonus which led to the tea riots at Boston, and which hurried on indirectly the War of Independence, by which England lost a greater empire in the West than the one which she was beginning to win, by the genius and skill of Clive and Warren Hastings combined, in the East.

At the same time Lord North brought in a bill which effected a great alteration in the constitution of the Company. The chief principles of this important measure were the formation of a Supreme Court of Judicature at Bengal, consisting of a chief justice and three puisne judges appointed by the Crown, with great and extended powers in civil and criminal causes over natives and English residents in India alike; and also, what proved of unspeakable importance to Hastings on a memorable occasion, it was entirely independent of the Calcutta Council. The constitution of the Council was entirely remodelled. Henceforth it was to consist of a governor-general with four councillors nominated by the Crown, for the first five years having supreme authority over the other presidencies, after which the right of nomination was to be vested in the Court of

Directors, but still subject to the approval of the home Government. It was also enacted that no person serving in India under the Company or the Crown should be allowed to receive presents from any of the native princes or others on any pretence whatever; and that the Governor-General, members of the Council, and judges of the Supreme Court should be forbidden to enter upon any commercial pursuits. Such, in brief, was the "Regulating Act," as it was termed, which was to come into operation in England on October 1st, 1773, and in India on August 1st, 1774.

In proceeding to the choice of the first Governor-General of India, there was no difference of opinion as to the person best qualified for this important and difficult post. When, therefore, the Government nominated Warren Hastings to the office of Governor-General, it met with the unanimous approval of all parties concerned. Clive pronounced him to be the right man in the right place; and cordially offered his congratulations on the appointment, though he expressed a doubt, which the result fully justified, whether his colleagues in the Council would act in harmony with him. And here was the blot, which Clive's profound knowledge of India enabled him to see at a glance, in the working of the new Act. All the four councillors were to have nearly co-extensive powers with the Governor-General, who was only to be allowed a casting vote in the event of the Council being equally divided. Very different from the subsequent construction of the Government, as it has lasted down to the present time, when the Governor-General's voice is supreme, as it ought to be, and the other members of the Council are in the position of assessors or advisers.

The four councillors named by the Crown, who were to govern the British Empire in India conjointly with Hastings during the next five years, were Mr. Barwell, a tried and experienced servant of the Company, then in India, General Clavering, Colonel Monson, and Mr. (afterwards Sir Philip) Francis. Of these three, the first two were mere military ciphers, or rather obedient tools in the hands of the resolute and violent Francis, whose character may be described in a few lines by those who were the best judges; and almost every action of his after life, from the moment of his landing in India until he descended into his grave, "Unwept, unhonoured, and unsung," displays his nature in the worst and most lurid light. Even Macaulay, who would fain throw a veil over the dark spots of his character, from the probability of his having been the author of "Junius," as well as for his association in after days with the illustrious Edmund Burke and other eminent Whigs before the disruption of the party, is obliged to confess that "Francis's hatred was of intense bitterness and long duration." Pitt told him to his face in the House of Commons, even though he sided with him in the matter of impeachment, that his "conduct both in India and in Parliament was most dishonest and malignant." While Hastings himself publicly charged Francis with having deceived him, and with having induced Barwell to quit India with insincere promises which were broken on the first opportunity. "I do not," said Hastings, in a minute recorded on the Consultations of the Government, "I do not trust to

Mr. Francis's promises of candour, convinced that he is incapable of it. I judge of his public conduct by his private, which I have found to be void of truth and honour."

Such was the character of the man who ruled the majority of the Council which presided over the destinies of the British Empire in India; and it is not too much to say that if the death of Colonel Monson had not intervened, and by this means restored Hastings to power, of which he had been so foolishly deprived, our rule in Hindostan might have come to an end as rapidly as it had been acquired, leaving behind nothing but the vision of a mighty and ill-starred dream.

No sooner had the new councillors arrived at Calcutta, than they commenced their quarrel by studied insults to the Governor-General, and by making the most ridiculous complaints to the directors at home; their first one being that Hastings had only allowed them a salute of seventeen guns from the batteries of Fort William, whereas their high-mightinesses considered themselves of sufficient importance to entitle them to a salute of four guns more.

No sooner were Francis and his two incompetent followers installed in office, than they instantly wrested the government out of the hands of Hastings, who was supported only by Barwell; condemned all his previous acts, without condescending to examine whether they were just or not; recalled the English resident whom Hastings had sent to Oude, and replaced him by a creature of their own; ordered Colonel Champion to return with his brigade, which

CALCUTTA.

Hastings was bound by treaty to lend to the Vizier of Oude, within the Company's territories, and instituted a severe inquiry into the conduct of the war. But for various incidents which happily were overruled for good, this incompetent trio in the depth of their ignorance and conceit would have lost all that Clive and Hastings had won in India. It was with the greatest difficulty that Hastings succeeded in persuading them to pause for a single day in the mad and reckless career on which they were determined to enter. Hastings reminded them that one of their own body was not then in Calcutta, and that his arrival was not expected until four days later; and he so far succeeded, that they consented to defer their next meeting until the 25th, but beyond this they refused to yield a jot. "These men," said Hastings in a letter to a friend, "began their opposition on the second day of our meeting. The symptoms of it betrayed themselves on the very first. They condemned me before they could have read any part of the proceedings, and all the study of the public records since, all the information they have raked out of the dirt of Calcutta, and the encouragement given to the greatest villains in the province, are for the purpose of finding grounds to vilify my character, and undo all the labours of my government."

The next step which this wretched trio attempted to take was still worse. In spite of the Governor-General's earnest remonstrances, they proceeded to exercise their new authority over the subordinate presidencies of Madras and Bombay in the most reckless manner, threw their affairs into confusion, and interfered, with an incredible mixture of feebleness and rashness combined, in the disputes of the Mahratta Government. At the same time they fell on the internal administration of Bengal, and attacked the whole fiscal and judicial system, without making the least attempt to establish any better way. The effect of their high-handed proceedings was that all protection to life and property was withdrawn, and that gangs of robbers plundered and slaughtered with impunity in the very suburbs of Calcutta. Hastings continued to live in the Government House, and even to take the lead at the Council-board in the transaction of ordinary business; for his opponents could not but be conscious of their own ignorance and incompetency. But the higher powers of government, and that which is of the most vital importance always and everywhere, especially in India, when the British Empire was gradually beginning to rise on the ruins of fallen dynasties—the act of patronage—had been taken from him.

The natives were not long in discovering the altered position of the Governor-General. They regarded him as a fallen man, and they acted as men of the basest character always will act on such occasions even unto the world's end. Macaulay, who himself, as a member of that very same Supreme Council of Bengal half a century later, was more competent than most men to express an opinion on the subject, declares that "An Indian government has only to let it be understood that it wishes a particular man to be ruined, and in twenty-four hours it will be furnished with grave charges, supported by depositions so full and circumstantial, that any person unaccustomed to Asiatic mendacity would regard them as decisive. It is well if the signature of the destined victim is not counterfeited at the foot of some illegal compact, and if some treasonable paper is not slipped into a hiding-place in his house."

Such was the position of Hastings at the mercy of his malignant and vindictive enemies. The power to make or mar the fortune of every one in Bengal had passed into the hands of Francis and the new councillors. Immediately charges of the vilest description began to pour in against the devoted Governor-General, and, to the unutterable shame and disgrace of all concerned, they were eagerly welcomed by Hastings' triumphant foes. It would have been strange if at such a juncture Nund Comar had remained quiet. That bad man was stimulated at once by malignity, avarice, ambition, and revenge. Now was the time to be avenged on his old enemy, to wreak a grudge of many years' standing, to establish himself in the favour of the ruling powers of the Supreme Council, and to become the greatest native in Bengal.

From the moment of their arrival, directly it was known that the new councillors were in deadly enmity with the Governor-General, Nund Comar began to fawn upon them with all the subtle arts of a wily Bengalee. He now put into the hands of Francis, with much ceremony, a paper containing a long list of the most foul calumnies against the Governor-General. By this document, Hastings was charged with putting offices up for sale, and of receiving bribes for suffering offenders to escape in the most unblushing manner. In particular, it was alleged that Mohammed Reza Khan had been dismissed with impunity, in consideration of a large sum of money paid privately to the Governor-General.

Although there was not a single iota of truth in any of these charges, Francis, with indecent haste, and with feelings congenial to the basest of human characters, read aloud this infamous paper to the Council. A violent altercation followed. Hastings refused to allow the Council to sit in judgment on the Governor-General, maintaining, with his accustomed dignity, that the Council-room was not the proper place for such an investigation, nor were Francis and his coadjutors, blinded as they were by malevolence and passion, the proper parties to be his judges. At the next meeting of the Council, another communication from Nund Comar was produced, in which he begged for permission to attend in person, and that he might be heard in support of his assertions. Hastings, feeling that he could not, without betraying the dignity of his office, submit to be confronted with such a scoundrel as Nund Comar, declared the sitting at an end, and left the room, followed by Barwell. Francis and his two obsequious followers kept their seats, voted themselves a council, and ordered Nund Comar to be brought in. The wretched man not only adhered to his original charges, but, after the fashion of the East, added a large supplement. Amongst others, he put in a letter purporting to bear the seal of the Munny Begum, the appointed guardian of the young Nabob, for the purpose of establishing the truth of his story. The seal and the letter were alike forged; the Munny Begum denied having written such a letter; and after the death of this infamous character there were found in his house counterfeit seals of all the leading men in Bengal. What would be thought in the present day if a majority of Her Majesty's Cabinet Council were to receive similar accusations against the Prime Minister of the day, made by a scoundrel with the gallows stamped on every feature, and without the slightest attempt to discover the truth, to declare that they were all genuine and true? And yet, such was the animosity of Francis and his followers, that they voted Hastings had corruptly received between thirty and forty thousand pounds, which he ought to be compelled to refund.

The general feeling among the English in Bengal was strongly in favour of the Governor-General. In talents for business, in knowledge of the natives, and in courtesy of demeanour towards his fellow-countrymen, Hastings was far superior to his unworthy persecutors. The officials of the Company were naturally disposed to side with the most distinguished of their own body, who had ruled mankind, both at Madras and Calcutta, with signal success, against a mere clerk from the War Office in London, which had been the previous occupation of Francis, who, profoundly ignorant of the native languages, as well as of the native character, took on himself to regulate every department of the administration. And as it was once said of an illustrious Roman, "Nihil erat quod non tetigit: nihil quod tetigit non ornavit," it may be said with equal truth of Francis, in an opposite sense, there was nothing with which he did not *meddle*, and in so doing there was nothing which he did not *muddle*.

The triumph of Nund Comar seemed to be complete. He held a daily *levée*, to which his countrymen resorted in crowds, to triumph over the fallen Governor-General ; and, to their shame be it said, to this *levée* Francis and the majority of the Council condescended to repair. The lengths to which they were prepared to go in their rancorous animosity against Hastings, and their readiness to accept the testimony of the villainous Brahmin, whose lies and forgeries had been detected and exposed over and over again, may be seen in the minute drawn up by Francis and his associates, bearing date April 11th, 1775, when, speaking of Nund Comar, and felicitating themselves on the able assistance which he had afforded them, they say, "Whatever might have been his motives, his discoveries have thrown a clear light upon the Honourable Governor-General's conduct, and the means he had taken of making *the very large fortune which he is said to possess*, of upwards of forty lacs of rupees (£400,000), which he must have amassed in two and a half years."

Happily we have the means of proving the falsehood of this insinuation, which implies that Hastings, by the most flagitious means, had amassed a fortune of £400,000 in the course of two and a half years. Warren Hastings remained at the head of the Government until 1785, having held the office of Governor-General for the space of thirteen and a half years, during which period, if he had been the base character which Francis and his colleagues pretended, he had ample opportunities of making a fortune ten times over the amount which they accused him of having made in two and a half years. Yet when he returned to England, and was subjected to the enormous expenses of the impeachment (caused by Francis having poisoned the mind of one of England's greatest worthies, the noble-minded Edmund Burke, together with the tergiversation of William Pitt at a critical moment), the whole of his fortune, which amounted to only £100,000, was entirely absorbed in the proceedings, which extended over a course of seven years; so that had not the East India Company come forward on his behalf (as indeed they were bound by every principle of justice to do), Warren Hastings, the first and most illustrious of the many great Englishmen who have held the office of Governor-General during the last 107 years, might have died a pauper in the workhouse!

But we must hasten to the *denouement* of this episode in Hastings' grand career, and which has left such an indelible stain on the name of Francis. The house of Nund Comar having been made an office for the purpose of receiving charges against the Governor-General, as well as an audience chamber to which the majority of the Supreme Council thought it decent to resort, the villainous Brahmin succeeded, partly by threats and partly by wheedling, in inducing many of the wealthiest natives of Bengal to send in complaints against Hastings. But he was playing a dangerous game. Nund Comar, with all his subtlety, did not understand the nature of the institutions under which he was living. He was sharp enough to perceive that the majority of the Supreme Council made treaties, raised taxes, bestowed places, and were filled with envy and hatred against the Governor-General. But the separation between the political and judicial mode of government was a thing of which he had no conception. It had never occurred to him that there was in Bengal an authority perfectly independent of the Supreme Council, an authority which could protect one whom the Council wished to destroy, and send to the gibbet one whom the Council desired to protect. Yet such was the fact. The Supreme Court was, within the sphere of its own duties, altogether independent of the Government. The judges, like the entire English colony in Calcutta, were hostile to the outrageous proceedings of the majority of the Supreme Council, and the time had now arrived for testing who was to be master in the coming struggle.

On a sudden the whole community at Calcutta, natives and Europeans alike, were startled by the news that Nund Comar had been arrested on the charge of forgery, and cast into prison. The charge was brought by a native merchant, and though by the law of England forgery remained a capital crime for more than half a century later, witness the death of Fauntleroy, it was thought so lightly of in India, and had been committed so frequently by the accused, that the natives were overcome with surprise and astonishment. But if the native mind was excited by this unexpected *coup*, that of Francis and his colleagues was ten times more so. They saw the only witness they could depend on for effecting the ruin of the Governor-General escaping from their hands. Their rage rose to the highest pitch. They protested against the proceedings of the Supreme Court, and sent repeated messages to the judges, commanding them to admit the wretched Nund Comar to bail. The judges returned resolute answers, and very properly refused to obey. All that Francis and his coadjutors could do was to prove their indecent animosity by heaping honours and emoluments upon the family of the accused.

In the meanwhile the time for the assizes drew near; a true bill was found against the prisoner, and Nund Comar was tried by Sir Elijah Impey, the Chief Justice, and the other judges, together with a jury composed entirely of Englishmen. An enormous amount of contradictory swearing, and the necessity of having every word of the evidence interpreted and carefully sifted, protracted the trial to an unusual length; and when at last a verdict of guilty was returned, and Nund Comar paid the forfeit of his life on the gallows, it was felt by all that Calcutta was well rid of one of the most consummate scoundrels that ever existed.

As Francis's few friends endeavoured to raise a cry charging the Governor-General and the Chief Justice with being the cause of Nund Comar's death, it may be well to point out that the proceedings in the House of Lords during the impeachment of the latter, some years later, proved them to be guiltless of such a charge. What are the facts of the case? Nund Comar had a fair and protracted trial before a body of twelve impartial English jurymen. All the judges concurred in the verdict. The Chief Justice had no power to stay the execution for a single day. The only party which had the power of reprieve pending a reference to the directors at home was the majority of the Supreme Council. Why did they not exercise this power? The Rev. G. R. Gleig, the biographer of Hastings, observes with great force, that "they had the matter entirely in their own hands. By a simple vote they might have suspended the execution. Why did they, who were so zealous in Nund Comar's cause prior to conviction, sit with folded arms and see their *protégé* put to death? In their despatches which succeeded the event, as well as in Burke's speeches during the trial of Hastings, some clue may be discovered. It might not suit the purpose of the majority to save the life of Nund Comar; it might suit that purpose that they were able, however groundlessly, to assert that 'the Governor-General murdered him through the hands of Sir Elijah Impey.' For even to this day the impression has not everywhere been removed, that Mr. Hastings was censurable for failing to effect that which he had no power to effect. The will of the majority was law. Had they willed a reprieve for Nund Comar, he must have received the benefit of it. On their heads, then, and not on that of Mr. Hastings, must the death of the culprit rest." ("Life of Hastings," ii., p. 5.)

CHAPTER XVIII.

THE NEW GOVERNMENT AT CALCUTTA, TO THE TREATY WITH THE MAHRATTA CHIEFS.

A.D. 1775-6.

WE have already seen that one of the first acts of Francis and his submissive colleagues, on their reckless determination to oppose the Governor-General in every possible way, was to recall his British brigade from Oude, notwithstanding the treaty which entitled the Vizier to its assistance, and by which the East India Company had profited so much. But though the war with the Rohillas, waged by the Vizier and his English allies, was to be reprobated, the sovereign of Oude was not only to be compelled to pay the whole expenses of the war, but he was to be bullied into earlier payments than he had stipulated for. Thus, if they considered the Rohilla war, as they termed it, "diabolical," they could still determine to profit by the devil's wages in grasping more of the Vizier's treasures than they were entitled to. It was in vain that Hastings and Barwell remonstrated; they were but two to three; and the determination of Francis was carried into instant execution. The Vizier, Shujah-ood-Dowlah, was so terrified by the injustice with which he had been treated by the majority of the Supreme Council, that he died a few months after, addressing in his last moments a touching letter to Hastings to implore his friendship and protection for his son.

The son, Asof-ood-Dowlah, succeeded without opposition to Oude and its dependencies. Francis with his majority had dismissed Mr. Middleton, the able Resident at the court of Oude, for no other reason than his having been appointed by Hastings, and sent a creature of his own in Middleton's place. The new Resident forced the young Vizier to accede to a new treaty incomparably more questionable than the previous one made by Hastings. By this treaty the East India Company guaranteed to Asof-ood-Dowlah the possession of Corah and Allahabad, but required in return that he *should cede to the Company the territory of Cheyte Singh, the Rajah of Benares, which was not his to cede, and what had been solemnly guaranteed to the Rajah by the Governor-General.* Hastings indignantly refused to sanction this treaty, which nevertheless met with the warm approbation of the directors at home, because it added between two and three millions sterling to their annual revenue of the territory which they plundered from Cheyte Singh, who, if it be allowable to make a pun on the name, was certainly in this instance *cheated* out of his own by the infamous Francis and his submissive allies.

Nor was their conduct towards the other presidencies much better. Though the provisions of the Act of Parliament, which gave the Supreme Council at Calcutta authority over the other presidencies at Madras and Bombay, were well intended and eventually beneficent to the British rule in Hindostan, for the two years in which the Supreme Council was ruled by the reckless and incompetent trio, the Act proved most detrimental and injurious to our empire there. The political state of Bombay at that time was as bad as bad could be. They had entered into the stormy sea of Mahratta politics, and the unhappy interference of Francis had only made matters ten times worse. The first temptation had been the rich island of Salsette, adjoining Bombay, which formerly belonged to the Portuguese, but who had been expelled from it in 1739, and which had been long coveted by the English in India, as well as by the directors at home. In the year 1773, after various attempts had failed, advantage was taken of the civil war which ensued on the assassination of Narráin Ráo, and the election of his uncle, Rughonath Ráo, or Rughoba, as he was more commonly called, as Péshwah. The odium of the assassination rested on Rughoba for a time, as a servant of his had done the deed in the confusion arising from a party of Narráin's soldiers, who were in arrears of pay, having mutinied and invaded the palace. But it was proved afterwards that the order to "seize" Narráin Ráo had been altered to "kill" him, and the Mahratta nation acquitted Rughoba of the murder. The Council of Bombay, however, gladly seized the opportunity of dispatching a considerable force to Salsette, which carried the principal fort by assault, and then took possession of the island.

To secure this valuable possession, and to obtain future cessions of territory in the neighbourhood of Surat, which may be considered as the cradle of the

British Empire in India, the Bombay Council concluded a treaty with Rughoba, whom for the nonce they accepted as the legitimate Péshwah of the Mahrattas, who were much divided in opinion whether the legitimate right or might rested with Rughoba or with a posthumous son of Narráin Ráo, called Mahdoo Narráin, who had been installed by Rughoba's opponents as Péshwah when a babe only forty days old. Rughoba, who made sure of the English support, granted without hesitation Salsette, Bassein, and other places, and the Bombay Council sent Colonel Keating with a force of over two thousand troops to assist Rughoba, who himself possessed a large force of Mahratta cavalry. On the 18th of May, 1775, Keating defeated a Mahratta army hostile to Rughoba, on the plains of Arras, and was on the point of taking possession of Poonah, the Mahratta capital, in conjunction with Rughoba, when the unwise interference of the meddlesome Francis prevented so desirable a result.

At this moment the reckless majority in the Supreme Council at Calcutta thought proper to show their power, and they did so in the same unhappy temper which they had displayed on other occasions. After rating the Council at Bombay as if they had been a set of schoolboys, Francis and his colleagues ordered them instantly to withdraw their army, haughtily informing them that they had no business to undertake such important matters without their sanction, and that they should send a servant of their own, Colonel Upton, to Poonah to pursue a different policy. When Colonel Upton arrived at the close of the year 1875, it was found that his instructions were to treat with the chiefs of the Mahratta confederacy, which the majority of the Supreme Council considered as likely to be the strongest in the end. But he was also provided with a letter for Rughoba, in case he should prove the winner. If the confederacy prevailed, the letter was to be burnt; if Rughoba, then the instructions to the confederated chiefs were to be treated in the same way. Such was the crooked policy of the meddlesome Francis and his incompetent allies.

Colonel Upton had only been a few days at Poonah ere he found the Mahratta chiefs were much in the same uncertain state of mind as the unworthy trio. "For," said he in his letter to the Calcutta Council, "the chiefs of this country are quite at a loss which side to take, and are waiting to see what the English will do"—which reminds us of the well-known epigram composed on the occasion of the Walcheren expedition, some forty years later, when the chiefs of the army and navy appear to have been in a somewhat similar degree of uncertainty:—

> "The Earl of Chatham, with his sword drawn,
> Stood waiting for Sir Richard Stra'hn;
> Sir Richard Stra'hn, longing to be at 'em,
> Stood waiting for the Earl of Chatham!"

The pertinacity of the Mahratta chiefs in insisting on the restoration of the island of Salsette, Bossein, and all that had been acquired by the recent treaty with Rughoba, removed the vacillations of the Supreme Council, who finally determined that the Péshwah recognized by the Bombay Council was to be recognized by them also; and that the cause of

Rughoba was to be supported, as they said, "with the utmost vigour, and with a general exertion of the whole power of the English arms in India." Rughoba, however, gained nothing by this pompous proclamation. His foes jockeyed him at the moment he thought he was sure of the prize; for the Mahratta chiefs at length agreed to yield Salsette, on finding the English were determined to have it; on which the majority of the Supreme Council instantly threw Rughoba overboard, and agreed to give up the claim to Bassein and the other territory, which the *then* lawful, but *now* unlawful Péshwah had given to the presidency of Bombay as the price of the English assistance. Hastings and Barwell had protested against this treaty; and the directors at home, finding that they had lost Bassein and the territories which Rughoba had conceded to them, and consequently some addition to the revenue which they eagerly sought, expressed their disapproval of the treaty likewise. Such was the fiasco caused in the affair of Rughoba by the blundering Francis and his incompetent allies.

In the meanwhile intelligence of the Rohilla war, and of the first disputes between Hastings and his colleagues, had reached London. The directors took the part of the majority, and severely condemned Hastings for sanctioning a war which appeared merely for the sake of pecuniary advantage; but they entirely forgot that if Hastings had by improper means obtained pecuniary advantages, he had done so, not for his own, but in order to meet their incessant demands for an increased revenue. To insist upon honesty in dealing with the natives, and also upon having what could not be honestly got, was then the constant practice of the directors at home. As Lady Macbeth says of her husband—

> "What thou wouldst highly,
> That wouldst thou holily; wouldst not play false,
> And yet wouldst wrongly win."

The Regulating Act of 1773, by which Hastings had been appointed Governor-General for five years, empowered the Crown to remove him on an address from the East India Company. Lord North, then Prime Minister, was anxious to procure such an address. Francis, with Clavering and Monson, the unworthy trio who had misgoverned India for the last two years, were men of his own choice. Lord North's wish was to remove Hastings, and put Clavering in his place. In the Court of Directors, parties were so evenly balanced that eleven voted for Hastings, and the same number against him. The Court of Proprietors was then convened to decide the point. Notwithstanding the most unscrupulous means were used by the Government to crush Hastings, when no less a number than forty-nine peers and privy councillors were counted among the crowd of proprietors by whose means the Government hoped to triumph—notwithstanding all this, so convinced were the great body of proprietors of the incompetence of Francis and his coadjutors, and that the Governor-General was the only man able to govern India in the critical state of their affairs, that Hastings triumphed by more than one hundred votes over the combined efforts of the directors and the Government. The ministers were

12

greatly exasperated by this defeat. Even the easy-going Prime Minister threatened to convoke Parliament without delay, and to bring in a bill for depriving the East India Company of all political power, and for restricting it to its old business of trading in silks and teas.

Colonel MacLeane, Warren Hastings' agent in London to defend his interests with the directors, considered that the Governor-General was in imminent danger of being turned out and branded with parliamentary censure. It seemed, therefore, that the time had come for securing an honourable retreat. Colonel MacLeane, in a long despatch dated November 10th, 1776, gives a full account of the negotiations which were carried on between Hastings' friends on the one part, and with the directors and the Government on the other. At a meeting held by the former at Haldon House, near Exeter, the seat of Sir Robert Palk, who was president of the Madras Council when Hastings was its most efficient member, terms were agreed upon for continuing the negotiation, and which eventually induced MacLeane to produce the resignation with which he had been entrusted by Hastings, to be used only in case of necessity. The instrument was not drawn up very clearly, but the directors were not particular. They accepted the resignation, fixed upon one of their own body, a Mr. Wheeler, unknown to fame, but acceptable to Lord North, to succeed Hastings, and sent out orders that General Clavering should exercise the functions of governor-general till Wheeler should arrive.

Hastings' friends had just cause for dissatisfaction

with Lord North. It was at the instigation of the Prime Minister that Hastings was nominated as the first Governor-General of India, the only man in England then qualified for so important a post, now that Lord Clive was sinking into his grave. From Lord North Hastings had received every encouragement at communicate freely with the king's minister; by Lord North he had been exhorted to bear patiently the annoyances to which the ignorance and prejudices of his colleagues might subject him; on Lord North therefore he relied with perfect confidence for the vindication of his policy and good name from the calumnies with which both were assailed.

In Lord North, however, Hastings was painfully deceived. Not that the easy-going Prime Minister was in anywise opposed to Hastings, and the result proved two years later that Lord North was conscious of Hastings' vast superiority to his inefficient colleagues; but General Clavering's parliamentary interest was very great, and Hastings had none at all. Lord North had not sufficient strength of mind to resist the pressure that was put upon him for the purpose of removing Hastings from the post which he was so well qualified to fill, and allowing Clavering to step into his place. But so palpable was Clavering's incompetency after two years' experience of his powers as member of the Supreme Council, that at the very time he was to supersede Hastings, the latter, writing home to a friend, under date of September 26th, 1776, after alluding to "the crude and confused ideas of General Clavering," says, "If Clavering is destined to be the scourge of God for the correction of this miserable people, he will need no aids to his own malevolence and ignorance for accelerating the ruin of this country."

Happily for the existence of the British Empire in India, Clavering never presided over the Council of Calcutta; and Francis's vindictive power passed away, leaving nothing behind but the shadow of a hideous and troubled dream. While the directors and proprietors at home were squabbling about Hastings, and the way by which they could rid themselves of the only man in their service fit to rule India, a great change had taken place in Bengal. Colonel Monson died the day before Hastings' letter was written, with the character of General Clavering given above. Thus only four members of the Supreme Council were left; Clavering and Francis on the one side, Hastings and Barwell on the other; and by the Regulating Act of Parliament the Governor-General had the casting vote. Thus Hastings, who had been during the last two years destitute of all power and patronage, became all at once master of the situation. He instantly proceeded to undo all the evils which Francis and the majority had attempted. Their measures were reversed; their creatures were displaced. A new valuation of the lands of Bengal, for the purpose of taxation, was ordered, and it was provided that the whole inquiry should be conducted by the Governor-General, and that all letters relating to it should run in his name.

Hastings, at the time when he had recovered the proper power which should always belong to the Governor-General, began to revolve in his mind some of those vast plans for the consolidation of the British Empire in India—plans which, though he was not permitted to carry into effect himself, he lived to see realized before his death in 1818. He saw that our empire had already become the pivot round which all the states of Hindostan were revolving. He cast his eyes over the map of India, and beheld three detached countries, each of them greatly superior in population to European kingdoms of the first class in the middle of the eighteenth century; viz., the Mahrattas, a powerful confederation of principalities; Hyder Aly, now king of Mysore; and Mohammed Ali, sovereign of the Deccan; with many smaller states, all of them intent on watching the growth of the British Empire, which already consisted of so large a portion of the north of India, ruled by a handful of Englishmen, and all eager to overwhelm it on the very first opportunity. Nevertheless the directors at home desired the Governor-General to hold entirely aloof from these states, and to have no communication with them, friendly or otherwise. It was easy to issue such orders, but impossible for Hastings to obey them, because the same authority required him to exercise the most rigid economy in their military establishments, on the efficiency of which the existence of their power depended. Hastings knew that all the resources of the three presidencies would not suffice to keep together such an army as would enable him, single-handed, to maintain the British Empire in India, were it seriously attacked. If the French should only send an adequate force to India, round which the native powers could rally, our empire might be as speedily overthrown as it had been created. How did Hastings act in this supreme hour of trial and danger? With that far-sightedness which is never found except among statesmen of the highest order, he conceived the idea of that system of subsidizing the native princes, out of which the greatness of the British Empire in India may be said to have arisen. He resolved to contract such intimate alliances with the minor states contiguous to the English territories in Bengal, and to maintain at their expense such a force as should at once protect them from both foreign and domestic violence, and place him in a position to cope with any or all of the greater powers, in the event of their making war against the rising British Empire in India.

CHAPTER XIX.

WARREN HASTINGS GOVERNOR-GENERAL DE FACTO AND DE JURE. THE MARCH ACROSS INDIA.

A.D. 1776—1779.

WHILE Hastings was meditating his vast designs for the consolidation of the British Empire in India, the *Ripon*, which arrived at Calcutta in June, 1777, brought the intelligence that he had ceased to be Governor-General; that his resignation had been accepted; that Wheeler, as we have seen in the preceding chapter, had been appointed in his place, and that until Wheeler arrived the chair was to be filled by General Clavering.

Had Hastings still been in a minority, as he had been during the two previous years, he would probably have retired without any further struggle; but happily for England, by the death of Col. Monson, which gave him the casting vote, he was now the master of British India. He declared that he never had given such positive instructions to his agent, Colonel MacLeane, which could warrant the steps taken at home. He had repeatedly told the directors he would not resign, and with that declaration he could not see how they could have received his resignation. He subsequently stated that though

Col. MacLeane had not acted in accordance with his instructions, he would nevertheless have considered himself bound by that act of resignation, had not General Clavering attempted to seize the supreme power by violence. The General sent for the keys of the fort and treasury, took possession of the records, and held a council with Francis as his sole companion; while Hastings took the chair in another apartment, and Barwell sat with him.

Thus there were two parties, each claiming supremacy, and each possessing some plausible show of right. There was no authority entitled to their obedience within fifteen thousand miles. It seemed as if there was no way of settling the dispute but by an appeal to arms; and from such an appeal, conscious of his integrity, and of his deservedly great influence over the English in India, Hastings was not inclined to shrink. He directed the officers of the garrison at Fort William, and of all the neighbouring stations, to obey no orders but his. At the same time, with admirable judgment, he offered to submit the case to the Supreme Court, and to abide by its decision. Nobody could be treated as a criminal for obeying what the judges should solemnly pronounce to be the lawful government. The boldest man would shrink from taking arms in defence of what the judges should pronounce to be usurpation. Francis and Clavering, after much quibbling and trying to shirk the challenge, at length agreed, though most unwillingly, to abide by the award of the Supreme Court. The court pronounced that the resignation was invalid, and that Hastings was still Governor-General under the Regulating Act of 1773;

and the two defeated members, finding that the sense of the whole community in Calcutta was against them, sullenly acquiesced in the decision.

Happily for the security of the British Empire in India, when Wheeler arrived shortly afterwards, expecting to be Governor-General, and through disappointment and feelings of jealousy sided with the vindictive Francis, General Clavering was removed from the scene of dispute by death; and thus Hastings, supported by Barwell, and possessing still the casting vote, remained master of the situation. Shortly after a marked change took place in the feeling both of the Court of Directors and the ministers of the Crown. All designs against Hastings were dropped; and when his original term of five years, as settled by the Regulating Act, expired, he was quietly re-appointed, to the satisfaction of every patriotic Englishman throughout the world. The fact was, that the fearful dangers to which the British Empire in every quarter was now exposed made Lord North, with his feeble administration, and the Court of Directors alike unwilling to part with a Governor-General whose talents and experience were well known to them, and who had proved himself, now that the star of Chatham and Clive had set, and that of the younger Pitt had not yet risen, the first English statesman of that age.

The crisis was indeed formidable. The great and victorious empire to which George III. had succeeded only eighteen years before, by the most senseless misgovernment, had been brought to the verge of ruin. In America a civil war was raging, caused by the folly of the home administration, and which ended by the loss of that magnificent empire to the British crown. The great powers of Europe, humbled to the dust a few years before by the genius of the elder Pitt, were now rejoicing in the prospect of a signal revenge. The time was approaching when England was to be assailed by the combined fleets of France, Spain, and Holland, and to be threatened by the armed neutrality of the Baltic; when our maritime supremacy was to be in jeopardy; and when the British flag was scarcely able to protect the British Channel. It was then a happy thing for our country, as Macaulay justly declares, that "at this conjuncture, the most terrible through which England has ever passed, Warren Hastings was the ruler of her Indian dominions."

Some months before war was declared in Europe between England and France, the Calcutta Council were alarmed by the news that a French adventurer, calling himself the Chevalier St. Lubin, had arrived at Poonah, the seat of the Mahratta confederacy, with letters and presents from Louis XVI.; and that a treaty hostile to England had been concluded between France and the Mahrattas. Hastings had long reflected on the best means of defending the British Empire in India, and had come to the conclusion that our greatest danger would come from such a union, and that any attempt of the kind ought to be opposed instantly, and with the utmost vigour.

At this critical juncture Hastings received intelligence that a fresh quarrel had broken out among the Mahratta chiefs at Poonah, who constituted a sort of regency; and that a powerful faction, headed by Succaram Bapoo, had declared for Rughoba, whom, as we have before seen, the Supreme Council, when ruled by Francis, had treated so iniquitously, having thrown him overboard after having declared strongly in his favour. No sooner, however, had Hastings recovered his power, and Rughoba's party were appealing to the English for assistance, than Hastings proposed in Council that every assistance should be given him in men and money, and that an army should be sent at once from Calcutta to Bombay. This necessary measure was of course opposed by Francis and Wheeler, but happily for our Empire in India, Hastings was master of the situation, and the plan was adopted without delay.

The question then arose how to get the army from Calcutta to Bombay. If sent by sea, it would have to go round nearly the whole of the immense peninsula of India, and it was not the season for such a voyage, neither were there transports sufficient to convey the troops, nor men of war to give them convoy. The bold idea of a march overland had never yet presented itself to the mind of any Englishman in India, whether soldier or statesman. Hastings, who had studied the capacity of the Sepoys, and had a high opinion of their steadiness and powers of endurance, and had long desired an opportunity of displaying the might of the Company to some of the potentates in the interior, confidently determined upon the land march right across the peninsula, a feat which Alexander the Great had evidently intended more than two thousand years before, but which, through the mutiny of his troops, he was unable to perform.

The army was composed of about 7,000 native troops, commanded by 103 English officers, and accompanied by over 30,000 camp followers; and this numerous host had to march upwards of one thousand miles through unknown territories, where, as the event proved, nearly every kind of obstacle had to be overcome. The command was entrusted to Colonel Leslie, who, having nothing of the spirit or genius of Clive, showed himself quite incapable of carrying out so bold a plan. The army began its march June 12th, 1778, and had not proceeded far when a letter from the English Consul at Cairo brought the intelligence to Calcutta that war had been proclaimed both in London and Paris. Francis and Wheeler, with the incompetency of little minds, proposed that the army should be instantly recalled to Bengal; but Hastings determined that the plan should be carried out, as he was convinced that Calcutta and the river Hooghly might very well be defended without it.

Nothing more clearly displays the vast superiority of Hastings over Francis than their respective actions on this trying emergency. The death of Captain Crawford, one of the best officers on the march, had given Francis an opportunity of recording on the minutes, with the most unblushing mendacity, that three hundred of the Sepoys had already fallen victims to the hardships of the march, whereas up to that time not one single native soldier had died. And such was the unpatriotic nature of his character, and, as Hastings wrote, such "the artifices by which this dangerous man endeavoured to support a sinking cause," that he sent letters to the native princes of

India to inform them of the way in which General Clavering had been dispossessed of the presidential chair which he had unlawfully seized, with the view of inducing them to place no confidence in the present Government, and as it were inviting its subjects to disobey its authority.

Clive, however, could not have acted with more resolute determination or more admirable foresight than did Hastings on this memorable occasion. After ordering the army for Bombay to continue its march as fast as possible, he proceeded to protect Bengal without a moment's delay. The French factories at Chándernagore, on the Hooghly, were seized. Orders were sent to Madras, that Pondicherry, which the French had craftily fortified, contrary to the terms of the treaty, should be instantly occupied. Near Calcutta, works were thrown up which rendered the approach of a hostile fleet impossible, while a competent marine establishment was formed for the defence of the river. Nine new battalions of Sepoys were raised, and a corps of native artillery was formed out of the hardy Lascars of the Bay of Bengal. Having made these admirable arrangements, the Governor-General with calm confidence pronounced the presidency secure from all attack, unless indeed the Mahrattas should march against it in conjunction with the French, which was nigh impossible by the masterly expedition which he had sent overland to the assistance of Bombay.

Colonel Leslie, the commander of the expedition, had been told to consider himself under the orders of the Bombay Council directly he crossed the river Jumna; but the vacillations of the Council, and the incompetency of Leslie himself, speedily proved that he was not equal to the occasion. Hastings then decided upon replacing him by Colonel Goddard, the second in command, whose brilliant success it will be now our pleasing duty to record. Freed from the orders of the incompetent authorities of Bombay, who had hampered his predecessor in the same manner as the Dutch commissioners had Marlborough during his campaign in the Netherlands, or the Spanish Junta Wellington, during the early part of the peninsular war, Goddard continued his march, and crossing the Nerbudda river, soon reached the city of Nagpoor, which Hastings, with a prospective glance, had declared to be the exact and proper centre of all our possessions and connections in India.

By the 1st of December, Goddard had established friendly relations with the Mahrattas of Berar, and soon after he received despatches from Bombay, informing him that the Council had at length sent a force, nearly five thousand strong, under the command of Colonel Egerton, to march on Poonah, and expected that he would meet it in the neighbourhood of that city. By the beginning of January, 1779, Egerton had reached a place called Wargam, within sixteen miles of Poonah, where he was ordered to form a junction with Goddard's army. But here a halt was suddenly called, as a large body of Mahratta horse, many thousand strong, was drawn right across their front.

Unfortunately for the credit of the expedition, the Bombay Council, in the depth of their unwisdom, had sent two civil commissioners to share the authority and direct the movements of Egerton. The civilians allowed themselves to be overcome with unmanly fears, and under the pretext that it would be difficult to feed the troops if they advanced, although they then had provisions for eighteen days, they ordered a retreat. The Mahratta cavalry attacked them, destroyed between three and four hundred of Egerton's force, and carried off the greater part of their baggage and provisions. The two commissioners fell into a state of despair, and Egerton declared it was impossible to lead the army back to Bombay. A deputation was sent to the Mahratta chiefs to know on what terms the army might be allowed to depart in peace, very much in the same way in which an English army, seventy years later, was obliged to submit to Akber Khan, on its retreat from Cabul in the last Afghan war. The Mahratta chiefs demanded that Rughoba should be delivered into their hands. When this was complied with, they asked another price for permitting the army to retreat; viz., that the English should agree to give up all the acquisitions they had made in that part of India since the year 1756, when Clive and Admiral Watson had captured Gheriah and destroyed Angria's piratical fleet; and that orders should be sent to Colonel Goddard to take his army back to Bengal. Egerton and the civil commissioners consented, and signed a treaty to that effect. The Mahratta chiefs, not yet satisfied, then demanded hostages, intimating that they must be men of importance. The army wished that the two commissioners, whose feeble conduct had produced this danger, should be delivered up; but it was finally arranged that two other civilians should be sent to the Mahratta camp. Then, and not till then, the dishonoured army was allowed to depart in peace.

In the meanwhile Goddard had continued his brilliant march on Poonah, in full confidence that he should meet with Egerton's force near that city; but when he reached Boorhaunpoor, on the river which flows into the gulf of Cambay, beside the city of Surat, and nearly one thousand miles from his starting-point at Calcutta, he was compelled to halt, by the most perplexing and contradictory orders sent him by the Bombay Government. According to one dispatch he was told to return to Bengal, in compliance with the recent treaty made with the Mahrattas; by another he was told not to pay any attention to what had been done, while the incompetent commissioners omitted to give him the slightest hint of the disgrace which had befallen the Bombay army.

In this uncertain state Goddard remained at Boorhaunpoor until the beginning of February, 1779, when he learned the true state of affairs. Happily for him and the gallant force under his command, he was no Egerton, nor had he any civilians with him to lead him astray; but with the resolute determination of a Clive he resolved not to be bound by a treaty made by cowards and drivellers, who had no right to include him in their disgrace; so he bravely pushed forward with all possible speed, making for Surat, where he would be in an English settlement, with the sea open to Bombay, and ready to act as occasion might require. Goddard and his Sepoys performed the two hundred and fifty miles' march from Boorhaunpoor to Surat in nineteen days, and entered the latter city amid the acclamations of his wondering fellow-countrymen.

Goddard's army had achieved a triumph in their successful march right across the country, from east to west, more valuable than half a dozen victories. They had left a moral impression on princes and peoples which would not soon be effaced. "Be assured," wrote the Governor-General, with just pride, on hearing of Goddard's success, both in the march to Surat and subsequent victory over the Mahratta army, "that the successful and steady progress of a part, and that known to be but a small part, of the military force of Bengal, from the Jumna to Surat has contributed more than perhaps our most splendid achievements to augment our military reputation, and to confirm the ascendant of our influence over all the powers of Hindostan. To them, as to ourselves, the attempt appeared astonishing and impracticable, because it had never before been made or suggested. It has shown what the British are capable of effecting."

The disgraceful capitulation of Egerton's army at Wargam, the greatest disaster which had befallen the English since their first establishment as a substantive power in the East, was speedily felt in all parts of India. A spirit of dissatisfaction on the part both of the Nizam and Hyder Ali, which had long been suspected, began to show itself. The Rajah of Berar hung back from the projected alliance. The party among the Mahrattas most hostile to the English took fresh courage, and the most dependent of all their allies manifested a change of bearing. Moreover, ample use was made of the reverse by the vindictive Francis, both in the council chamber at Calcutta and also in his letters to the directors at home. He reminded them that he had all along been opposed to the war. He moved, in a formal minute, that Colonel Goddard's army should be recalled to Calcutta, and predicted that the result of persevering in the existing line of policy would bring utter ruin upon the Company's affairs in every part of India.

Happily for England, the prognostications of Francis proved utterly false. The policy was continued, and came triumphant out of the ordeal. Rughoba, escaping from the confinement at Poonah, which the hostile Mahratta chiefs had imposed upon him, took refuge at Surat. At the beginning of the year 1780, Goddard, deservedly promoted to the rank of general, took the field again with his brave and hardy Sepoys. In a few days he reduced the fortress of Dubhoy, and carried by storm the important city of Ahmedabad, the ancient capital of Gujerat. He was suddenly recalled southwards by the intelligence that a Mahratta army under the two great chiefs, Scindia and Holkar, was approaching the city of Surat. On the 8th of March, Goddard had brought his small force within sight of the Mahratta army, which was 40,000 strong; but, undeterred by their superior numbers, Goddard, like Clive at Plassey, determined to attack them at once. On account of their great superiority in cavalry, Scindia and Holkar were for some days enabled to avoid a battle; but early in the morning of the 3rd of April, Goddard, with a select portion of his army, surprised them in their camp, and inflicted on them a decisive defeat. Fleeing in the greatest confusion to the Ghauts, the Mahrattas left Goddard undisputed master of all the country between the mountains and the sea.

Such was the issue of General Goddard's splendid march across India from Calcutta to Bombay; one quite equal, if not superior, to another which has excited such deserved admiration in our own day, the march of Sir Frederick Roberts from Cabul to the relief of Candahar.

CHAPTER XX.

THE WARS WITH HYDER ALI AND TIPPOO SAHIB.

A.D. 1780—1799.

WHILE General Goddard was inflicting so decisive a defeat on the Mahratta army, Hastings had succeeded in forming an alliance with the Rajah of Gohud, a Hindu prince, who possessed an extensive country on the banks of the Jumna, between the territories of Holkar and the kingdom of Oude. At the suggestion of Goddard, Colonel Popham was detached from his army with a small force, with which he not only drove out the Mahrattas from the dominions of the Rajah, but took by storm the fortress of Lahar, the capital of Cutchwagar.

On the news of his success reaching Calcutta, Francis of course protested against any extension of the war; but Hastings, who still retained the casting vote, determined to reinforce him as a meritorious officer who was capable of shaking the power of both Scindia and Holkar in the midst of their own country. Before, however, the reinforcements arrived, Popham, withe xtraordinary skill and daring, took by escalade the fortress of Gwalior, one of the very strongest and most important places in all India, built upon a lofty

AGRA.

and almost perpendicular rock, and defended by a numerous garrison. Although in former times it had been taken more than once during the various wars between the Mussulmans and the Hindus, so strongly had it been fortified by the Mahratta chiefs, that it was considered to be impregnable. As it was only fifty miles from Agra, which was then Scindia's capital, no sooner was it captured by the British than the Mahrattas abandoned all the neighbouring country, and carried their feelings of dismay as far as the capital itself.

Thus the most brilliant successes had been obtained by those two meritorious officers, General Goddard and Colonel Popham, and the Mahratta war promised a complete triumph, when Hyder Ali, who had been concerting schemes with the French at Pondicherry for the space of seven years, determined on opening a campaign against the English. In the summer of 1780 he quitted Seringapatam at the head of an immense force numbering upwards of 85,000 men of all arms, assisted by a small corps of 400 Europeans, chiefly Frenchmen and a few other adventurers.

Before proceeding it may be well to give a brief sketch of the rise of the extraordinary man who had long proved such a thorn in the side of the English. About thirty years before this time, when Clive had just commenced his wondrous career, a Mohammedan soldier of the lowest rank began to distinguish himself in the wars of southern India. His birth was humble; his father had been a petty revenue officer, and his grandfather a wandering and howling Dervish; and as for education he had none. But though thus meanly descended, and unable to read even the letters of the alphabet, no sooner had this adventurer been placed at the head of a small body of troops than he approved himself a man born for conquest and command. Among the crowd of chiefs who were then struggling for a share of the sick man's inheritance in the fast decaying empire of the Moguls, none could compare with him in the qualities of the soldier and statesman. Out of the fragments of the old principalities, which had gone to pieces in the general ruin, he succeeded in forming for himself a great, compact, and vigorous empire, of which he became the first sovereign. Though a tyrant and oppressor of no common order, he saw the utility of protecting his people against all oppression except his own. He was in extreme old age, but his intellect was as clear, and his spirit as high as in the prime of manhood. Such was the great Hyder Ali, the founder of the Mohammedan kingdom of Mysore, and the most formidable enemy with whom the English conquerors of India have ever had to contend.

Had Hastings been governor of Madras, Hyder Ali would have been either made a firm friend or vigorously encountered as an enemy. Unhappily the Council of that presidency provoked their powerful neighbour's hostility without adequate preparation to meet it. On a sudden, in the summer of 1780, an army nearly 100,000 strong, far superior in discipline and efficiency to any other native force that could be found in India, poured down from the highlands of Mysore into the plains of the Carnatic. Hyder Ali was at first triumphant everywhere. The Sepoys in many garrisons flung down their arms. Portobello on the coast, and Conjeveram, close to Madras, were captured and plundered; the people were fleeing in all directions towards the English presidency. The inhabitants of Madras could see by night, from the top of Mount St. Thomas, the eastern sky reddened by a vast semicircle of blazing villages. Blacks and whites alike gathered under the guns of Fort St. George, as the only place where they could be safe; and the beautiful villas, to which our countrymen had been in the habit of retiring after the daily labours of government and trade, were now left without an inhabitant; for bands of the fierce horsemen of Mysore had already been seen prowling among the tulip trees and gardens of the English residents.

To complete the embarrassments of the presidency of Madras, the arrival of a French armament on the coast, to recover Pondicherry and co-operate with Hyder, was confidently reported. Nevertheless, there were means of assembling an army which might have defended the presidency, and even driven the invader back to the mountains of Mysore. And had Hastings been at Madras, in place of the incapable President Whitehill, this would undoubtedly have been done. Sir Hector Munro was at the head of one considerable force; Colonel Baillie was advancing with another, amounting to about 2,500 men. Hyder, without attacking Munro, sent his son, Tippoo Sahib, with a select division of his army, to attack Baillie, whose progress had been delayed by a flood in the river Cortella. Tippoo attacked him, but without result; and Baillie, seeing no means of advancing, requested Munro to march with his whole force, consisting of about six thousand men, to his assistance. Had this been done, one of the greatest disasters that ever befell the British arms in India would have been avoided; and many valuable lives would not have been thrown away. Instead of this, Munro despatched Colonel Fletcher, with only eleven hundred men, to join Baillie, which, after some difficulty, he succeeded in doing.

Their united forces, which amounted to less than four thousand men, were speedily surrounded by the gigantic host of Hyder Ali, over eighty thousand strong, with upwards of sixty cannon. The bravery and steadiness of the Sepoys when commanded by British officers was never more signally displayed than on this memorable occasion. Though worn out by forced marches, and almost sinking with hunger, they repelled charge after charge of Hyder's numerous cavalry; they would have come victorious out of the contest, and Hyder would have retreated, had it not been for the French staff around him. At 7.30 p.m., after the contest had lasted for many hours, and Hyder's troops were commencing to retreat without orders, two tumbrels exploded, killing a number of men, and leaving the English almost without ammunition. Still they continued fighting until nine, when all the Sepoys that remained were broken and cut to pieces. The English survivors, less than four hundred in number, and most of them wounded, gained the summit of a hill, and formed in square; when, after resisting many attacks, Colonel Baillie went forward to ask for quarter, waving his handkerchief and ordering his men to lay down their arms. It is said that Baillie committed a mistake in supposing that his signal was favourably answered;

but the painful result was a cowardly butchery of one half of the English, and a horrible captivity of the rest. Of the eighty-six British officers engaged in the battle, no less than thirty-six were killed and thirty-four desperately wounded. It is melancholy to reflect that had Munro, who was within two miles, only moved up directly he heard the cannonade, the army of Hyder Ali would have suffered a disastrous defeat; instead of which, with a scandalous incapacity, if it does not deserve a severer designation, Munro threw his heavy guns into a tank, so as to render them entirely useless, and then, without firing a shot, retreated with his whole army in precipitate confusion to Madras. Thus perished a reputation which, sixteen years before, had risen high at the battle of Buxar, with scarcely a larger force than he then had at his disposal, when he overthrew the confederate forces of Meer Cassim and the Vizier of Oude, upwards of thirty thousand strong, took from them one hundred and thirty cannon, and by this brilliant victory had the whole of Bengal at his feet.

Thus in three weeks from the commencement of Hyder's invasion the British Empire in Southern India had been brought to the verge of ruin. Only a few fortified places remained to us. The glory of our arms had departed by the disastrous defeat of Baillie and the shameful retreat of Munro. Then it was that the fertile genius and serene courage of Hastings achieved their most signal triumph. A swift ship flying before the south-west monsoon brought the evil tidings in a few days to Calcutta. In twenty-four hours the Governor-General had framed a complete plan adapted to the altered state of affairs. The struggle with Hyder was a struggle for life and death. All minor objects must be sacrificed to the preservation of the Carnatic. The disputes with the Mahrattas must be accommodated. A large military force and a supply of money must be instantly forwarded to Madras, in response to the earnest supplication of the Council of that presidency, who declared that without money everything must be lost, and a death-blow given to the British Empire in India.

But these measures would have been insufficient, unless the war, hitherto so grossly mismanaged, were placed under the direction of an able commander. Hastings wisely determined to resort to the extreme measure of sending Sir Eyre Coote to replace the incapable governor of Fort St. George, and of entrusting that distinguished general with the entire management of the war. In spite of the sullen opposition of Francis, who, happily for the security of the British Empire in India, was shortly about to leave the scene of his ill fame, the Governor-General's wise and firm policy was approved by all the other members of the Supreme Council. The reinforcements were sent off without delay, and reached Madras before the long-expected French fleet had arrived in the Indian seas. The effect was quickly perceptible. In place of driving the English into the sea, as Hyder Ali, in anticipation of Napoleon some thirty years later, vainly boasted he would do, he now found the conqueror and his French ally, Sir Eyre Coote, in the field against him. In January, 1781, Coote commenced the campaign by marching on Wandiwash, where, twenty-one years before to a day, he had obtained his great victory over the French under Lally, where he found Lieutenant Flint with only one day's ammunition remaining for the hundred men who composed the garrison. After relieving the garrison, Coote, on his march from Porto Novo to Cuddalore, with about 8,000 men, encountered Hyder at the head of 80,000. His troops had only four days' provisions, which they carried on their backs, and Hyder's position was a very strong one. Nevertheless, Coote did not hesitate to attack him. A road which had been cut through the jungle and sandhills, intended for a flank attack upon the British, was happily discovered in time, and by this a part of Coote's army advanced, while two other divisions in line passed the sandhills in front. The battle was hotly contested for upwards of six hours, and ended in a complete defeat of Hyder's army, by which he lost fully 10,000 men, while Coote's force was only weakened by 300 in killed and wounded. Ten weeks after this brilliant victory Coote again defeated Hyder severely at the pass of Sholinghur, destroying not less than 5,000 of Hyder's cavalry in their charges on the British guns. Sir Hector Munro, with a force made up of seamen, marines, and other detached parties, was sent in the end of October to besiege the Dutch fortress of Negapatam. After a siege of three weeks, the garrison, which numbered nearly 7,000, and far in excess of the besieging force, capitulated, with its numerous and valuable military stores; and thus Munro was enabled to wipe out the disgrace he had incurred by failing to assist Baillie in his desperate hour of need.

To Hyder's perception the western coast of India

was by far the weakest portion of his territory; open to attack from the English by sea, and by the Mahrattas on land, with whom he now discovered the English were making peace. At this juncture, when experience had shown him that even with the aid of his French and Dutch allies he could not face the British, Hyder was thrown into dismay by learning the result of Hastings' masterly and successful policy on the conclusion of the treaty between the English and the Mahrattas. He expected to have the Mahratta confederacy soon upon him, and the Mahrattas on a previous occasion had proved more than a match for him. His health, which had been visibly declining for some time, was now much shaken by suspicions of conspiracy and murder against those who surrounded him. Nevertheless he was persuaded by the French general, Bussy, that his affairs in the Carnatic were far from being hopeless, and he prepared to co-operate with him in an attack upon Negapatam.

Sir Eyre Coote, completely shattered in health, had resigned his command to General Stuart, who reinforced Negapatam, at the same time sending four hundred British to co-operate with the Bombay army under General Goddard, who was preparing to invade the kingdom of Mysore. Tippoo had been sent by his father to the Malabar coast, with twenty thousand men, and accompanied by a French corps four hundred strong. Colonel Mackenzie was invading Mysore from the south. When midway between Calicut on the coast and Hyder's capital of Seringapatam, he met Tippoo and the French, and inflicted upon them a decisive defeat, the honour of the day being conceded to that pride of Highland regiments, the gallant 42nd. At this juncture Tippoo received the intelligence of his father's death, which induced him to hurry to the capital to look after his interests; for he had brothers and cousins who might claim a share in the kingdom of Mysore.

Hyder Ali, whose death took place in the month of December, 1782, had long been failing; and his last moments are thus curiously described by his faithful biographer, Meer Hussein: "He had directed that water might be made ready for him to bathe; and although the physicians objected to his bathing, his servants turned the doctors out of his tent, and Hyder took his bath. Then, having put on clean clothes, he repeated prayers and invocations on his fingers, rubbing his face at the same time. After that he despatched two thousand cavalry to ravage the country of the Poligars, and five thousand horse for a like purpose to Madras. Then, after taking a little mutton broth, he lay down to rest. That same night his ever-victorious spirit winged its flight to Paradise." Hyder was over eighty at the time of his death; and notwithstanding his advanced age, and the existence of a large carbuncle on his back, which eventually carried him off, in his last eventful campaign he had been almost as active as ever. His strange character and the romantic events of his career are fully detailed in Colonel Wilk's "History of Mysore;" and with the exception of Sivajee, the founder of the great Mahratta confederacy a century before, there is not one of the many adventurers who rose to power in India on the breaking up of the empire of the Great Mogul, who can be compared for ability or success with Hyder Ali, the founder of the kingdom of Mysore.

Had the Madras army at this critical period been commanded by such a general as Clive, a blow would have been struck against the Mysorean host, now that it was deprived of its head, before the arrival of Tippoo Sahib, and the war would have been brought to an honourable close in a very different manner from what eventually proved to be the case. But the Madras army was now under the command of General Stuart, who is described as a "perverse, disobedient, and incapable officer," and who certainly allowed the opportunity to slip by without attempting a single hostile movement.

When Tippoo succeeded to the kingdom of Mysore, on the death of Hyder Ali, he possessed an efficient army of a hundred thousand men, a treasury containing nearly £4,000,000 sterling, and a mass of jewels and other valuables estimated at an immense amount. With these resources, with a passion for war, and secure of the French alliance, Tippoo scorned all overtures for peace with the English—overtures which his wiser father would certainly have entertained, had he only lived a few weeks longer. He commenced the campaign at the beginning of 1783, by investing the strong fortress of Bednore,* which had been previously captured by the gallant 42nd Highlanders under the command of Colonel Macleod, and before which he was detained upwards of five months. The defence of Bednore by the Highlanders forms one of the most interesting episodes in the history of our Indian wars; and finding no

* See Appendix.

hopes of relief, the garrison, with General Mathews, who had taken up his quarters in the fort, was compelled to capitulate on honourable terms. Those terms were shamefully violated by Tippoo, under the false pretence that Mathews had purloined some of the public treasure which he had agreed to leave in the fort. The brave garrison, in place of being sent to the coast, as Tippoo had engaged, were bound in chains, and thrown into the dungeons at Seringapatam, where General Mathews, with several of his officers, at a later period, was deliberately put to death.

From Bednore Tippoo proceeded to Mangalore with his whole army, 100,000 strong. The place was garrisoned by 700 British soldiers and nearly 3,000 Sepoys, under the command of Colonel Campbell, who made a noble defence until February, 1784, when, unable to obtain provisions, and reduced to the utmost extremity by famine, he was obliged to capitulate, and in this instance allowed to march out with the honours of war to Tellicherry. Tippoo had lost by sickness and desertion nearly half of his immense army before the weak walls of Mangalore; but considering the place as a sort of charm, on the possession of which the fortunes of his house depended, he was rendered so happy by the possession of the place, that he allowed the garrison to quit the fort unmolested, and adhered to the terms of the capitulation. But even then Campbell would not have capitulated, though reduced to such dire distress by famine, had he not known that the Madras Council were determined to make peace with Tippoo, and to restore not only Mangalore, but also every place on the Malabar coast which had been taken from him by the prowess of the British arms.

There is little doubt but that another campaign would have finished up Tippoo Sahib entirely; as two other British armies, one under the command of Colonel Fullerton, an officer of high merit, amounting to nearly 14,000 Sepoys, were preparing to invade the kingdom of Mysore; but the infatuated conduct of Lord Macartney, President of Madras, and his imbecile Council, prevented so desirable a result. Although Bengal had had its Clive and Hastings, together with subordinate officers of merit, and Governor Hornby of Bombay, with his stout-hearted Council, had eventually guided that presidency through a momentous crisis during the Mahratta war, Madras, with the exception of Mr. Saunders, (for Warren Hastings during his three years' residence in that presidency was only a subordinate member of Council,) had never possessed a chief of political capability or resolution.

It is impossible, even after the lapse of a century, to read without a sense of humiliation and shame the absurd proceedings of Lord Macartney and his ever-incapable Council. They sent commissioners to Tippoo, with the most abject offers of submission, notwithstanding Hastings' indignant protest that the only way to treat with such a monster as Tippoo had proved himself to be, was to dictate peace, as Hyder had done to Madras fifteen years before, in 1769, at the gates of Seringapatam. "How will you manage the beast," asked the celebrated missionary Schwartz of Colonel Fullerton, "now that you are about to quit the reins?" How, indeed! It is melancholy to

TIPPOO SAHIB.

have to record that, as the English commissioners proceeded to Tippoo's camp, they were insulted and mocked at every stage. At Mangalore, gibbets were erected opposite their tents; and such was their fright, that after a detention of some weeks previous to their admission to Tippoo's presence, they planned to escape to the English ships lying in the roads. Nor was it until Tippoo was in actual possession of Mangalore, that he would condescend to notice the matter at all. At length, on March 11th, 1784, as Tippoo Sahib proudly caused it to be inscribed on the walls of his palace in Seringapatam, "*The English commissioners stood with their heads uncovered, and the treaty in their hands, for two hours, using every form of flattery and supplication to induce compliance. The vakeels of Poonah and Hyderabad united in the most abject entreaties, and His Majesty, the Shadow of God, was at last softened into assent.*"

The basis of the treaty was the restitution of mutual conquests; and directly it was executed, the English commissioners hurried back to Madras, leaving the release of the prisoners to be effected by the officer who commanded their escort, and who executed his difficult task with wisdom and discretion. No less than 180 officers of all grades, 900 English soldiers, and nearly 2,000 Sepoys, were rescued from the dungeons of Seringapatam; while the accounts of their barbarous treatment, and of the cold-blooded murder of General Mathews and his companions, excited mingled feelings of horror and compassion. And, if possible, there is something worse to be recorded still; for by the treaty the poor Malabar Hindus, whom the Madras Council had incited to rebel against the King of Mysore, and to whom protection had been solemnly promised, were now given over and restored to the dominion of one of the most ferocious and vindictive princes that ever ruled over the myriads of Hindostan. Such was the unworthy treaty to which the feeble rulers of Madras consented, as a termination of their struggle with the monster, Tippoo Sahib. And the people of Mysore had to submit to his terrible rule for fifteen years longer, until judgment overtook him on April 6th, 1799, by the celebrated siege of Seringapatam, when the kingdom of Mysore, formed by the genius of his father, Hyder Ali, passed away for ever, and henceforth formed a portion of the mighty and ever-growing British Empire in India.

CHAPTER XXI.

THE GOVERNMENT OF WARREN HASTINGS.—THE EPISODE OF CHEYT SINGH, THE RAJAH OF BENARES.

A.D. 1780-1.

NOTWITHSTANDING the humiliation to which the English commissioners had been compelled to submit by Tippoo Sahib, in concluding the treaty agreed to by the incompetent Council of Madras, the result on the whole was a most advantageous peace for England. The real danger in the Carnatic was passed by Coote's great victory at Porto Novo. The French power in India had been overthrown, vast acquisitions of territory had been made, and the impression had been produced among nearly all the native princes that the power of the British Empire in India was irresistible. The extent of these operations was magnificent in the extreme ; for it embraced the three sides of the vast triangle of India, from Calcutta down the eastern coast, including the Northern Circars and the French settlements of Pondicherry, to Cape Comorin ; and from Cape Comorin along the western coast, through the newly formed Mysorean kingdom of Hyder Ali, up to Bombay and Surat ; and the splendid march of General Goddard right across India, from Calcutta to Surat, which resulted in his triumph over the Mahratta confederacy, may be said to have completed the territorial triangle.

By this means the British Empire in India was saved, when our empire in the far West, through the incapacity of the home Government, was irrecoverably lost. No patriotic Englishman can even now contemplate without dismay the effect which would have been produced in Europe, if the loss of our Indian Empire had been added to the loss of the thirteen states of North America; and that this had not happened was owing, under Providence, to the wonderful genius, the resolute daring, and the serene courage of one man—the illustrious Warren Hastings, the Governor-General of Bengal.

Hastings' great principle of action was that the Carnatic must be rescued, and India saved, at all costs; and as the first step towards such preservation it was necessary to obtain the funds, which the Madras Council implored him to send them, without delay. If the expenses of the three separate wars with the Mahrattas, the Franco-Dutch, and Hyder Ali, had not strained the Bengal treasury to the utmost, it is certain that Hastings' administration in a financial point of view would have been as successful as he or the directors at home could have desired. His early success both at Madras and Calcutta, before he received the appointment of Governor-General, proved his capacity as a financial administrator; and his improved systems of rental and collections of revenue had been at least as successful as could be expected in the commencement of an important change. Still the drain on the treasury had never ceased; and while the Bombay and Madras presidencies could supply next to nothing, but were a heavy burden on the Calcutta exchequer respecting the means for carrying on the wars which were confined to the territories of those two presidencies, the demands for more money to be sent to England, for the use of the proprietors of East India stock, were loud and incessant. Moreover the debt in Bengal had now again reached more than a million sterling, while the credit of the Company was no better than when Hastings found it, and when he subsequently showed by his masterly operations how a deficit of two millions could be converted into a surplus of the same amount.

The testimony of Hastings himself on this point, together with his prognostication of the growth of the British Empire in India, deserves to be remembered. Writing to his friend Sulivan, one of the chief directors, in April, 1779, he says: "I came to this Government when it subsisted on borrowed resources, and when its powers were unknown beyond the borders of the country which it held in concealed and unprofitable subjection. I saw it grow into wealth, and again sink into a decline that must infallibly end it, if a very speedy remedy be not applied. Its very constitution is made up of discordant parts, and contains the seeds of death in it. I am morally certain that the resources of this country, in the hands of a military people, and in the disposition of a constant and undivided form of government, are both capable of vast internal improvement, and of raising that power which possesses them *to the dominion of all India* (an event which I may not mention without adding that it is what I never wish to see); and I believe myself capable of improving them, and of applying them to the real and substantial benefit of my own country." (Gleig, ii., p. 275.)

Hastings, when called upon by the Council of Madras for money, money, money, to enable them to resist the terrible invasion of Hyder Ali, was placed in a most difficult and delicate position. He could not increase the burdens of the British provinces, for they were already taxed to the uttermost. He dared not withhold the Company's investments, for then no dividends could have been paid, and the outcry on the part of the shareholders would have been tremendous. He was very unwilling to re-establish a bonded debt, the absorption of which had redounded so much to his own credit, and had proved so beneficial to his employers. Something, however, must be done, otherwise the ruin of the Company's affairs, together with the loss of our Indian Empire, must be regarded as certain. Under these circumstances, Hastings resolutely and wisely determined to utilize the privileges which the constitution of the country and the customs of the Mogul Empire gave him, and to call upon his dependent chiefs, the rajahs and nabobs and greater zemindars, like a European sovereign of the middle ages, for such aid as the critical condition of the British Empire in India might render indispensable. Several of the neighbouring princes, who owed their political existence to the power of the British arms, were known to possess hidden treasures of a vast amount. The plan was to compel them, by firm and necessary pressure, to disgorge some of these treasures, for their own as well as England's good, as it was well known, although they owed everything to the English, they would not willingly or freely part with a sou, even when they saw themselves threatened with destruction.

Oude and Benares, though nominally independent states, were to all intents and purposes tributary to the British power, and they would not have hesitated to have so acknowledged themselves. Shujah-ood-Dowlah, the Viceroy of Oude, who is described as a prince who "wanted neither pride nor understanding," would have been proud to be called the Vizier of the King of Great Britain, and had, as Hastings wrote to a friend, actually offered to "coin his money in the name and with the effigies of George III." If this offer of sovereignty had been accepted; if the East India Company, as representing the English nation, had frankly proclaimed themselves what they were *de facto*, the rulers of Oude and Benares; if, when they obtained dominion over these principalities, they had assumed their proper style and title, in place of calling themselves protectors, allies, and the like, with a false moderation of language which deceived no one, Lord Clive and Warren Hastings would have been alike relieved from an occasional false position, and actions scarcely warranted by their *nominal* relations with native princes would have been reconcilable with the law of nations.

Hastings' first design, in order to procure means for carrying on the war in the Carnatic, was on Benares, a city which in wealth, population, dignity, and sanctity, was among the foremost in Asia. The schools and temples drew crowds of pious Hindus from every province where the Brahminical faith was known. Hundreds of devotees came thither to die; for it was believed by the superstitious Hindu that a particularly happy fate awaited those who died in the sacred city and passed into the sacred river. Commerce likewise flourished to a greater extent than in any other city of India. All along the shores of the mighty Ganges lay great fleets of vessels laden with rich merchandise. From the looms of Benares went forth the most delicate silks that adorned the courts of St. James and Versailles; and in the bazaars the muslins of Bengal and the sabres of Oude were mingled with the jewels of Golconda and the shawls of Cashmere.

This rich capital had long been under the rule of the Rajah Cheyt Singh, whose ancestors had rendered homage to the emperors of Delhi. During the anarchy which ensued on the breaking up of the Mogul Empire, the lords of Benares became independent of the court of Delhi, but were compelled to submit to the authority of the Vizier of Oude. Oppressed by their formidable neighbour, they invoked the protection of the English. That protection was cordially given by Hastings; and at length the Nabob, by a solemn treaty, ceded all his rights over Benares to the East India Company. From that time the Rajah was the vassal of the Government at Calcutta, acknowledged its supremacy, and engaged to send an annual tribute to the Governor-General of Bengal.

In 1778, on the breaking out of the war with France, Cheyt Singh, the Rajah of Benares, had been called upon by the Governor-General, with the acquiescence of the directors at home, to pay in

BENARES.

addition to his tribute an extraordinary contribution of £50,000. This was done in accordance with the prevailing custom throughout India, of the rajahs, zemindars, and tributary states being compelled to contribute to the wants and necessities of the supreme power. In the following year a similar sum was exacted; and on the third occasion when a similar demand was made, Cheyt Singh, in the hope of obtaining some indulgence, offered the Governor-General a bribe of £20,000. Hastings took the money, but not for himself; he handed it over for the benefit of Colonel Carnac's division of the army during the Mahratta war, and thus enabled him to inflict a severe defeat on Scindia, in the night attack of March 24th, 1780; which proved of great use in the result of the war. Hastings' enemies have accused him of endeavouring to purloin this gift, and to apply it to his own use; but they little knew the noble nature and character of the man which they so frequently attempted to blast. And it is in no improper spirit that we find Hastings at this time writing to a friend among the directors, under date of November 10th, 1780, to complain of the way in which he was treated by those in authority at home; being accused, among other high crimes and misdemeanours, of rapacity in the acceptance of presents, and malversation of the public money of which he had the charge! "Your colleagues," he writes, "have been so much habituated to pass their censures on my actions, and to discountenance those to whom I have shown any degree of confidence, or who have given proofs of their attachment to me, that it will possibly occur to them that in this instance I have been guilty of a flagrant breach of orders in seducing one of their servants from the station which they had allotted to him. Such is the treatment which I have experienced with respect to Elliott, Bogle, Richard Sumner, and Sir J. d'Oyly, men of eminent merit, and universally respected, but, unfortunately, known to have attached themselves to me. Perhaps the spirit which dictated these malevolent acts may at length have subsided, and it may be allowed me at a time like this, and after the labours of so many years, performed almost with my own hands, to make one election of my own assistant in the first and most arduous department, under the superior administration of the British Empire. Few are the privileges which I have hitherto received or assumed. I have never called the members of another presidency to compose the government of this; my name has received no addition of titles, my fortune of jagheers, nor my person any decorations of honour. I was introduced into this government without any cost of ships to transport me, nor has any provision been assigned me of a domestic surgeon, nor a domestic chaplain. Neither my constitution nor religious principles have been a charge to the Company. These and other distinctions have been the lot of others, my inferiors; nor upon my honour has my envy been excited by them. I only mean by this comparison to furnish you with an answer, which ought to shame those who require one." (Gleig, ii., p. 328.)

Honour to the noble utterer of such righteous indignation, the much-maligned and misrepresented Governor-General Hastings, who by his wise acts and lofty disregard of everything which conflicted with the path of public duty, must be regarded as the second founder and consolidator of the British Empire in India.

But we must return to Hastings' dealing with the Rajah of Benares, when the stern necessities of the war which Hyder Ali, with his French allies, were raging against us in the Carnatic, compelled him to require more pecuniary aid from his wealthy vassal, Cheyt Singh. He was called upon to contribute to the public service five lacs of rupees, with a contingent of two thousand horse for the defence of the British Empire; which, considering the Rajah's known wealth and his complete dependency upon the Company, was neither unjust nor extortionate. Nevertheless, Cheyt Singh, after the fashion of his countrymen, shuffled, solicited, and pleaded poverty. Hastings was not to be so easily put off. He added to the requisition a fine for delay, and sent troops to exact the money.

Finding the matter was more serious than he expected, Hastings resolved to visit Benares in person. Cheyt Singh received the Governor-General with every mark of reverence, came many miles with his Guards to escort the illustrious visitor, and expressed his deep concern at the displeasure of the English. Hastings made known to him the demands of the Government of Bengal. The Rajah, in reply, attempted to clear himself from the accusations brought against him. Hastings, whose long experience in dealing with Eastern potentates enabled him to detect at once the Rajah's position, was not to be put off with such artifices. He took the strong measure of ordering him to be arrested, and placed under the custody of two companies of Sepoys.

In taking this strong measure, Hastings scarcely acted with his usual judgment. Possibly he may not have been aware that the national and religious prejudices with which the English were regarded throughout India were peculiarly intense in the capital of Brahminical superstition. Hastings, before attempting to arrest the Rajah in the midst of his own subjects, should have assembled a force capable of bearing down all opposition. This had not been done. The handful of Sepoys who attended Hastings were not sufficient to contend with the fanatical rabble of Benares. The streets surrounding the palace were filled by an immense multitude, of whom a large proportion wore arms. The tumult became a fight, and the fight a massacre. The officers defended themselves with the usual courage of Britons against overwhelming numbers, and fell, as became them, sword in hand. The Sepoys were all killed; the gates were forced; and the captive Rajah, neglected by his gaolers during the confusion, discovered an outlet which opened on the steep bank of the Ganges, let himself down by a string made of the turbans of his attendants, discovered a boat, and escaped to the opposite side of the river.

If Hastings had thus placed himself in a situation of extreme peril, he extricated himself with more than his usual ability and presence of mind. The house in which he had taken up his abode was blockaded on every side by the insurgents, and he had only fifty men with him. But his serene courage remained unshaken. Cheyt Singh from the other side of the river sent apologies and liberal offers of submission. Hastings abstained from noticing them. Some subtle and enterprising men undertook to pass through the surging crowd, and convey the intelligence to the English cantonments. It is the custom of the natives to wear large earrings of gold. When they travel, the rings are laid aside, lest the precious metal should tempt some gang of robbers; and in place of the ring a quill or a roll of paper is inserted in the orifice, to prevent it from closing. Hastings placed in the ears of his messengers letters rolled up in the smallest possible compass, very similar to the plan adopted ninety years later at the siege of Paris by the German armies, when the pigeon post was made so effective for conveying Parisian news to the outside world. Some of the letters were addressed to the officer commanding the troops at Chunar, to acquaint him with the dangers that threatened. By the same means he was enabled to satisfy the mind of Mrs. Hastings and the officials at Calcutta of his own personal safety. And what is still stronger evidence of his own calm presence of mind, he sent through the same channel instructions to Colonel Muir, who was at that time negotiating a treaty of peace with Scindia, the powerful Mahratta chief, framed in that situation of extreme danger, with as much composure as if he had been writing in his palace at Calcutta.

Matters, however, were not yet at the worst. Colonel Morgan, an English officer of more spirit than judgment, eager to distinguish himself and to relieve the Governor-General, who was beloved by the army, both British and Sepoys alike, made a premature attack upon the insurgents at Ramnagur beyond the river. His troops were entangled in narrow streets, and assailed by a furious population. He fell with many of his men, and the survivors were forced to retire. The horizon in consequence became darker than ever. Hastings escaped by night to Chunar, a fortress on the Ganges, about seventeen miles distant from Benares, and there set himself to arrange the plan of the campaign against a still extending rebellion.

The fiasco at Ramnagur produced the effect which has never failed to follow every check, however slight, sustained in India by the British arms. For hundreds of miles round the whole country was in commotion. The entire population of Benares took arms. The infection spread to Oude. The people of that province rose against the Vizier, refused to pay their imposts, and put the revenue officers to flight. Cheyt Singh soon found himself at the head of forty thousand troops, and his hopes began to rise. In place of imploring mercy as a vassal, he began to talk as a conqueror, and threatened to sweep the British usurpers out of the whole of Hindostan. But the English troops were assembling fast. The officers and privates alike regarded the Governor-General with enthusiastic attachment, and flew to his aid with an alacrity which, as Hastings subsequently boasted with just pride, had never been surpassed. Colonel Popham, who had greatly distinguished himself the preceding year by the capture of the great fortress of Gwalior, as we have already recorded, and in whom Hastings reposed the greatest confidence, took the command. Cheyt Singh's large army was speedily put to the rout; thirty thousand men immediately quitted his standard. The defeated rajah fled to Bideghur; and thence, with all the treasure he could find means to transport, into the district of Bundelkhund, leaving his own country for ever. Bideghur surrendered to Popham on November 9th, 1781, when half a million sterling was captured, which, under the misinterpretation of a private letter written on the occasion by Hastings to Popham, was divided as prize money among the troops at once, even before Hastings knew that the place had been taken. Cheyt Singh's nephew was appointed to succeed him; but the Rajah of Benares was henceforth to be, like the Nabob of Bengal, a mere pensioner; while his fair domain was added to the ever-growing territory of the British Empire in India.

CHAPTER XXII.

CONCLUSION OF HASTINGS' GOVERNMENT.

A.D. 1782-5.

MACAULAY, in his brilliant and interesting "Essay on Warren Hastings, observes, after the Court of Directors had refused to obey the resolution of the House of Commons, which required the recall of the Governor-General, as being the vote of only one branch of the legislature, that, "Being thus supported by his employers, Hastings remained at the head of the Government of Bengal till the spring of 1785. His administration, so eventful and stormy, closed in almost perfect quiet. In the Council there was no regular opposition to his measures. Peace was restored to India."

An attentive perusal of Hastings' letters, which are so fully given in Gleig's "Memoirs of Warren Hastings," the very book under review on which Macaulay has based his essay, scarcely supports such a conclusion, with the exception of the last sentence, that peace was restored to India as the result of the masterly policy of the Governor-General. According to the following letters written by Hastings, putting aside the ceaseless quarrels between Lord Macartney, the incapable Governor of Madras, and Sir Eyre

Coote, the able general whom Hastings had sent to rectify the blunders of the Madras Council, it would seem that the Governor-General was anything but supported as he should have been by the Court of Directors at home, or that the members of the Supreme Council, Messrs. Macpherson and Stables, whom they had sent out to supply the vacancies at Calcutta, allowed him that supremacy in conducting the administration which his position, his experience, and his success fully warranted. Hence, in a letter to his agent, Major Scott, of February, 1783, he writes as follows: "Three days ago I received the resolutions of the Court of Directors, condemning my conduct in the affairs of Benares as a breach of treaty, and justifying Cheyt Singh. Are these men aware, in their eagerness to vilify me, they sow the seeds of distrust and rebellion among their own subjects, and that a declaration so authentic in the favour of a rebel, now residing under the protection of the chief of the Mahratta State, at the crisis of our negotiations with him, might tempt the former to resume his pretensions, and the latter to espouse them; and that a slight spark would be sufficient to blow up our possessions and those of the Vizier, if it fell on so combustible a ground? What is to follow these resolutions? An order to restore Cheyt Singh? The conclusion is inevitable; for if we are bound by treaty with him, if he faithfully performed all his conditions of it, and we have broken our engagements with him, and the Court of Directors solemnly pronounce this at their judgment, they must render him justice, or they are the violators of public faith by their own avowal.

"It will not be expected that I should obey such an order, and how can I oppose it without exposing my person, fortune, and reputation to the most fatal extremities? And how can I elude it, but by resigning the trust which imposes on me so infamous a duty? . . . I trust to Lord Shelburne (Prime Minister) and to the injunctions of Lord Ashburton and Sir Robert Palk. In the meantime I hope that my narrative, which I find must have arrived in England within a few days of the passing of these resolutions, will have completely defeated them; for if there ever was a demonstration produced by argument, I have demonstrated the falsehood of Cheyt Singh's pretences to independency, and those of his advocates who assert that we were bound by any treaty or any engagement differing from that of a common zemindary. While the Court of Directors assume the style and form of the late parliamentary resolutions, they may affirm what they please, with the preface that '*It appears to this Court*,' for who can contradict them whilst they have the dishonest discretion to conceal the grounds of the assertion? . . .

"I shall bear with patience and forbearance every article of abuse that is yet to come; but the right of judging when I ought to quit the service because I can no longer retain it with effect or with credit, I shall certainly exercise; and at all events I shall stay till I know the result of the present deliberation in Parliament concerning India. I wish to see the war closed in the Carnatic, and the defeat and capture of the French; and this I trust will be effected before the month of October, if Coote gets safe to the coast and lives. When this work is accomplished, I care not what they may do with me in England." (Gleig, iii. 36—40.)

Of his coadjutors which the Court of Directors had sent him from England to help him in the most arduous task which has ever befallen the lot of any statesman since England became a nation, he thus writes to his agent in January, 1784, after speaking of their want of resolution, their fickleness, promising one day to support the Governor-General, and the next day retracting their consent :—

" In short, I can confidentially mention as a certain fact that the members of the Board see less danger in doing nothing than in acting and seeing a standing Committee of the House of Commons on the watch for matter of crimination against us all, and determined, right or wrong, to condemn whatever is done ; a powerful party, covetous of our places ; a weak administration (Lord Shelburne's), courting support from all quarters, and this government affording a wide field of profitable patronage ; they do not choose to add to the number of their enemies the connections of Lord Macartney, or give them fresh and strong ground of attack. This Mr. Wheeler has confessed. As to the other two, they received an early hint from their friends not to attach themselves to a fallen interest, and they took the first occasion to prove that if I was to be removed, their removal was not to follow as a necessary consequence of their connection with me, by opposing me on every occasion, on the most popular ground, on the plea of economy and obedience of orders, which they apply indiscriminately to every measure which I recommend ; and Mr. Stables, with a spirit of rancour which nothing can equal, but his ignorance has so acted throughout. His friend, with the most imposing talents, and an elegant and unceasing flow of words, knows as little of business as he does; and Mr. Wheeler is really a man of business. Yet I cannot convince him of it, nor persuade him to trust to his own superiority. He hates them, and is implicitly guided by them, and so he will always be by those who command him, and possess at the same time a majority of voices." (Gleig, iii. 145.)

Two years later, in writing to his intimate friend Mr. Anderson, after his arrival in England, he sums up the defence of himself, while dwelling on the extraordinary difficulties under which he laboured during the whole of the time that he was at the head of affairs, and engaged in consolidating the British Empire in India, which had been founded by the genius and skill of Clive. In this confidential communication to an intimate friend, which, as his biographer remarks, was evidently never meant for any other eyes than those of his correspondent, the principal points dwelt upon are these:—

When Mr. Hastings was appointed to be the head of the Bengal Government in 1772, he found it deeply in debt, and without resources. He constituted all the offices now extant, divided the departments of the Council, instituted new courts of civil and criminal justice. With great labour he reduced the expenses of every department, and formed a complete system of economical establishments. He first converted the funds of salt and opium from private emolument to the profit of the East India Company, and in the course of a few years he converted a deficit of £2,000,000 sterling into a surplus of the same amount. He rigidly obeyed the orders of the Court of Directors in revoking the authority of Mohammed Reza Khan, for which he received their thanks, while the same men united to support Mohammed against him. He freed the provinces from the yearly incursions of the Seniasses, who never failed to visit them before his time; and from the second year of his accession they have abandoned them entirely. *He received the thanks of the whole body of the directors for the first acts of his government, and received the reproaches of the same body, under exactly the same signatures, as soon as the new Council proclaimed themselves his enemies.*

In 1773, he established an alliance between the two states of Bengal and Oude, on conditions of such equal advantage that the representatives of both parties were quite satisfied; and had the succeeding governments pursued the same line, Oude would have been a shield of defence and a source of wealth to Bengal, while it derived reciprocal support and means of wealth from it. In the Rohilla war he did what every state similarly circumstanced should do. The invasion of the country threatened ruin to those of our ally who gave a solemn pledge in writing for the payment of £200,000 for the expense and risk incurred in their protection. They obtained their safety, and refused to pay the price of it. We made war with them, defeated them, with the death of their ungrateful and perfidious leader, and annexed their dominion to that of Oude, which from that period became thoroughly defensible. *The directors, as usual, allowed the justice of our proceed-*

ings, and approved them, but condemned both when Francis and his allies appeared on the scene.

After speaking with becoming indignation of the infamous conduct of Francis during the whole period of his having a seat in the Supreme Council, from October, 1774, down to December, 1780, Hastings continues: "When intervals of accidental authority enabled me to act, I employed them in forming and setting in motion the greatest and most successful measures of my government. When these were impeded by frequent changes of influence, I still contrived to keep them in existence, and again gave them energy when my power returned. My antagonists sickened, died, and fled. I maintained my ground unchanged; but my difficulties did not end here. New coadjutors became new enemies, with the same encouragement from the directors, but without the same personal consequence. Mr. Wheeler, Mr. Macpherson, and Mr. Stables were, as soon as they could stand without me, my successive, and lastly, my united opponents. Mr. Wheeler has declared to me that he was enjoined to oppose me, and complained that he was deserted. Mr. Stables pleaded the advice of one friend, and Mr. Macpherson that of another, not to link themselves to a fallen man, but save themselves by showing that the same policy which sought my removal did not require theirs. Yet even when they were all three in force against me, I awed them into a surrender of a wretch (Cheyt Singh) whom they had scandalously protected in the most infamous of all oppressions, and compelled them to yield the charge of a province which he had reduced to the brink of ruin, with the national honour linked with it; and in spite of their wishes, for they durst not act against me, I succeeded. I need not expatiate on this subject; you know it all as well as I do."

After giving a masterly analysis of his government during the wars with the French, Hyder Ali, and the Mahrattas, Hastings winds up this personal defence of himself in a confidential communication to an intimate friend as follows: "After adopting with lawful pride the words of Augustus respecting Rome, 'Urbem lateritiam recepi, marmoriam reliqui,' if I might be allowed to point out the best features of my own character in office, I should place these in the catalogue: integrity and zeal, affection for my fellow-servants, and regard for the country which I governed; official regularity, accuracy, and collateral provision (you must find out the meaning of these words) in the creation of new offices or systems of policy, in instructions for political negotiations, and in the construction of treaties; sincerity and unreserve in my dealings with the chiefs in connection with our Government; a study to choose agents most fitted for their trusts, confidence liberally given to them, and their conduct guarded from the hazard of every responsibility which belonged in right to myself; and lastly, patience, longsuffering, confidence, and decision. My dear David, let no man see this. I am ashamed of my own praises, bestowed so lavishly by my own pen; but I mean this only as hints to help your sounder judgment and clearer recollection. Adieu, my dear friend. Yours ever most affectionately, WARREN HASTINGS." (Gleig, iii. 301—311.)

Passing by the necessary egotism of Hastings'

defence of himself it is impossible to deny the enormous merit of his services in the preservation of our empire in the East during the terrible crisis through which England passed at the very time when he was at the head of the Government of India. She indeed still maintained her place in the foremost rank of European powers, and the manner in which she had defended herself against fearful odds had inspired surrounding nations with a high opinion both of her spirit and her strength. Nevertheless, in every part of the world, except one, she had been a loser. Not only had she been compelled to acknowledge the independence of thirteen colonies in America, and to conciliate the Irish by giving up the right of legislating for them, but in various parts of the world she had been compelled to cede the fruits of her victories in former wars. Spain regained Minorca and Florida, and France regained Senegal, as well as several West Indian islands. The only quarter of the globe in which England had lost nothing was that in which her interests had been committed to the care of Hastings. In spite of the utmost exertions, both of her European and Asiatic enemies, the fickleness of the Court of Directors at home, the incompetency of the two subordinate governments of Bombay and Madras, as well as the ceaseless opposition of Francis and his bitterly hostile allies, the power of the British Empire in India had been vastly extended on every side. And that our influence had been thus extended, nay, that the capitals of the three presidencies had not been occupied with hostile armies, and the horrible scenes of the Black Hole at Calcutta had not been repeated, was owing, as the general voice of the English in India proclaimed, to the skill and resolute courage of one man, the first and greatest of our governor-generals, the illustrious Warren Hastings.

His internal administration gives him a title to be considered as one of the most remarkable statesmen whom this country has ever produced. If we were required to give the names of the greatest men who have borne their share in the government of our empire during the eighteenth and nineteenth centuries, and to limit the number to that of the famous sages of Greece, we think the majority would unhesitatingly place the name of WARREN HASTINGS on this illustrious list; and some perhaps would give him the foremost place of all. From a careful study of Hastings' character, the difficulties with which he had to contend, the opposition he had to encounter, and the wonderful results which he obtained, we are inclined to place the name of Hastings, if not *facile princeps*, at least *primus inter pars*, amongst the illustrious band of England's seven great men; for, as Mill, the historian of India, and for many years secretary to the East India Company, and not too much disposed in Hastings' favour, after reviewing his career, admits, "there was not one of the chief rulers whom the Company had employed, who would not have succumbed under the difficulties he had to encounter." It should not be forgotten that amongst his many great deeds, not the least difficult was the dissolving the double government in Bengal, and of transferring the direction of affairs from native to English hands. Out of anarchy he brought order. The whole organization, by which justice was dispensed, revenue collected, and peace maintained, throughout a territory not inferior in population to the greatest of the European monarchies, was formed exclusively by Hastings alone. And as Macaulay, one of the best of judges, seeing that within half a century after Hastings' departure he himself became a member of the Supreme Council at Calcutta, has justly observed, "Whoever seriously considers what it is to construct from the beginning the whole of a machine so vast and complex as a government, will allow that what Hastings effected deserves high admiration. To compare the most celebrated European ministers to him seems to us as unjust as it would be to compare the best baker in London with Robinson Crusoe, who, before he could bake a single loaf, had to make his plough and his harrow, his fences and his scarecrows, his sickle and his flail, his mill and his oven. The just fame of Hastings rises still higher when we reflect that he was not bred a statesman; that he was sent from school to a counting-house, and that he was employed during the prime of his manhood as a commercial agent, far from all intellectual society. Nor must we forget that all, or almost all, to whom, when placed at the head of affairs, he could apply for assistance, were persons who owed as little as himself, or less than himself, to education. A minister in Europe finds himself, on the first day on which he commences his functions, surrounded by experienced public servants, the depositories of official traditions. Hastings had no such help; his own reflection, his own energy, were to supply the place of all Downing Street and Somerset House. Having had no facilities for learning, he was forced to teach. He had first to form himself, and then to form his instruments; and this not in a single department, but in all the departments of the administration."

When to this just testimony of an impartial historian we add that Hastings and his subordinates were a little company of foreign traders, placed in the midst of an enormous population speaking many languages, of different races and religions, at a distance from home so great that it required sometimes nearly a year before news reached him; that during his entire administration he was at one time rancorously opposed by his foes who sat in council with him, and at another but feebly supported by his professed friends at home; that in the wars which occurred in the subordinate presidencies of Bombay and Madras, during the time of his being governor-general, he had to deal with the most incompetent set of councillors in those two presidencies; and that, had it not been for the vigorous policy by which Hastings was enabled to overrule their acts and correct their blunders, both would have been brought to the verge of ruin: when, moreover, we reflect that, during the whole period of his administration, he was either opposed, condemned, or very feebly upheld by the directors of the Company which sent him to India, as well as intrigued against by the king's ministers, from Lord North, the Prime Minister, downwards, we are surprised at the success which attended Hastings' rule under such disadvantages; and we are not going too far when we give him the first place among the great statesmen of the age in which he lived, and to whom, under Providence, is alone due the existence of our British Empire in Hindostan,

Like another great man in the estimation of the world, whose rise and fall Hastings witnessed long after he had retired into private life (we refer, of course, to the first Napoleon, who has been accused, and with more justice, of far greater crimes than his bitterest foes ever brought against Hastings), he was unsurpassed in the art of inspiring large masses with confidence and attachment. If he had made himself popular with the English residents in India by giving up the natives to extortion and plunder, or if, on the other hand, he had conciliated the natives and alienated the English, there would have been no cause for wonder. What is so astonishing in Hastings is, that being the chief of a small number of foreigners, who exercised boundless power over a vast population, he made himself beloved both by the subject many and by the dominant few. The affection felt for him by the civil branch of the service was singularly warm, and never failed him; while the army at the same time loved him as much as they loved Clive, and as armies have seldom done any but the greatest chiefs who have led them to victory.

While such was Hastings' influence over the hearts of his countrymen, he enjoyed among the natives a popularity such as no other future governor—though the list includes the names of such great men as Wellesley, Moira, afterwards Marquess of Hastings, and Bentinck—has been able to attain. He spoke the vernacular dialects of Bengal with ease, and was intimately acquainted with their feelings and customs. Even when he was constrained to act in defiance of their opinions, he gained more in their respect than he lost in their love; and he wisely avoided everything which could shock their national or religious opinions.

Comparing the security in which the Bengalese were living under the rule of Hastings' government with that of the previous native princes, the oldest man in the province could never recall to mind a season of equal prosperity. For the first time within living memory, the province was placed under a government strong enough to prevent others from robbing, and not inclined to play the robber itself. These things, notwithstanding the charges brought against him, and the ceaseless attempts to discredit his government so persistently made by his unworthy foes, inspired goodwill and confidence on the part of the natives towards a ruler who had done so much for their worldly good. Moreover, the constant success which had attended Hastings' policy, the way he had triumphed over his foes, and the manner in which he had extricated himself from every difficulty, made him an object of superstitious awe by the more than royal splendour which he occasionally displayed, and which captivated a people who had much in common with the simplicity of children. "Even now," wrote Macaulay in 1841, "after a lapse of more than fifty years, the natives of India still talk of him *as the greatest of the English*,* and nurses sing children to sleep with a jingling ballad about the fleet horses

* A similar testimony is borne to another of England's greatest men, who has been as much the subject of unjust accusation and foul calumny after death, as Hastings was in his lifetime. A Turkish historian, after describing Cromwell as "the mightiest of the kings of the Franks," on the occasion of his ambassador having been insulted and locked up in a stable on account of his firm adherence to truth, pays this merited compliment to our national character: "These cursed ambassadors," says

and richly caparisoned elephants of SAHIB WARREN HOSTEIN."

And the same great historian sums up his character in the following words: "Though we cannot with truth describe Hastings either as a righteous man or as a merciful ruler, we cannot regard without admiration the amplitude and fertility of his intellect, his rare talents for command, for administration, and for controversy, his dauntless courage, his honourable poverty, his fervent zeal for the interests of the state, his noble equanimity, tried by both extremes of fortune, and never disturbed by either."

May we not say with the utmost confidence, in conclusion, that it has been, under Providence, by the genius and skill of such heroes as CLIVE, WARREN HASTINGS, and last, but not least, the late LORD LAWRENCE, that England has won and still retains a greater empire than Rome possessed at the zenith of her power—an empire on which it has been often said with truth "the sun never sets;" and the brightest jewel in the imperial crown will be universally admitted to be what is so well known by the significant term of—

THE BRITISH EMPIRE IN INDIA,

which said crown has been so long and so becomingly worn by Her Majesty the Queen-Empress Victoria, the most benevolent and constitutional monarch the world has ever seen, whom God preserve to reign over us for many years to come. AMEN!

the Turk, "*especially the English*, are very stiff-necked; as the English in their business will not depart from their word, though it cost them their head; by which we see that this coarse rudeness is a necessity of their nature."

CHAPTER XXIII.

AFGHANISTAN.

AT the close of the last century, Zemaun Shah, son of Timour, and grandson of the illustrious Ahmed Shah, reigned over the great Douranee Empire, which then included Afghanistan, Beloochistan, and Scinde, with many other miscellaneous tribes besides, having Cabul for its capital, and including a population of about fifteen millions, very much the same in point of numbers with the kingdom of Prussia after the War of Independence and the Waterloo campaign. And it is not a little curious to contrast the fortunes of the two great military states of central Europe and central Asia, then and now. Prussia, since the overthrow of Napoleon I. in 1815, and Napoleon III., in 1870, has become the greatest military power in the world, with a population of nearly fifty millions of subjects; whereas the Douranee Empire during the same period has not only been entirely broken up and dispersed; but the only kingdom which can have any claim to being its representative, viz., that of Afghanistan, is now so thoroughly disorganized, that when peace is made after the useless war in which we have unhappily been engaged in that country during the last two years, the utmost which the Afghans can hope for is to possess the remains of an ancient empire, with a population of, perhaps, two or three millions. And the problem still awaits solution as to how the once great kingdom of Afghanistan is hereafter to be governed.*

It may be of some interest if we endeavour to give a brief sketch of how this has come to pass; which is explained by the history of the country, during the present century, presenting a continual struggle between rival competitors for power, with scarcely any intermission of anarchy, war, and internecine horrors, very similar to what occurred in our own country during the Wars of the Roses. Very little appears to be known of the Dourances until the time of Nadir Shah, the great King of Persia, who reduced them to submission in the early part of the last century. After the death of Nadir, in 1747, Ahmed Shah, the chief of the tribe called Abdaullees, seized the government, and was crowned at Candahar; and in consequence of the dream of a Mohammedan saint, he changed the name of his tribe from Abdaullees to Dourances, while he himself assumed the name of Shah Dooree Douran.

Ahmed was an enterprising warrior, and likewise distinguished as a patron of literature. He extended his conquests as far as Delhi; and his life was chiefly passed in a series of campaigns against the Mahrattas and the Sikhs. He was succeeded by his son, Timour Shah, in 1773, whose chief characteristic was the reverse of his father's activity, which rendered him quite incapable of retaining in submission the various tribes which his father had conquered. The only important event of his twenty years' reign

* This was written before the accession of Abdul Rahman, in 1880.

PALACE OF LAHORE.

was in leading an army of 100,000 men from Cabul against the King of Bokhara, who before long offered acceptable conditions of peace. On Timour's death, in 1793, a fearful struggle ensued between his sons for the throne, which was at first obtained by his eldest son, Zemaun, who, after a turbulent reign of between seven and eight years, was eventually overthrown by his brother Mahmoud, with the help of Futteh Khan, the chief of a tribe called the Barrekzyes.

It was during the reign of Zemaun Shah that the English may be said to have come into contact with Afghanistan; for in and during the chief part of this present century that nation has been more or less a thorn in the side of England. For many years Zemaun's threatened descent on Hindostan had kept our Indian officials in a chronic state of unrest. But he never advanced farther than Lahore, and was then compelled precipitately to retire. Sir John Kaye, in his valuable "History of the War in Afghanistan," observes: "We, who in these times trustingly contemplate the settled tranquillity of the north-western provinces of India, and remember Zemaun Shah only as the old blind pensioner of Loodhianah, can hardly estimate aright the real importance of the threatened movement, or appreciate aright the apprehensions which were felt by two governor-generals of such different personal characters as Sir John Shore and Lord Wellesley."*

* Vol. i., p. 3. Sir John Shore wrote in 1797: "Report speaks of an intended invasion of Hindostan by Zemaun Shah, and with respect to his intention is entitled to credit." Lord Wellesley, two years later, spoke of the threatened invasion "creating the liveliest sensation

At the commencement of the present century, little was known in India, and nothing in England, about the Dourance Empire, the nature and extent of its resources, the quality of its soldiers, or the character of its ruler; the empire which then extended from Herat in the west, to Cashmere in the east, including an extent of territory of over ten degrees. Bounded on the north and east by immense mountain ranges, and on the south and west by vast tracts of sandy desert, it opposed to the advance of a foreign enemy defences of a formidable character. Its people were a race of vigorous mountaineers, brave and independent, but of a turbulent and vindictive character; their delight was in a constant succession of internal feuds; their chief happiness seemed to be nothing but strife. Among such a people civil war has a natural tendency to perpetuate itself. Revenge, as among the ancients, was a virtue with them; the heritage of retribution passed from father to son, and murder became a solemn duty.

The main strength of the Afghan army was in their cavalry. After Nadir Shah had settled the Douranee tribes in Western Afghanistan, he parcelled out amongst his military dependants, in imitation of William of Normandy, seven centuries before, the lands which had been held by a motley race of native cultivators. It was the policy of

throughout India;" adding, "Every Mohammedan, even in the remotest region of the Deccan, waited with anxious expectation for the advance of the champion of Islam." Had this been attempted half a century earlier, how different might have been the condition of the British Empire in India!

Ahmed Shah and his successors to elevate these powerful tribes, by bestowing on them a multitude of privileges at the expense of their less favoured countrymen. Upon the misery and humiliation of others the Douranee tribes throve and flourished. The principal offices of state were in their hands, and their own lands were exempt from taxation. The only demand made upon them was that they should furnish a certain amount of soldiers to the army; and the principle of their military tenure was that for every plough used in cultivation the owner should contribute a horseman for the service of the state.

The two principal tribes of the Douranees at that time were the Popubzyes and the Barukzyes. The former possessed the chief influence, while the latter were the more numerous; to which tribe belonged Futteh Khan, who played so prominent a part in the affairs of Afghanistan during the early portion of this present century. He was the son of Poyndah Khan, an able statesman and a gallant soldier, whose wisdom in council and experience in war had long sustained the tottering fortunes of Timour Shah. On the death of that weak sovereign, he had supported the claims of his eldest son, Zemaun Shah, who, with as little wisdom as gratitude, had in course of time preferred the services of a man of less honesty and ability, and became a tool in the hands of Wuffadar Khan. Poyndah Khan was disgraced, and from a powerful friend became the resolute enemy of the reigning family. He conspired against the king; his designs were discovered, and he paid the penalty of his treason with his life.

POYNDAH KHAN* died, leaving a family of twenty-one sons, of whom FUTTEH KHAN was the eldest. He was one of those remarkable characters who occasionally appear in history, especially when troublous times are in the ascendant; and during the next seventeen years which followed the deposition of Zemaun Shah he played his part with such skill and success as to have deserved the title of "Ameer-maker," quite as much as the Earl of Warwick did that of "King-maker" during the Wars of the Roses in the fifteenth century. The sons of Poyndah Khan had the murder of their father to avenge, and they rested not till the fatal obligation had been faithfully fulfilled. Futteh Khan had fled to Persia, and there leagued himself with Zemaun's younger brother, Mahmoud, who, with the assistance of the Barukzye Sirdar, determined to strike a blow for the sovereignty of Cabul. With a few horsemen they entered Afghanistan, and, raising the standard of revolt, pushed on to unexpected conquest. Their numbers quickly increased; and, with a few thousand cavalry of the Barukzye and Achekzye tribes, Mahmoud invested Candahar for thirty-three days,

* It may enable the reader to comprehend the leading chiefs of the Afghans with whom England has had to deal during the present century, if we insert here a brief genealogy of Poyndah Khan's descendants :—

1800. POYNDAH KHAN, *ob.* 1803

- Futteh Khan, *ob.* 1818.
- Dhost Mohammed, *ob.* 1863.
  - Akbur Khan.
  - Afzul.
    - Abdul Rahman.
  - Azim.
  - Shere Ali, *ob.* 1878.
    - Yakoob.
    - Ayoob.

1880.

when Futteh Khan, with a handful of resolute men, escaladed the fortress, put the panic-stricken garrison to flight, and Prince Mahmoud became master of the place.

At this period Zemaun Shah was on his way towards Hindostan, with a view to invade what remained of the once mighty empire of the Great Mogul. He had advanced as far as Peshawur, when intelligence of the fall of Candahar reached his camp. All idea of invading Hindostan was speedily abandoned, and everything now gave place to the one necessity of saving the kingdom from the grasp of his brother. Zemaun Shah marched against his opponents only to be defeated. His troops were commanded by one Ahmed Khan; when Futteh Khan, watching his opportunity, seized the person of Ahmed's brother, and threatened to destroy him if the chief refused to come over bodily with his troops, and swell the ranks of the rebels. Ahmed Khan at once made his election, and joined the insurgent force. From that moment the cause of Zemaun Shah became hopeless. He and his chief minister fell into the hands of the enemy, and Wuffadar Khan, with his brothers, was put to death. The king received still more cruel treatment, being doomed only to political extinction. Between a blind king and a dead king there is no political difference. The eyes of a conquered sovereign are punctured with a lancelet, and then *de facto* he ceases to reign. They blinded Zemaun, and cast him into prison, and the Douranee empire owned his brother, Prince Mahmoud, at its head.

The year following Zemaun's deposition, another

brother by the same father and mother, Shah Soojah-ool-Moolk, whose name was very familiar in England forty years ago, proclaimed himself king, and marched from Peshawur upon Cabul, where he was severely defeated by Futteh Khan, and fled to the Khyber Hills. The destinies of the royal claimants to the sovereignty of the Dourance Empire were for the next seventeen years in the hands of this powerful Barukzye chief. His energies and influence alone upheld the drooping power of Mahmoud, until, after various unsuccessful attempts,* Shah Soojah obtained a victory over Futteh Khan, and was thus enabled to enter Cabul in triumph, and to confine his rebel brother Mahmoud ; while, to his honour be it said, he abstained from retaliating the cruelty which Mahmoud had displayed towards their mutual brother Zemaun. Shah Soojah's own account of his treatment of Mahmoud, which is given in the Appendix of Elphinstone's *Cabul*, is thus recorded. After speaking of his recovery of his capital, he says: "Mahmoud was so disheartened at the news of our victory, that, after swearing on the Koran he would not again be guilty of treachery, he sent some of his principal attendants to request the royal pardon, which we granted, and had him conveyed from the outer to the inner fort with all the respect

* Shah Soojah at one time was reduced to such straits, very similar to the condition of the Great Mogul Babur three centuries before, which is mentioned at the commencement of this treatise, that at one time he was reduced to the condition of a pedlar, trying to support himself by the sale of some of the crown jewels which he had preserved, and with difficulty finding a purchaser. At another time he pursued the occupation of a bandit, giving various receipts to those travellers whom he had met and plundered.

due to his rank. We then entered the Balla Hissar with regal pomp, and seated ourselves on the throne of Cabul."

From this time for many years to come the strife between the royal brothers and their children was fierce and incessant. In his son Kamran the deposed Shah Mahmoud found a willing ally and an active auxiliary. To the reigning monarch, Shah Soojah, it was a period of endless disquietude. The Dourance monarch could not meet his engagements without weakening himself by making large assignments upon the revenues of different provinces of his empire; and even then, as is generally the case all over the world, many interested friends were turned by disappointment into open enemies. But the chief error of his life was when he failed to propitiate the great Barukzye chief, Futteh Khan. On the accession of Shah Soojah he had been freely pardoned, and, to use Oriental phraseology, he was "allowed to salute the step of the throne." The king did not estimate aright the value of the alliance, and while refusing the moderate demands of the Barukzye chief, he gave the preference to his rival, Akrum Khan. Disappointed of what he conceived his just rights, Futteh Khan then deserted the royal standard, just as, three centuries and a half before, the Duke of Buckingham turned against Richard III., when refused his claims to the great inheritance of the Bohuns.

Futteh Khan chose his time wisely and well. In 1804, the year following Shah Soojah's conquest of his brother Mahmoud, the king had set out with an army to overawe Peshawur and Cashmere on the march. Futteh Khan, who accompanied him, excused himself on the plea of some physical infirmity from keeping pace with the royal *cortége.* Thus disguising his defection, he fell in the rear, and as Shah Soojah advanced, returned to foment a fresh rebellion. Before long he succeeded in inducing Prince Kyser, the son of the blinded Zemaun Shah, who had been entrusted by Shah Soojah with the government of Candahar, to rise against his uncle, and proclaim himself king. Kyser and Futteh Khan marched upon Cabul, but were defeated, when the son of Zemaun at once made his submission, and was forgiven; Soojah in this instance proving himself far more lenient than the ordinary run of Afghan princes, having been persuaded by Mooktoor-ood-Dowlah, another of his brothers, against his better judgment to pardon the royal rebel.

Futteh Khan, having his plans frustrated in this direction, repaired to Herat, where he succeeded in persuading another of Timour Shah's sons, Haji Ferooz, to put in his claim to the throne of Cabul. Ferooz accordingly took up arms, when his brother, Shah Soojah, sent a force against him commanded by the recently pardoned Prince Kyser, who had, however, instructions to offer him such terms as would be likely to succeed. And such proved to be the case. Soojah's terms were at once accepted, while Futteh Khan, quitting his cautious *protégé* in disgust, once more retired to one of his castles at Gerishk, where Prince Kyser soon after contrived to seize him. Anxious to curry favour with his uncle, Shah Soojah, and to gratify his revenge on account of the treatment which his father, Zemaun Shah, had received from his brother Mahmoud when supported by Futteh Khan, Kyser was about to put the latter to death now that he had him in his power. Futteh Khan, however, contrived to obtain a private interview with his captor; and such were the powers of persuasion which this wonderful man possessed, that the young Prince Kyser not only spared his prisoner's life, but entered with him into a fresh plot against Shah Soojah's throne.

Futteh Khan was again allowed to retire to his fortress of Gerishk; from whence, after maturing his plans, he marched on Candahar, where he found his ally, Prince Kyser, under the influence of a powerful Sirdar named Kojeh Mohammed Khan, who dissuaded him from rebellion. Futteh Khan, in anger at Kyser's wavering disposition, renounced all connection with the Prince, and engaged to deliver Candahar to his cousin, Prince Kamran, the son of Mahmoud, who at once marched for that city. Kyser, before fleeing, requested a last interview with Futteh Khan. They met secretly by night, and though the interview commenced with mutual recriminations, it terminated in a manner scarcely credible amongst Europeans. Kyser reminded Futteh that he owed his life to his leniency, while the latter in return recapitulated his favours to Kyser, and complained of neglect. Kyser, upon this, swore to follow him implicitly, whereupon Futteh relented, and finally swore to support him under all circumstances. The following morning they marched out together from Candahar to oppose Prince Kamran, who was rapidly approaching the city.

Futteh advanced with his division of the allied forces, and informing Prince Kamran of his altered views, kindly advised him to retire. As soon as Kamran discovered that his opponent was serious he bid him defiance, upon which Futteh, without waiting for Kyser's troops to come up, charged and utterly routed him. In the meanwhile Shah Soojah had conquered Cashmere, when Kojeh Mohammed, having recovered his influence over the vacillating Prince Kyser, contrived to dissolve the recent alliance between him and Futteh Khan, and the latter once more retired to his castle at Gerishk. Here he contrived to renew his intercourse with Prince Kamran, after which he marched against Prince Kyser, and drove him from Candahar into Beloochistan. Shah Soojah, hearing of these events, marched against the combined forces of Prince Kamran and Futteh Khan. After some reverses, Soojah succeeded in defeating them, when Kamran fled, and Futteh, as usual ever fruitful in resources, managed to make his peace with and joined Shah Soojah.

In the autumn of 1808, when the British Government in India were sending forth embassies both to Cabul and Lahore, Mahmoud, Futteh Khan's first *protégé*, who had been deposed and imprisoned by his brother, Shah Soojah, but not blinded according to the cruel custom usually practised by victorious Afghan chiefs, contrived to make his escape. At the same time Shah Soojah's chief minister, feeling that his influence was on the decline, rebelled against his sovereign, and proclaimed Prince Kyser king of Cabul. Shah Soojah, however, quickly defeated the rebels, and entered Peshawur in triumph.

In the meanwhile the mission, which the British Government were sending forth for the first time to the sovereign of Afghanistan, was making its way to the court of Shah Soojah-ool-Moolk. Mr. Elphinstone, the ambassador, had been originally instructed that he was empowered to receive from the King of Cabul proposals having for their basis the employment of the power and resources of that state against the advance of any European army, whether French or Russian ; the former being then our chief bugbear, just as much as the latter is in the present day. The mission proceeded through Bahawalpore and Mooltan ; and into whatsoever city they entered, the most marked civility was shown to the British ambassador. But one thing was wanting to render the feeling towards them a pervading sentiment of universal respect. It was discovered soon after crossing the frontier, that a more liberal display of the signs of manhood on the face would elevate the representatives of Great Britain greatly in the eyes of a people who uniformly wear the beard and moustache. In February, 1809, the mission entered Peshawur, where Shah Soojah was then residing. Crowds of wondering inhabitants came out to gaze on the representatives of the nation which had reduced the Great Mogul to a shadow, and not long before had conquered the kingdom of Mysore, and overthrown the power of Hyder Ali and the warlike Tippoo Sahib. Seated on rich carpets, fed with sweetmeats, and regaled with sherbet, every attention was paid to the European strangers. The hospitality of Shah Soojah was profuse. Though his fortunes were then at a low ebb, and very shortly were about to become still lower, he managed to send provisions to the mission for

2,000 men, with food for beasts of burden in proportion. And when the eventful day of presentation arrived, they found the King, with that love of outward pomp so pleasing to the Oriental mind, sitting on a gilded throne, crowned and plumed; his dress a blaze of jewellery, conspicuous among which was to be seen the famous Koh-i-noor diamond, which became subsequently such a source of misery to himself, and which, after having undergone such romantic vicissitudes, is now in the possession of Her Majesty Victoria the Queen-Empress of India.

To return, however, to the fortunes of the "ameer-maker," Futteh Khan. At the very time that Shah Soojah was receiving the first British embassy in his royal city of Peshawur, Mahmoud having escaped from his prison, succeeded in forming a junction with his old friend Futteh Khan, when he determined again to assert his claim to the sovereignty of Afghanistan. They jointly defeated the forces which Shah Soojah sent against them, and they entered Cabul in triumph. Soojah was next defeated in person by Futteh Khan, when he fled, first to the hills, and subsequently sought the protection of Runjeet Singh, the Maharajah of the Punjaub. It soon became very evident that Runjeet Singh coveted the possession of the great Douranee diamond. On the second day after his entrance into Lahore, Shah Soojah was waited upon by an emissary from Runjeet, who demanded the jewel in the name of his master. The fugitive monarch, asking for time to consider the request, hinted that after he had partaken of his master's hospitality, he might be disposed to grant it. On the day following, the same messenger appeared and received a similar reply. Runjeet Singh, determined to possess himself of the matchless Koh-i-noor, resorted to other measures in order to extort it from its luckless owner. The means employed shall be related in Shah Soojah's touching words of the transaction. After recounting the privations to which he was reduced by the infamous behaviour of Runjeet, even wanting the necessaries of life, he says: "After a month passed in this manner, confidential servants of Runjeet Singh waited on us, and asked again for the Koh-i-noor, which we promised to deliver as soon as a treaty was agreed upon between us. Two days after this, Runjeet Singh came in person, and after friendly protestations, and swearing by the Grunth of Baba Nanuck and his own sword, wrote the following treaty: 'That he delivered over certain provinces to us and our heirs for ever; also offering assistance in troops and treasure, for the purpose of again recovering our throne.' He then proposed himself that we should exchange turbans, which is among the Sikhs a pledge of eternal friendship, and we then gave up to him the Koh-i-noor diamond."

Having thus possessed himself of the coveted jewel, Runjeet Singh proceeded to prove himself one of the basest characters among the Oriental princes with whom we have had to deal in Hindostan. After he had stripped the fugitive monarch of everything he possessed that was worth taking, "even after this," says the wretched Soojah, "he did not perform one of his promises." After a series of romantic adventures, extendingover a course of years, which prevents our recording them here, the discrowned monarch of Afghanistan, in the year 1816, sought and found a resting-place under the mighty ægis of the British crown; and for some years Shah Soojah gratefully accepted our hospitality for himself and family, in Loodhianah, the neighbourhood of which became famous in after years for Sir Harry Smith's decisive victory over the Sikh army.

After Shah Soojah's flight, in the year 1809, and Mahmoud's capture of Cabul, by the assistance of Futteh Khan, the "ameer-maker," that enterprising soldier and distinguished statesman virtually ruled Afghanistan, under the name and authority of Shah Mahmoud. He captured Herat from Haji Ferooz, the brother of Mahmoud, and vigorously repulsed an attack on that famous city which is of some interest to us at the present time, when the Shah of Persia had sent his troops to demand tribute of its inhabitants.

A few years later, A.D. 1818, Mahmoud having become jealous of his great prime minister, Futteh Khan, as is too commonly the case with Oriental despots, most ungratefully seized and blinded, under circumstances of peculiar atrocity, the man who had twice placed him on the throne. Upon this the family of Futteh Khan flew to arms to avenge him, when the partisans of Mahmoud attacked the illustrious Futteh, blinded as he was, and literally cut him to pieces. Thus died this remarkable man, the ameer-maker of the Douranee Empire, whose versatile talents gave the ascendency to whatever party he joined; and though his perfidy and want of principle were notorious, there is this to be said in extenuation, that he possessed them in common with every one of his countrymen, and what seems vice to us was accounted a virtue by them.

Among the twenty brothers of Futteh Khan was one many years his junior, whose infancy was wholly disregarded by the great Barukzye Sirdar. The son of a lowly woman of the Kuzzilbash tribe, he was looked down upon by the high-bred Douranee ladies of his father's household. The lad had begun life in the menial office of a sweeper at the sacred edifice, which is traditionally supposed by the Afghans to contain the remains of the antediluvian saint, Lamech, the father of Noah! Permitted at a later period to hold office in his brother's household, he saw everything, heard everything, watched silently, bided his time patiently, and when the hour came he played his part on the stage of life, as one of the most remarkable characters in central Asia with whom our Indian officials have come in contact. On one occasion he slew, in broad day, in one of the crowded thoroughfares of Peshawur, one of the enemies of Futteh Khan, and galloped home to report the deed to his all-powerful brother. From that moment his rise was rapid; he became the favourite of the chief minister of Shah Mahmoud, and took his place among the chivalry of the Douranee Empire.

Such was the rise of the famous warrior DHOST MOHAMMED, who in after years was the cause of so much anxiety and distress to the British Empire. Nature had designed him for a hero of the true Afghan stamp and character. His youth was stained with many crimes which he lived to deplore. It is to the credit of Dhost Mohammed, that in the vigour of his years he looked back with contrition upon the excesses of his early life, one of which, the plunder of the harem of Ferooz-ood-Deen, at Herat, was accompanied with acts of peculiar atrocity. But such acts, partly caused by a neglected childhood, he struggled manfully in after years to remedy and repair. When he had attained the height of his reputation, it may be safely said that there was not to be found in central Asia a chief so remarkable for the exercise of self-discipline and self-control.

The assassination of the illustrious Futteh Khan was the signal for the dismemberment of the Douranee Empire. The murder of his father, Poyndah Khan, nearly twenty years before, had shaken the Suddozye dynasty to its base; the assassination of the son soon made it a heap of ruins. From this time the rise of Dhost Mohammed was rapid. He succeeded in speedily making himself sovereign ruler of Cabul, with the reputation of being an enlightened prince. Kamran, the son of Shah Mahmoud, seized Herat. Candahar became subject to the Sirdars. The ameers of Scinde made themselves independent; while Runjeet Singh took advantage of the general confusion to make large encroachments on the Afghanistan monarchy, which was then falling rapidly to pieces, very much in the same manner as Turkey is in the present day.

To come to the events of our own generation. In 1835, Runjeet Singh crossed the Indus, and occupied the province of Peshawur up to the mouths of the Khyber Pass. Dhost Mohammed, hoping to recover Peshawur, caused a holy war to be proclaimed against the Sikhs, and a large force, descending the passes, appeared before the city. The agents of

Runjeet Singh, had, however, been successfully at work with that golden bait which is so irresistible with the Oriental mind, and succeeded in persuading the governor of Peshawur to desert his brother, on which the Afghan army broke up and dispersed. Dhost Mohammed then applied to Lord Auckland, Governor-General of India, for assistance, who replied that he would send an officer to "discuss questions of commerce," but declined any interference with the Punjaub. Left thus to his own resources, Dhost Mohammed sent another army under the command of his son, the famous Akbur Khan, by whom, on the 30th of April, 1837, the Sikh army was completely defeated near Jumrood, at the entrance of the Khyber Pass.

Lord Auckland's envoy, Lieutenant (afterwards Sir Alexander) Burnes, reached Cabul in the September of that year, where he was hospitably received by Dhost Mohammed, who, according to the Afghan mode of political reasoning, naturally concluded that Burnes' mission, though professedly confined to trade, meant in reality a discussion on the affairs of the Punjaub and Afghanistan. The Ameer had recently discovered that a morbid dread of Russian influence existed at that time with the British rulers in India. Dhost Mohammed skilfully contrived to fill Burnes' mind with apprehensions of Russian intrigue, which was confirmed by news from Persia, when, a few weeks later, Captain Vickovich, an aide-de-camp of the Russian general at Orenburgh, arrived at Cabul, December 19th, 1837, with a letter from Count Simonich, the Russian ambassador at the court of Persia. Had Burnes only considered for a moment the impossibility of any advance by Russia against our Indian empire, he would scarcely have written to Lord Auckland, as he unfortunately did, to say that "much more vigorous proceedings than Government might wish or contemplate are necessary to counteract Russian or Persian intrigue in this quarter than have yet been exhibited." It is not too much to say that this fatal letter has been the primary cause of all troubles in Afghanistan from that day to this year of grace 1881.

The Indian Government, on receiving this despatch, sought to detach Dhost Mohammed from the interests of Russia and Persia. The Ameer declared himself willing to embrace the British alliance, if the Governor-General would protect him from Runjeet Singh; but if not, he must look to Persia for assistance. In an evil hour it was determined that our relations with the Sikh ruler did not permit of our giving the Ameer of Afghanistan any assistance in that direction, neither could we permit him to find assistance in any other quarter; so the only remaining course, as it then appeared to our Indian rulers, was to dethrone Dhost Mohammed, and to reinstate Shah Soojah, who had been for twenty-eight years a fugitive from the kingdom he claimed, in order to impose a bar, as it was fondly hoped, to the progress of Russia, and to secure British influence throughout central Asia.

Had Lord Auckland possessed the talents of even any of the second-rate governors whom England has sent forth to govern the vastly extended British Empire in India, he would surely have adopted the wise, and, as Meadows Taylor points out in his

"History of India," "the only safe and consistent course;" he would have been content with guarding the line of the Indus, and have abandoned central Asian politics to the native princes, there being no call upon us to interfere in any way. This was the course which all the great Indian statesmen from that time until now have considered the wisest to pursue. But unhappily in 1838, as again in 1878, when history so closely repeated itself in our dealings with Afghanistan, it was thought advisable to plunge into the vortex of Afghan troubles; and so, on October 1st, 1838, the celebrated manifesto was sent forth from Simla, explaining the action of the British Government as best they could. Of this manifesto, Meadows Taylor justly affirms that "it is as weak in argument as it is untrue in the assumptions in which it indulged; unfair to Dhost Mohammed, and unjust to the people of Afghanistan, in forcing upon them an unpopular monarch already expelled from his throne, and whose repeated attempts to regain it had been resented and defeated; and, in regard to the object of the expedition, altogether as delusive as it was dangerous and inexpedient."

With the exception of Sir John Hobhouse, then President of the Board of Control, every Indian statesman of consideration, including the Duke of Wellington, the Marquis of Wellesley, Lord William Bentinck, and the Hon. G. Elphinstone, disapproved of the war in the strongest terms, just as the late Lord Lawrence, and those who are best qualified to judge, with the exception of Sir H. Rawlinson, have on the present occasion. But the die was cast, war was declared, and one of the best appointed forces that had ever assembled in India, under the command of Sir Willoughby Cotton, commenced its march from Ferozepoor towards the fated capital of Afghanistan. Another force marched from Bombay under the command of Sir John Keane, who took the supreme command of both armies, and entered the country by the Bolan and Khojuk passes in the beginning of 1839. Shah Soojah, at the head of his own troops, entered Candahar without opposition, where he was formally enthroned in May of that same year.

In the following month Sir John Keane recommenced his march from Candahar to Cabul, which he reached with Soojah, who made a triumphant entry into the capital after an exile of over thirty years. Dhost Mohammed surrendered to Sir William McNaghten, and eventually obtained an allowance of £20,000 a year from the Indian Government. Sir J. Keane was raised to the peerage, and all appeared prosperous. Alas! how little did our rulers foresee the rising storm! In the beginning of 1841 the mine exploded. Sir W. Cotton, who had hitherto commanded in Afghanistan, resigned, and was succeeded by General Elphinstone, an aged and infirm general, totally unfit for the post he was thus suddenly called on to fill. The British troops had evacuated the Bala Hissar, and were cantoned without the walls of the city; while Sir Alexander Burnes, who was in charge of Cabul, and the envoy, Sir W. McNaghten, were unable to perceive any cause for alarm, treating all the warnings which they had received respecting a plot against the Feringees, as the Europeans were termed, with complete disdain. On November 1st, at a secret meeting of the chiefs in Cabul, Abdoolla Khan, who had been grossly insulted by Burnes, proposed that his house should be attacked the next day. Burnes was warned of the conspiracy by some native friends; but though he was implored by Osman Khan, Soojah's chief minister, to proceed to a place of safety, he turned a deaf ear, and remained. His house was attacked the next day, and in a vain attempt to escape in disguise both he and his brother Charles were literally cut to pieces by the mob, and his escort perished to a man; just as history has been repeating herself in that same city of Cabul, when in 1879 Sir Louis Cavignari and his gallant band perished in the same way.

Akbur Khan, the son of Dhost Mohammed was now the avowed head of the insurgent chiefs. Five weeks after the massacre of Sir Alexander Burnes, a meeting took place between him and Sir W. McNaghten, in order to discuss the terms of the British troops evacuating Afghanistan, when it was agreed that Dhost Mohammed should return with his family, Shah Soojah was to retire with the English, and Akbur Khan agreed to escort the army through the dangerous passes on their return to India.

With lamentable want of discretion, Sir William McNaghten, at the very same time that he was endeavouring to make terms with the all-powerful Akbur Khan was conducting a miserable set of intrigues with the Ghibzai and other chiefs of an entirely opposite character from that which he had agreed to with Akbur Khan. The only defence which the envoy could make for such double dealing was, as he said, "the lives of fifteen thousand human beings were at stake, and he did the best that he could to secure them." But all to no purpose. The result was melancholy and distressing in the extreme. On the 23rd, Sir William again met Akbur Khan, and before going to this second conference he confided his plans to General Elphinstone, who warned him, and remonstrated against the whole proceeding, but in vain. It is probable that Akbur Khan only intended to carry off the whole party, but the result was of a very different and tragic nature. A question from Akbur Khan, asking the envoy if he was ready to carry out the proposals of yesterday, opened the business of the conference. The Afghans were closing around the party, and the suspicions of the officers who had accompanied McNaghten were aroused, and they naturally remarked that if the conference was a private one, the intruders ought to be removed. With a movement of doubtful sincerity, some of the Afghan chiefs lashed out with their lips at the closing circle; but Akbur Khan said their presence was of no consequence, as they were all in the secret with him.

Scarcely were these words uttered, when Sir William McNaghten and his companions were violently seized from behind. The movement was sudden and surprising. A scene of terrible confusion ensued. The officers of the envoy's staff were dragged away, and compelled each to mount a horse ridden by an Afghan chief. Trevor slipped from his insecure seat, and was instantly cut to pieces by the infuriated Ghazees, while Lawrence and Mackenzie, the other two officers of the staff, reached Mahmoud Khan's fort alive.

In the meanwhile Sir William McNaghten was struggling desperately with Akbur Khan. The look of wondering horror that sat upon his upturned face will never be forgotten by those who witnessed the terrible scene. The only words he was heard to utter were, "For God's sake"—the last spoken on earth by one who has been justly described as "one of the bravest gentlemen that ever fell a sacrifice to his erring faith in others." He had struggled from the first manfully, and now these last struggles cost the envoy his life. Exasperated beyond control by the resistance of his victim, whom he intended only to seize, Akbur Khan pointed the pistol, which had been given him only a few minutes before by the envoy, and shot him through the body. Thus perished Sir William Hay McNaghten by the hand of the favourite son of Dhost Mohammed—murdered in the execution of his duty, just as Sir Alexander Burnes before him, and Sir Louis Cavagnari after him, three noble representatives of the British Empire, were treated by the wild and savage Afghans, notwithstanding their office, always considered sacred by most nations from the beginning of the world.

The English troops in the cantonments, almost within sight of the terrible scene, would have at once attacked the city of Cabul, as they ought to have done, in order to avenge the murder of the envoy, but were prevented by their weak and incompetent commander, who, after making a useless and most disgraceful treaty with his murderer, commenced that fatal retreat on January 6th, 1842, which ended so disastrously for a British army. The entire force consisted of 4,500 soldiers, including the 44th of the line, and 12,000 camp followers. The first day they had only advanced four miles, as snow lay deep on the ground, and the cold was intense. On entering the Khoord Cabul pass, they found it lined by Ghilzais, who poured a deadly fire upon the confused and struggling mass, and there upwards of 3,000 fell. Two days later there only remained of the whole army fifty artillerymen, 250 of the 44th, and 150 cavalry, with about 4,000 camp followers.

Akbur Khan now promised to save the remainder of the combatants, if they would lay down their arms; but the offer was indignantly rejected, and the broken remnant of the army pushed on to Jugdulluk. Here ensued another conference with Akbur Khan, who detained General Elphinstone and Brigadier Shelton, who attended it, as hostages for the evacuation of Jelalabad. After this, the wreck of men and officers passed on to Gundamuk, which was reached exactly a week after the doomed army had commenced its fated march, when it was found that only twenty officers and forty-five men remained; and while Major Griffiths, of the 37th native infantry, the chief of that little band, was endeavouring to obtain terms from the Afghan Sirdar who had sent overtures for that purpose, the little party was overwhelmed by a rush of bloodthirsty Ghilzais, and destroyed almost to a man. Captain Souter, of the 44th, who had wrapped the colours of his regiment around him in order to preserve them, just as the two British officers who earned such deserved fame in attempting to preserve their colours after the disaster at Isandwala, and a few privates were taken prisoners. The rest were all massacred at Gundamuk.

A few, however, had pushed on in advance of the column. One by one they fell by the way, until the number was reduced to six, who reached Futtehabad alive. They were then only sixteen miles from Jelalabad. A prospect of salvation opened out for all, but only one was suffered to escape. Some peasants of the neighbourhood came and offered the fugitives food. They thought that a little food would strengthen them to toil on to the end of their painful journey; and the agonies of hunger were hard to endure. But there was death in delay. While the wearied officers tarried for a few minutes to satisfy the cravings of nature, some of the armed inhabitants of the place sallied out and attacked them. Two of them were instantly cut down; the others rode off, but were pursued and overtaken, and three of the remainder were slain. Dr. Brydon alone escaped to Jelalabad to tell the dreadful tale. Wounded and worn out by famine and fatigue, he had struggled onward, mounted on a jaded pony, till the fortress appeared in sight, when a party came out to succour him and to bring him in alive.

So perished the last remnant of a British army which had left Cabul only a few days before, numbering between four and five thousand combatants, with twelve thousand camp followers; destroyed partly by the rigours of the climate, or massacred by the relentless tribes of Afghanistan. It was as complete a destruction as that mighty army of six hundred thousand men, though commanded by such a genius as Napoleon I., which had been entirely destroyed thirty years before, in the retreat from Moscow; and yet so infatuated are some of the writers of the British press in the present day, so reckless are they in their hatred of Russia, that, incredible as it may appear to those who remember the awful judgment which befell the armies of Napoleon in 1812, when the news reached England of the assassination of Sir Louis Cavagnari at Cabul, in 1879, the *Morning Post* * attained the climax of vapouring by declaring that if Russia dared to interfere in our dealings with the Afghans, though the Government had been repeatedly warned against the attempt to force upon them an English resident at Cabul—"*Though it were necessary to march to Moscow, the thing should be done!*"

However much we may feel surprised that any one in his senses should give utterance to such bombast, it is still more surprising to find professing Christians giving utterance to similar sentiments in relation to Afghanistan. There are in this country two bodies of men, happily not very influential in the political world, respectively named the "Patriotic Association" and the "Israel Identification Society," who seem determined, *coûte que coûte*, that England must annex Afghanistan to the British Empire. The

* The *Morning Post* is happily the least influential paper on political matters of any of the London press; and such, we may conclude, it ever has been, judging from what Lord Macaulay wrote of it in 1831, in his brilliant review of "Samuel Johnson." When speaking of a duel fought by the editor of the *Morning Post*, in 1777, the great historian observes, "It certainly seems almost incredible to a person living in our time, that any human being should ever have stooped to fight with a writer in the *Morning Post*."

latter, by its representative in the press, the *Banner of Israel*, when commenting on an article in the *Times* of June 21st, 1880, respecting Afghanistan, and declaring that there was "no real remedy short of annexation for settling the Afghan difficulty," had the boldness to affirm that the English were "foolish Israelites, who did not know their glorious pedigree, nor what honour God means to put upon them in spite of themselves; and how He means to force them, *not only to incorporate Afghanistan, but also all the earth besides!*" It is a pity that this writer did not remember the solemn lesson conveyed in the Scripture story of Ahab and Jezebel coveting the vineyard of Naboth the Jezreelite, before exhibiting his fanaticism, recorded above, that England is to annex "Afghanistan and all the earth besides." The *Guardian*, which is one of the best informed and best written papers in England, especially on foreign affairs, takes a very different view of our dealings with Afghanistan from that of the unknown *Banner of Israel.* With a prescience to which its weekly contemporary has no pretensions, notwithstanding its many prophetic boastings, all of which, hitherto, have notoriously failed, the *Guardian*, in its issue of February 4th, 1880, before the late Government had decided upon an appeal to the nation, justly observed that "The invasion of Afghanistan, taken with the acts which originally led to it, and with its consequences, is one of those great and inexcusable miscarriages which are enough in themselves to destroy the reputation of a Government, if they do not prove *immediately fatal to its existence.* Placed between two powerful empires, the Afghans, a fanatical race, passionately jealous of their independence, and desirous only of maintaining it, are suspicious of both, and always ready to incline to the one most likely to protect them against the other. The proper course to be pursued towards such a people was surely pointed out by the most ordinary considerations of prudence. We have chosen a course which is exactly the reverse of it. . . . This is a policy, take it altogether, on which the verdict of history will certainly be severe." Has it not been so already? Three months had not elapsed after these words had been penned, before the electorate of England had pronounced, in a voice that could not be mistaken, their entire disapproval of Lord Beaconsfield's policy in general, and his treatment of Afghanistan in particular. It may be confidently affirmed that the chief cause of the overthrow of the late Government was the second invasion of Afghanistan, so unwisely adopted by our late rulers, and, with the exception of Sir Henry Rawlinson, so contrary to the advice of every statesman in England or India, who was competent to express an opinion on the matter.

From the days of Lord Canning until the viceroyalty of Lord Lytton, every one of our Governor-Generals of India have pronounced against the policy of Lord Beaconsfield in Afghanistan. Lord Canning expressed himself most pointedly against such a species of madness after the experience of 1842. Lord Mayo condemned it. Lord Northbrook resigned sooner than make himself responsible for endeavouring to carry it out. And the greatest of them all, the late Lord Lawrence, withstood to the last moment of his life the fatal act of the triumvirate Lords

Beaconsfield, Salisbury, and Lytton, in plunging England into the fathomless gulf of Afghan politics. At the time when that illustrious Oriental statesman was striving to avert the Afghan war, he wrote with all the authority of his intimate acquaintance with the policy adopted on our north-western frontier ever since the first invasion of Afghanistan in 1840. During the last twenty-eight years, he said that he had personally taken more or less an active part in carrying out that policy, and had during these years met and conferred with almost all the principal Afghan leaders, including Dhost Mohammed and his sons. He admitted that Russia had been led to advance step by step in Asia in a course which was obviously parallel with our own progress in India. In place of recommending what has been erroneously called "masterly inactivity," he gave the following sage counsel, which it would have been well for us, and have saved the country about £30,000,000, if the late Government had possessed the wisdom to follow.

"I am still in favour," said Lord Lawrence, "of the policy which has hitherto prevailed. Let us do what may be necessary, in a reasonable way, to conciliate the Afghans. Let us watch events, and deal with them as they occur. This is no inactive, no negative policy, in the true sense of the term. It is really, I submit, a watchful and defensive policy. The employment of natives beyond our frontier is, I consider, a far more safe, and at least an equally effective, mode of obtaining information, and is *free from the risks of employing Englishmen in such places.* We have acted on this principle with fair success for the last twenty years."

Lord Lawrence expressed his firm conviction, founded on experience, that the Afghans as a nation would not tolerate the presence of British officers in Afghanistan. And in reference to the proposed mission to Cabul, and the war which it was certain to involve, he justly asked a question which his would-be detractors have never attempted to answer: "Are not the *moral* considerations very strong against such a war? Have not the Afghans a right to resist our forcing a mission on them, bearing in mind to what such missions often lead, and what Burnes' mission in 1836 did actually bring upon us?" Then he asked one or two more pointed questions, to which the disasters of the last two years have afforded a terrible reply: "What are we to gain by going to war with the Ameer? Can we follow the policy of 1838-9 *without, in all probability, incurring similar results?*"

In the same strain spoke Shere Ali's very able envoy, Noor Mohammed Shah, who died in harness at Peshawur, March 26th, 1878, after having used every argument he could think of to induce the Government not to send an English envoy to Afghanistan. "In the first place," he said, "the people of Afghanistan have a dread of this proposal, and it is firmly fixed in their minds, and deeply rooted in their hearts, that if Englishmen or other Europeans once set foot in their country, it will sooner or later pass out of their hands. . . . Therefore, since the opinions of the Afghans are such, the protection of the English in the midst of the hill tribes is difficult, nay, impossible, because the whole army and the subjects of the Government are of these mountain people.

Besides, there are some people who, out of hostility to the Ameer, would secretly kill some of the Sahibs, in order to mar the friendship of the governments. Was not the Commander-in-Chief of the Ameer's army murdered by these very people in the midst of twenty thousand of his troops?

"Now the Ameer would have to protect the Sahibs with his army. But if he could not protect the life of his commander-in-chief, then in what manner could he protect the life of any other person?

"Again, if at any time a disturbance or revolution should occur in Afghanistan, the Sahibs would be certainly destroyed, and this is a point which needs no explanation, for it is well known; because in times of disturbance in Afghanistan, from the days of Timur Shah to the present day, very many of the noblest men of Afghanistan itself have perished, and many of their greatest chiefs and leaders have been murdered.

"Therefore, *in case the Sahibs be killed*, what would be the consequence? Eternal reproach and bitterness against Afghanistan would be the result, and their friendship with the English Government being thus destroyed would naturally produce enmity."

Notwithstanding the wise counsel of Sheer Ali's envoy, Noor Mohammed Shah, and the strong opposition of a far greater man in the person of the late Lord Lawrence, notwithstanding the overwhelming experience gained by the invasion of Afghanistan in 1838, the Indian Government, under the guidance of Lord Lytton and the home Government of Lords Beaconsfield and Salisbury, committed the unpardonable blunder of invading Afghanistan for the second time, in order to force an unwilling people to receive a political mission which our rulers were warned would be at the sacrifice of the lives of all connected with it. And so the event has proved only too true. What would have been said if Christians had had influence enough with the Government to induce them to send a band of missionaries to Cabul to instruct the natives in the principles of the Gospel, and the same sad results had followed? The world would have uttered its maledictions loud enough then at the mad and reckless policy of our rulers. And yet there are professing Christians in the present day who are not only ready to justify Lord Beaconsfield's action towards Afghanistan, but anxious and ready to urge the present Government to follow their example in its lawless aggression, not only upon that unhappy country which has been so long torn with the dissensions and strifes of bloodthirsty partisans, but, according to the desire of some monomaniacs in the present day, upon "all the earth besides."

When Sir Henry Rawlinson, with the Russian bugbear in his head, urged on the Government a few years ago the necessity of advancing to meet the great Northern power in Central Asia, and the duty of occupying both Candahar and Herat—ridiculing the idea of anything like defeat from the despised Afghans, or their daring to murder any envoy which England might send to Cabul, terming such things "as puerile absurdities, the stale refuse of a bygone period of panic"—he spoke with the usual inaccuracy of the prophets of the present day. As recently as August of last year Sir Henry recorded his belief in the *Nineteenth Century* that we should be received with open arms as welcome guests in Candahar. On such grounds the opinion of Lord Lawrence was contemptuously set aside. No sooner had Lord Northbrook resigned, rather than carry out such a mad policy, and Lord Lytton taken his place in India, than he proceeded to occupy Quetta, near the Bolan Pass ; which act, though Quetta is beyond the borders of Afghanistan, at once, as every experienced Indian official expected, made an enemy of the late Ameer Shere Ali. Then came the favourite device of the "go-ahead" school. As a Russian General had been permitted for some time to reside at Cabul, a British Resident must be forced upon the ruler of Afghanistan, whether he liked it or not. We all know the result. If ever the truth of Lord Bolinbroke's aphorism, "History is philosophy teaching us by example," was contemptuously set aside, and a proverbial saying of our own time, "History often repeats itself," was fulfilled to the letter, it has been witnessed in our second invasion of Afghanistan. The massacre of the gallant SIR LOUIS CAVAGNARI, and the whole of the mission in the same city, which forty years before had witnessed the murder of Sir Alexander Burnes and Sir William McNaghten and other brave Englishmen—the disgraceful defeat at Kushk-in-Nakhud and the twenty miles' subsequent flight of a British army to the sheltering walls of Candahar, and the large number of English officers killed at a petty sortie from the fortress of that city—almost as disastrous as the retreat from Cabul to the Khyber Pass in 1842—all these things seem to declare that the judgment of God has been laid upon us for our second invasion of Afghanistan, unredeemed though it be by the successful march and the brilliant victory of Sir F. Roberts and his gallant companions on the field of Baba Wali Khotal.

But in order to show how blinded the Indian Government were at their supposed success in sending Sir Louis Cavagnari to Cabul, it is a well-known fact that on September 3rd, 1879, Lord Lytton, then Viceroy of India, telegraphed to the home Government, "All well in the Cabul embassy," while that very day the whole of the embassy were being ruthlessly cut to pieces by the infuriated Afghans; notwithstanding that warnings of danger had been given to the embassy as early as the 13th of August, when the Government telegram mentions "the turbulence of some regiments had caused excitement—now subsiding." Then follows an "all well" in the Government message of the 21st, and again the same on the 28th of August, and once more a final and fatal "all well" on the sad day of the massacre.

Never was so miserable a policy more signally and speedily punished as that of the late Government in its dealings with Afghanistan. Surely its promoters must feel something like remorse when they recall to mind the result of their ill-advised proceedings. Far sounder was the judgment of Sir Alexander Burnes, when we were first brought into contact with Afghanistan, than that of Lord Beaconsfield after the forty years' experience which England has had, and which the Government ought to have known, of the impolicy of their recent proceedings. "I hold," wrote Sir A. Burnes, "that the man who recommends the cantonment of a British or an Indian soldier west of the Indus is *an enemy to his country.*" Lord Beaconsfield's thoughtless reply was, "The scientific frontier." And what does this so-called "scientific frontier" mean? Speaking generally, it consists of the Khyber Pass, with its peaks nearly 1,500 feet high, many of them covered with perpetual snow, having in its rear a series of unhealthy, dangerous defiles, flanked on both sides by high mountains, inhabited by unconquered hostile tribes. It is said not to command any strategical point whatever, and its maintenance will be always difficult and costly. To occupy Afghanistan as Sir Henry Rawlinson desired to do, would have cost about three millions sterling annually, and an army of 30,000 men. To occupy the Khyber Pass as a "scientific frontier," would be as expensive in proportion, and more useless. General Hamley, in his lecture at the *United Service Institution*, on the "Strategical Conditions of our Indian North-West Frontier," expressed himself quite opposed to England taking such a position. "It covers nothing and commands nothing but the pass itself. There is much to be said against, nothing for, the occupation of a post beyond the Khyber, and that would be a source, not of strength, but of weakness." It is scarcely necessary to point out the remarkable inconsistency of Sir Henry Rawlinson, the only statesman of any reputation who supported the late Government in its invasion of Afghanistan, and who is so sensitive in regard to Russian encroachments in Central Asia, that he should see no impropriety in our forcibly seizing one position after another in a country to which we have no claim.

All this is a perfect justification of Lord Northbrook in resigning the viceroyalty of India sooner than attempt to carry out the intention of Lords Beaconsfield and Salisbury in invading Afghanistan. As far back as January, 1876, he told the home Government, "We are convinced that a patient adherence to the policy adopted towards Afghanistan by Lord Canning, Lord Lawrence, and Lord Mayo, which it has been our earnest endeavour to maintain, presents the greatest promise of the eventual establishment of our relations with the Ameer on a satisfactory footing."

But nothing would satisfy the infatuated Government of that day but a second invasion of Afghanistan. Unmindful of the experience of the past, the misery and the horrors of the first invasion of that torn and distracted country, regardless of the advice of the greatest Indian statesman of the age, as Lord Lawrence expressed himself in a letter to the *Times* before the war began, that "it was not for the honour of England that we should go to war with the Afghans because they would not receive our mission, and that such a war would be impolitic and unjust," Lord Beaconsfield's government determined at all risks to plunge into the vortex of Afghan politics, and to undertake a second invasion of that unhappy land. So reckless has been the policy of the late Government towards Afghanistan, that the following remarks of an influential provincial newspaper, the *Liverpool Daily Post* of last August 4th, are not too severe in their condemnation of the same :—

"The policy in Afghanistan was carried out to the

derogation of our national character. Begun in weak fears, it was carried on in ignorance, and by misstatements, misrepresentations, and perversion, such as happily the history of England does not elsewhere show. It has been most injurious to our character as a nation, and the interests of our Indian Empire. The revelations made as to the manner in which the *financial* part of the affair was managed for party purposes brand every one connected with it as *worse than blind.** Another matter connected with India, not to be forgotten, is their conduct with regard to the famine of 1877-8. It tells a sad story of inhumanity on the part of the Government. What shall be said of the party which allows itself to be led by men who, well forewarned of impending famine, do by their neglect allow one million and a quarter of our Indian fellow-subjects to die of famine? The men responsible for this were at the same time spending millions of money, disseminating and supporting a spirit of sham imperialism. It would have been far more profitable, to say nothing of humanity, to have spent the money squandered in bringing troops from India to Malta, in keeping alive those who were allowed to starve, although it might not have added so much to the honour and glory of Lord Beaconsfield and his party."

These remarks on the policy of Lord Beaconsfield are no less severe than true. But inasmuch as they will be doubtless credited to the spirit of party politics, rather than to the domain of historical accuracy, I give the testimony of one who is far removed from the sphere of English politics, as from the position

* See Appendix.

he has filled in the Government of one of the greatest states in the world, he is better able to judge of the policy of Lord Beaconsfield when in office, than any foreigner now living. General Grant, who has had a double term of office as President of the United States, after having travelled over the chief parts of the world, has given to America, in two large volumes, his opinions on men and things with that frankness which is so characteristic of the men of the far West. Speaking of Lord Beaconsfield's once-lauded policy on the Eastern Question, which has been one long-continued mistake ever since he sarcastically termed the unmentionable atrocities * perpetrated by the Turkish soldiers on the trodden-down Bulgarians as "mere coffee-house babble," General Grant thus expresses himself on the occasion :—

"The more I looked into *the Eastern Question*, the more I was drawn irresistibly to the belief that the Russian side was the true one. Perhaps I should say the side of Mr. Gladstone. On the Eastern Question there is more diversity in England than elsewhere. As I was travelling through the East, I tried hard to find something in the policy of the English Government to approve, but could not. I was fresh from England, and wanted to be in accord with men who had shown me as much kindness as Lord Beaconsfield and his colleagues had done, but it was impossible. *England's policy in the East is hard, reactionary, and selfish.* No one can visit those wonderful lands on the Mediterranean without seeing what they might be under a good Government. I do not care under which flag the Government flourished

* See Appendix.

—English, French, Italian, or Russian—its influence would be felt at once in the increased happiness of the people, toleration to all religions, and great prosperity. Take the country, for instance, that extends from Joppa to Jerusalem, the plain of Sharon, and the hills and valleys beyond. What a garden the French would make of that! Think what a crop of wheat could be raised there within easy reach of the best markets! As I understand the Eastern Question, *the great obstacle to the good government of these countries is England.* Unless she can control them herself, she will allow no one else. That I call a selfish policy. I cannot see the humanity of keeping those noble countries under a barbarous rule, merely because there are apprehensions about the road to India. If England went in and took them herself, I should be satisfied; but if she will not, why keep other nations out? It seems to me that the Eastern Question could be settled easily enough, if the civilizing powers of Europe were to sink their differences and take hold. Russia seems to be the only power that really means to settle it, and it is a mistake of England that she has not been allowed to do so with the general sympathy of mankind."

However much party politicians may dislike this just critique on the policy of Lord Beaconsfield in respect to the Eastern Question, and which some of the New York papers condemned at the time in far stronger terms, it affords a faithful representation of what his policy, whether at Constantinople or Cabul, appears in the eyes of distinguished foreigners who have exercised rule over mankind. If it has been so unwise and unrighteous in respect to the one, it has been still more so in relation to the other.

Mountstewart Elphinstone, a high authority on Indian politics, in his "Kingdom of Cabul," relates that on one occasion, when speaking to a fine old Afghan, after descanting on the blessings of security under a strong government, the old man replied with warmth, "We are content with discord, we are content with blood, but *we will never be content with a master.*" Our first attempt forty years ago to impose a "master" on Afghanistan, leading as it did to the annihilation of a British army, brought upon the British Empire in India the sharpest trial through which it has had to pass since the days of Clive and Hastings, save the subsequent mutiny of the Sepoys in 1857. Our second invasion of Afghanistan has inflicted on us disasters nearly as great, and will assuredly bring a stain on the British name which it will require years to efface, if the frantic cry for annexation, or, as some euphemistically prefer to term it, "appropriation,"* be carried into effect. As the Queen's proclamation, issued on November 1st, 1858, on her assuming the direct sovereignty of India, distinctly declares, "We desire no extension

* At a public dinner given to Mr. Lepel Griffin, a high Indian official, at Simla, previous to his being sent by the Viceroy to Cabul, on the withdrawal of our troops from that city, he spoke most hopefully of the Cabul settlement, observing that "Abdul Rahman was rapidly creating a stable administration, and that his position was much strengthened by Ayoub's defeat. The criticism," he added, "on the withdrawal from Cabul was as foolish as it was unworthy of Englishmen. As to the talk about *annexation*, he could only thank God *that the destinies of the country were not yet entrusted to crack-brained enthusiasts*, who fancied it high and imperial policy for the Government to drag its coat through Asia for a barbarian to trample upon."—*Record*, October 11, 1880.

of our present territorial possessions; and while we will permit no aggression upon our dominions or our rights to be attempted with impunity, *we shall sanction no encroachments of those of others. We shall respect the rights, dignity, and honour of native princes as our own.*"

Let us now see how Lord Beaconsfield adhered to the letter or the spirit of this solemn promise on the part of the British crown. Notwithstanding the existence of such a promise, and the well-known opinion of nearly all the older statesmen, such as the late Duke of Wellington, Lord Hastings, Lord W. Bentinck, Lord Metcalfe, Sir John Malcomb, etc., etc., together with those of a later date, whose names have been already mentioned, who have been steadily opposed to the policy of absorption and aggression, there are always some to be found of a low range of intellect and principle who are perpetually craving after annexation of that to which we have no right whatever, any more than Ahab had to Naboth's vineyard, such as the typical Oriental abroad, or the Anglo-Israelite at home. In our own day the Russophobia is the pretext alike in the East as it has been in the West. "In India," says Sir John Kaye, the distinguished historian of the first Afghan war, "every war is more or less popular." The morality of the question never seems to enter into their calculations. Thus, when Lord Auckland's proclamation to invade Afghanistan in 1838 was issued, it was universally condemned for its flagrant injustice. Sir John Kaye has justly remarked, "If it were not pronounced a collection of absolute falsehoods, it was described as a most disingenuous distortion of the truth." And the same high authority, in his "History of the Sepoy War," when condemning the conduct of Lord Dalhousie (whose policy of reckless annexation was one of the main causes of that terrible insurrection) for his glaring disregard of the most solemn engagements on the part of the British Government against such appropriations, observes, "This temper was cherished and sustained by the prevailing sentiments of *the new school of Indian politicians*, who laughed to scorn the doctrines of the men who built up the structure of our Indian Empire, and by the utterances of a press which expounded the views of this school, and insisted upon the duty of *universal absorption.*"

The first invasion of Afghanistan was urged on by the mere will of two men—the late Lord Palmerston, the moving spirit at the time of the Government in England, galvanising the action of Lord Auckland, the feeble Governor-General—without the advice and against the judgment of the most experienced Indian statesmen at home and abroad, just as forty years later Lords Beaconsfield and Lytton have adopted a similar policy in the second invasion of that torn and distracted country.

To take a brief chronological survey of our dealings with Afghanistan, we must remember that twelve years after Dhost Mohammed had been permitted by the Indian Government to return to his native land, and to resume his rule over the Afghan race, from which Lord Auckland had so fatally sought to dispossess him, the Ameer, in 1855, made friendly overtures to the late Lord Lawrence, then Chief Commissioner of the Punjaub. The result was a treaty of perpetual peace and friendship between the British Government and the Ameer of Afghanistan and his heirs. In this treaty we solemnly engaged to "respect those territories of Afghanistan now in his Highness's possession, and *never to interfere therein;*" while Dhost Mohammed engaged to do the same towards us. Within two years after this treaty was made, the Sepoy mutiny broke out, when it was well known that the whole Afghan nation clamoured to be let down the passes, that they might join the rebels in a meritorious extermination of the infidel English. And how did the Ameer behave on that occasion? To his everlasting credit, he behaved nobly as a man of honour true to his word, and much better than many a nominal Christian ruler has done, and would have done, on a like occasion. As Mr. Dunlop told the House of Commons in 1861, "When our empire in India was tottering, Dhost Mohammed might have avenged himself by merely gathering troops in Cabul, and so creating an alarm, which would have prevented Sir John Lawrence sending reinforcements to Delhi, and thus have imposed upon us the necessity of reconquering India. But he abstained from taking such a step, thus contrasting the noble conduct of a Mohammedan chief with the tortuous policy of a so-called Christian state."

In 1863, Dhost Mohammed died. And as the law of primogeniture is not recognised by the Moslems, Dhost Mohammed, passing over his two eldest surviving sons, Afzeel, the father of Abdul Rahman, and Azim, left the throne to his youngest son, Shere Ali. For some reason or other, the Indian Government delayed the recognition of Shere

Ali for six months, which delay gave time for his elder brothers to conspire and rebel against him, and for the next four or five years civil war raged in the land of the Afghans. Although Shere Ali often sought the assistance of the Indian Government, Lord Lawrence, then Viceroy of India, wisely abstained from all interference in the internal convulsions of that unruly race, as Dhost Mohammed had advised him to do. In a speech which he made in the House of Lords in 1877, he said: "At the time of the treaty of 1855, the Ameer warned me against lending the support of the British Government to the conflicting pretensions of his sons, and advised me to allow them to fight it out." This advice Lord Northbrook rigidly followed; and it was only when Lord Beaconsfield unhappily resolved on another policy that the Viceroy felt compelled to resign sooner than carry out the designs which he foresaw with a seer's prescience would prove so disastrous to the British name. As long as India was governed by Lords Lawrence, Mayo, and Northbrook, we had no trouble with Afghanistan. No sooner had Lord Lytton succeeded the latter, than our troubles with that country began.

How friendly the ruler of Afghanistan was towards us may be seen by the noble letter of sympathy which Shere Ali addressed to the Indian Government on the assassination of Lord Mayo in 1872. "By this terrible and unforeseen stroke," he writes, "my heart has been overwhelmed with grief and anguish. The unvarying friendship and kindness displayed towards me, by him who is now *in the spirit land*, had induced me to determine to accompany his Excellency on his return to England, so that I might obtain the gratification of a personal interview with Her Majesty the Queen." If, as it has been alleged by the supporters of the late Government, Shere Ali had become embittered against England since that date, what has made him so? The answer is not difficult to find. During the viceroyalty of Lord Northbrook there were no disquieting rumours from Afghanistan; but no sooner had he been replaced by Lord Lytton, than a change came over the spirit of our dream. Almost from the very day when Lord Beaconsfield's nominee took the reins in his hand all has gone wrong.

Lord Northbrook had declined to station an armed force in Beloochistan, lest "it might have the effect of arousing suspicions in Afghanistan as to our intentions." Lord Lytton thought otherwise, and within six months after his arrival occupied Quetta, a town nearest the frontier of Afghanistan, which commands the western entrance of the Bolan Pass, and is on the high road to Candahar and Herat. The conclusion of Lord Lawrence on this high-hand proceeding is thus expressed: "The occupation of Quetta was a direct challenge to the Afghans, and an exceedingly unwise step, if we desired to cultivate friendly relations with them."

The policy pursued by Lords Beaconsfield and Lytton was evidently to pick a quarrel with the ruler of Afghanistan, for the purpose of obtaining what the ex-Premier in one of his mysterious communications to the citizens of London, at a Guildhall feast, cynically termed "a scientific frontier," and which could only be obtained by the invasion of the country, and the violent seizure of so much of it as would secure this unrighteous and shameful greed. It is scarcely necessary to show how such a policy has been carried out in contempt of all considerations of justice and morality, on the infamous principle that the end justifies the means, and that everything is lawful, however contrary to Christian ethics, which conduces to our supposed convenience and safety in India.

The fact of Russia having sent an embassy to Cabul has been merely seized upon as a pretext for exciting sufficient prejudice and passion at home to enable the Indian Government to commit a violent act of rapacity already decided on. We have in this another instance of the habit of equivocation which was so common with the late Government during their tenure of office. When the Duke of Argyll, in June, 1877, called the attention of the House of Lords to the rumours then prevalent, that the Government of India had determined upon a complete change of policy as regards Afghanistan, Lord Salisbury said in reply, that "our relations with the Ameer of Cabul have undergone no material change since last year," though the change was sufficiently great to make all the difference between peace and war. And when, later in the session, a similar question was asked in the House of Commons, Sir Stafford Northcote replied that he could speak with confidence on the determination of the Government respecting our Indian policy. "I have always demurred," he added, "to the idea that the best way to meet danger is to advance *beyond our frontier*, and have always held that the true lines we ought to lay down for ourselves are these, to strengthen ourselves *within our frontier*, and to do so by a combination of measures, moral and material. The occupation of Quetta, if taken from a military point of view, would be a false move." Lord Beaconsfield's view of "morality" must, however, have been of a different complexion from that of the excellent and virtuous Sir Stafford Northcote; as his policy was "*not* to strengthen ourselves within our frontier," but to "advance beyond our frontier," and to create his so-called "scientific frontier" by proceedings which have brought shame and disgrace on the British name.

This fatal system of equivocation, which Mr. Richard, M.P. for Merthyr Tydvil, has described as "the dishonourable characteristic of the late Government," was further seen in the way in which the Government first allowed the news of Major (afterwards Sir Louis) Cavagnari's reception by Shere Ali's representative to be made public. It was sufficient, not only to throw the jingo press, headed by the *Daily Telegraph*, into a whirlwind of passion, but even to mislead papers of a higher order and a more Christian spirit, and to make them call for instant war on the once friendly Ameer of Afghanistan. First it was intimated that the answer sent by Shere Ali through Nawab Gholam Hassein Khan was "the most impertinent communication addressed to the British Power in India since the days of Tippoo Sahib." Having thus effectively poisoned the public mind at home, another version of Shere Ali's reply was put forth, which gave a very different complexion to the message. "The Ameer had been anxious for the friendship of the British Government, but that of late years their policy had been changeable. Lord Mayo pursued one policy, and Lord Lytton another, and each new viceroy reversed all that had been done by his predecessor. He is open to make a new treaty, not being bound by any Russian alliance, explaining at the same time that the Russian embassy had not been invited to Cabul." Notwithstanding this frank explanation, which ought to have been accepted by any one blessed with a particle of Christian principle, the greedy lust of new territory, couched under the euphemistic expression of a "scientific frontier," was too strong to be resisted, and the second invasion of Afghanistan was decided upon and carried out.

So dead to all principle were the promoters of this wanton war, that the Indian correspondent of the *Times* was rash enough to write, "*It is feared* that, acting under the wise suggestions of his present diplomatic advisers, the Ameer may couch his reply in such ambiguous terms as will prevent *the immediate prosecution of vigorous measures!*" What those vigorous measures meant, let one of the so-called "society's journals" speak for itself and those who support such a bitter travestie of English morality. It expressed its opinion on our dealings with Afghanistan and Russia in these words: "There will be no peace in Europe until the power of Russia is trampled in the dust; and if Lord Beaconsfield will not lead us to the encounter, let him stand aside, and we will find one who will. Not only is the country ripe for action, but we understand that the most exalted personage in the realm considers that immediate war between England and Russia is unavoidable." We may let this pass as the mere ravings of political insanity, since it is as impossible to argue with such as it would be with a mad bull. And it is but justice to Lord Beaconsfield to say that he did not share the opinions of his would-be bloodthirsty supporter; for in the year 1876 he told the House of Commons, "I am not of that school who view the advances of Russia into Asia with those deep misgivings some do. I think that Asia is large enough for the destinies of both Russia and England. . . . Far from looking forward with alarm to the development of the power of Russia in Central Asia, I see no reason why she should not conquer Tartary, any more than why England should not have conquered India." The great outcry by the Russiaphobists, in the present day, is that Russia has made aggressions and annexations in spite of repeated promises to the contrary. This is an exact description of the growth of our British Empire in India; and we live in far too large a glass house to make such charges of any effect; for we have gradually acquired possession of the whole of Hindostan, not only in defiance of emphatic declarations at every step, that we did not desire any further extension of territory, but sometimes in flagrant violation of solemn treaty obligations. Our defence is that we have been driven to such a course in spite of ourselves, and that, on the whole, our dominion has been a blessing to the people. Just such is the plea of Russia, and we have no more right to charge Russia, as is so frequently done, with flagrant duplicity and hypocrisy, than we have to charge our own Government with the same offence. No reasonable person can deny but that the progress of Russia in Central Asia has on the whole been favourable to civilization, though doubtless of a lower standard than our own. They have abolished slavery everywhere, and have introduced order where previously nothing but anarchy and violence reigned. And when the Russian occupation of Khiva was discussed in the House of Commons, Sir Charles Wingfield, a high authority on Indian matters, expressed a hope that "Russia will not retire from Khiva, as I wish to see this nest of robbers, those scourges of humanity, reduced to order and civilization."

Lamentable in the extreme has been the conduct of the late Government in their dealings with unhappy Afghanistan. The official defence of their policy has been now some time before the country in the usual parliamentary papers; and while it is curious to note how the Government and its supporters have continually shifted their ground to find a plausible reason for the second invasion of Afghanistan, it is clear that it may be traced back to the determination of the late Government to effect a change of policy towards the Ameer Shere Ali as soon as they came into office. From the resumption of friendly relations between England and Afghanistan, through the treaty made by Sir John Lawrence with Dhost Mohammed in 1855, it had been the settled policy of every viceroy of India, approved and confirmed by successive Governments at home, *not to force British residents on Afghanistan.* The subject had been frequently mooted during the reigns of Dhost Mohammed and his son Shere Ali. But the objections to such a measure whenever proposed were so well grounded and reasonable, that the last four viceroys, Lords Canning, Lawrence, Mayo, and Northbrook, felt that if we wished to maintain a friendly understanding with the rulers and people of Afghanistan, it would be the height of folly to insist on that condition. Lord Canning is reported to have said, with the experience of the terrible disasters of the first invasion of Afghanistan fresh in his mind, that if the Ameer asked him to appoint a British resident at Cabul he would not consent so to do.

From the time of the accession of the late Government, this wise course has been practically set aside. A policy diametrically opposed to it has been adopted, and the consequences of their ill-advised acts have now been manifest to all mankind. Lord Beaconsfield and his party had only been a few months in office when Lord Salisbury, the Secretary for India, wrote in peremptory terms to Lord Northbrook to take immediate steps for procuring the establishment of a British resident, first at Herat, and then at Candahar. The Viceroy telegraphed that his Council were strongly opposed to such a measure. Lord Salisbury haughtily rejoined that he would only allow them a few months' grace to carry his orders into execution. The Blue Books contain the despatches of Lord Northbrook, which give the testimony of a cloud of witnesses against the unwisdom of forcing British residents upon a fanatical race like the Afghans, especially as the Ameer himself had objected, with such sinister memories of the past, he could not be answerable *for the safety of British officers residing or travelling in the country;* as the Ameer and his advisers very naturally argued "the appointment of such residents would be merely a preliminary step to annexation." General Taylor observes, "They believed that if they were to allow the thin edge of the wedge to be put in, we should very soon split up their country into our own hands, and they have spirit enough to prefer managing matters for themselves."

Finally, Lord Northbrook and his Council urged with overwhelming force that to insist on placing British residents in Afghanistan would be a direct breach of engagement. Lord Mayo, at the Umballa Conference, gave his solemn promise to the Ameer on this point, as the Indian Council in their despatch to the Duke of Argyll, then Secretary for India, say, "*We distinctly intimated to the Ameer that no European officers would be placed as residents in his cities.*" And Lord Mayo, in a confidential despatch to the Duke, sums up what the Ameer is not to have in these words: "*No treaty, no fixed subsidy, no European troops, officers, or residents.*"

But it was all useless. Lord Salisbury, undeterred by the testimony of the Viceroy, the Council, and every statesman of note in India, and by their convincing appeals to reason, experience, and common sense, to say nothing of what was due to the honour of the British name, was determined to have his own way; and so with the craft more like that of a Jesuit than of an Englishman who regards the sacred nature of a promise, he suggested that Lord Northbrook, *as a first step* towards forcing a British resident on the unwilling Shere Ali, should try to get a temporary embassy to the Afghan capital. At the same time Lord Salisbury instructed the Viceroy to *conceal his real object:* "There would be many advantages in *ostensibly* directing it to some object of small political interest which it will *not be difficult for your Excellency to find, or if need be to create!*"

Lord Salisbury's ears ought to have tingled with shame when writing such a despatch, and making such a proposition to a man of honour, which has necessarily entailed so much disgrace on the British name. Lord Northbrook, sooner than make himself the tool of such an unworthy proceeding, resigned office; his last words of advice to the reckless Government at home was to remind Lord Salisbury that "there was an entire concurrence of opinion among all those who could be supposed to have the means of forming a correct judgment of the sentiments of the Ameer, that he is most unwilling to receive British officers as residents in Afghanistan, that his reluctance is consistent with loyal adherence to the interests of the British Government, and that such being the case, we considered it would be a great error to urge upon him the establishment of a British agency at Herat or Candahar at the present time, because it would be a deviation *from the patient and conciliatory policy which had hitherto guided our relations with Afghanistan.*"*

Such was the concluding advice which a British nobleman gave to an unworthy Government on resigning office sooner than carry out its wanton and reckless behests. And what has been the result of this mad policy of Lord Salisbury? No sooner was Lord Lytton, the new viceroy, installed in office,

* See Appendix.

than everything was changed. A policy of active intervention, of aggression and menace, was openly substituted for that mode of dealing with the Afghans, which so many Indian statesmen had adopted and hitherto pursued with such satisfactory results. Before long the Viceroy sent the following communication to Shere Ali, by means of his vakeel, whom the Ameer had sent to greet him. He was instructed to inform him that "the moment we (the British rulers of India) cease to regard Afghanistan as a friendly and firmly allied state, what is there to prevent us from providing for the security of our frontier by an understanding with Russia, *which might have the effect of wiping Afghanistan out of the map altogether?*" And then, after alluding to the family dissensions between the unhappy Ameer, Shere Ali, and his eldest son, Lord Lytton contemptuously remarks, "This is the man who pretends to hold the balance between England and Russia, independent of either! His position is *rather that of an earthen pipkin between two pots.*"

What could be expected from the ruler of our British Empire who displayed such a spirit as this, when attempting professedly to observe friendly relations with the Ameer of Afghanistan? Or what good was likely to follow the proposed conference between the Viceroy's agent, Sir Lewis Pelly, and the Ameer's minister, Noor Mohammed, at Peshawur? It took place, however, at the appointed time; and though the Ameer's representative showed the greatest reluctance to admit the Viceroy's imperative condition of the admission of a British resident in Afghanistan, he never absolutely refused it. Noor

Mohammed died during the conference; and immediately Lord Lytton instructed his agent to withdraw, on the ground that there was no basis for further negotiation; notwithstanding, as Sir Lewis Pelly frankly admitted, that "a fresh envoy was already on the way from Cabul to Peshawur, and it was reported that this envoy had been authorised to *accept eventually all the conditions of the British Government. The Viceroy was aware of these facts when he instructed our envoy to close the conference.*" (Afghanistan Papers, pp. 170-1.)

Such were the high-handed proceedings and the tortuous policy of the late Government which led to the second invasion of Afghanistan.* And when we reflect on the way in which it was brought about by the flagrant abuse of that moral principle which distinguishes between right and wrong—the disregard of all advice afforded by those Indian statesmen who were most qualified to give it—the contempt shown for national pledges, by doing the very thing we were

* One of the monthlies has recently remarked that "there has been much in our dealings with Afghanistan to call for national humiliation on our part; much especially in relation to the war so lightly entered upon but two years since, that can make it no matter of surprise to Christian hearts that we should, as the result of our aggressive policy, have met in that country with so much trouble and disaster. But none the less, when the nation sees its error, and sincerely desires to repair it, may we anticipate that even warlike measures rendered inevitable by previous mistakes, but no longer entered on for aggressive purposes, will be attended with a blessing from on high. . . . . Sir F. Robert's triumph has seldom, if ever, been surpassed, and may well reassure those who are apprehensive on the score of our military prestige in the East. That prestige is now decisively assured, and the way is clear for the establishment of a higher kind of prestige founded upon the adoption of a policy marked by humanity, equity, and truth."—*Evangelical Christendom*, October, 1880.

engaged not to do—all these, and many other things besides—we cannot wonder at the disasters which have befallen us during our late war with Afghanistan. The judgment of God has been pronounced against us as clearly as it was against the late Louis Napoleon in the campaign of Sedan. And the decisive overthrow of Lord Beaconsfield's Government by the Electorate of England in the spring of 1880 was a striking comment upon the words which the censor of old addressed to the wrong-doing ruler of Israel, "Them that honour me, saith the Lord, I will honour, and they that despise me shall be lightly esteemed."

APPENDIX.

A.

Appendix, p. 122.

LORD MACAULAY, in his brilliant essay on Warren Hastings, says, "At fourteen he was first in the examination for the foundation. His name in gilded letters on the walls of the dormitory still attests his victory over many *older* competitors." This is scarcely correct, nor is it so stated in Gleig's Life of Warren Hastings, which work Macaulay was then reviewing. Gleig merely says that he distanced "all his competitors," without any mention of the word "older." Warren Hastings was just fourteen and a half when he got his election, and as no boy was allowed to compete after fifteen, he can scarcely be said to have beaten "many older competitors." The author himself entered Westminster School within ten years after Warren Hastings' death; and though upwards of half a century has passed away since that time, he can readily recall to mind the traditionary reverence with which the king's (now queen's) scholars of Westminster School regarded "the gilded letters" of Warren Hastings' honoured name on the college walls.

B.

Appendix, p. 206.

THE savage character of Tippoo Sahib has been well illustrated by an ingenious piece of mechanism which once belonged to him, and which was found in his palace on the capture of Seringapatam. This "tiger organ," as it is termed, which is still to be seen at the Museum of the East India House in London, represents a tiger standing over a prostrate man, whose figure and dress indicate a British officer. His screams, with the accompanying growls at intervals of the ferocious beast, are imitated by an internal apparatus resembling that of an organ, and acted upon by the turning of a handle on the outside, which is skilfully made to appear as one of the black stripes of the animal's skin. The man's arm is likewise raised by the action of the machinery in a supplicating attitude before he utters his cry. The classical reader will naturally be reminded of the brazen bull, in which Phalaris, the tyrant of Agrigentum, is said to have burnt the victims of his cruelty. One could wish that the well-known epistles which bear his name, and which present his character in so very different a light, were true ; but the masterly dissertations of Bentley, proving their spuriousness, appear to forbid such a pleasing hope.

C.

Appendix, p. 277.

LORD SALISBURY, as Secretary for India, previous to his removal to the Foreign Office, is one of those who are virtually responsible for our invasion of Afghanistan, and so far responsible for the glaring financial blunder, amounting to over £10,000,000, connected with the cost of the Afghan war. Yet this was the same man who, when in the House of Commons, had the temerity to criticise the splendid budget of 1861, introduced by Mr. Gladstone, one of the greatest financial ministers England has ever known, in the following insulting terms. Lord Robert Cecil said, "He had described the policy of the Government on a former occasion as only worthy of a country attorney; but he was now bound to say that he had done *injustice to the attorneys*, as, though they were very humble men, he believed they would have scorned such a course as that of her Majesty's ministers." Mr. Gladstone did not deign to notice his specimen of aristocratic temper, but treated the utterance with silent contempt.

D.

Appendix, p. 278.

THE following extract from a letter received by the Archbishop of Canterbury, from the Metropolitan of Servia, and signed by representatives of the Christian people of Bosnia and Herzegovina, will afford a faint idea of the "unmentionable atrocities" perpetrated by the Turks, and sanctioned by the Government of the Porte, as was recently proved by their rewarding the vile miscreant who was responsible for the massacre at Batak in 1876, instead of putting him to an ignominious death; but, as the *Times* of January 4th, 1877, speaking of the wretched government which has so long been permitted to rule over one of the fairest portions of the earth, says, "It is difficult for any tribunal to condemn a man who seems able to prove that *he has only obeyed orders;* but that a Mussulman of any rank should ever be hanged *for simply murdering*, no matter how many, *Christians*, is more than any man acquainted with the country and government could expect." Thus speak from their graves the long trodden-down Christians in their pitiable appeal professedly addressed to the English people: "It would only disgust you to be made acquainted with all the outrages which the Turks commit upon our persons. You would refuse to believe all the crimes of these savage hordes; but the Serb has had to bear the brunt of them for nearly five hundred years. What would you do, you English, if you had to keep guard night and day over wife and daughters, lest the Turk should seize upon them for the satiation of his vile passions? What if for a whim he forced you to eat the roasted flesh of your own child—the sole consolation which God had seen fit to leave you in this life of suffering and bitterness? Horror! Yet it is with this barbarous game that the Turks from time to time amuse themselves. You are fathers; you can at least understand the full atrocity of these ferocious deeds, to bear which the Serb has been condemned for centuries past, and which civilized Europe tolerates.

"But this is not all. After having ravished your daughter or your wife, after having forced you to taste the flesh of your child, the Turk will amuse himself with slashing your arms and your legs, flaying you alive, and will finish by impaling you, so that you may breathe your last sigh in agony such as only the Serb knows, and from which you in Europe are happily secure. . . . You cannot, for sheer disgust, believe these savageries, can you? For all that, they go on daily throughout the breadth of the Ottoman Empire. Ask your Consuls; they would not hide the truth from you. *Such* is the life to which Christians of Turkey are condemned."

Can we wonder, with the knowledge of these "unmentionable atrocities," that the noble-minded Lord Shaftesbury, the first philanthropist of the age, should publicly avow his conviction that "the Turkish Government is beyond remedy, and utterly incorrigible, and not in accord with the views of humanity? Looking to the interest of the commonwealth of mankind, I, for one, would rather see the Russians on the Bosphorus than the Turks in Europe." Or that the greatest statesman of the age should have urged, when in opposition, the duty of removing the Government which could overlook or perpetrate such atrocities "bag and baggage" from the scene of their disgrace? And now that he is in power, and doing his utmost to carry out the stipulations of the Treaty of Berlin, which Lord

Beaconsfield had not the courage, or, perhaps, the will, to attempt, see how mercilessly he is attacked by a licentious and unchristian press. The writer is old enough to remember the political disputes of the last half-century, but he cannot recall to mind anything so disgraceful or so indefensible as the conduct of a portion of the London and provincial press, headed by the *Daily Telegraph*, in their hatred of Mr. Gladstone, and the support which they unceasingly give to the degraded Government at Constantinople. Such conduct is not merely a disgrace to our professed Christianity as a nation, but a slur upon human nature itself.

E.

Appendix, p. 293.

THE differences between the conduct of Lords Northbrook and Salisbury, in respect to the two parties into which the Church of England is chiefly divided, and which constitute "two distinct religions," as Dr. Littledale truly declares, may be seen in this: the former is an annual subscriber of £100 to that excellent and admirable institution, *The Church Missionary Society;* the latter has exhibited his sacerdotal leanings in the nomination, I believe, of one or both of the most pronounced ritualistic bishops of the present day—the Bishops of Columbo and Bombay. The Rev. George Maxwell Gordon, who nobly fell when tending the wounded in the sortie from Candahar, was an heroic missionary of the Church Missionary Society, who fulfilled the active duties of a chaplain to the Bombay troops on that melancholy occasion, because the Bishop of Bombay had neglected his duty in not providing them with a chaplain when they marched to Afghanistan. Possibly, had he done so, the chaplain would have been worse than useless, if the story related by the *Bombay Guardian* be characteristic of his clergy in general. For it appears that a clergyman of that presidency, says the *Bombay Guardian*, "during last Lent, did penance by *running with bare feet* across a field of *stubble*, and got his feet so torn and full of thorns, that he had to lay up for several weeks, with his feet in *poultice bags*." Such is the extreme folly of an ascetic clergyman endeavouring to outvie the acts of a Hindu fakeer.

F.

Appendix, p. 103.

A MOST memorable day in the annals of our British Empire in India is the incident which took place on the overthrow of the Mogul Dynasty. After the capture of Delhi, Captain Hodson, with the permission of the Commander-in-Chief, on Sept. 21st, 1857, went forth accompanied by fifty native troopers to arrest Behaudur Shah, King of Delhi, and the last representative of the dynasty of the Great Mogul, who had taken refuge with his queen and princes of the imperial family at Hoomayoon's tomb, a magnificent structure in a suburb of Delhi, where the emperor of that name was buried, A.D. 1556. Concealing his troopers from the sight of the assembled thousands of fanatical Mussulmans who surrounded the tomb, Hodson sent emissaries to treat for the king's surrender, which, after two hours' delay, was at length arranged on a promise that his life should be spared. Then went forth the gallant English soldier, and stood in the open space near the beautiful gateway of the tomb with its milk-white domes, a solitary white man amongst so many thousands, awaiting the surrender of a king, and the total extinction of a dynasty, as Kaye in his interesting "History of the Sepoy War" terms it, "the most magnificent the world had ever seen." A grander historical scene was perhaps never witnessed than that of a single British warrior receiving the sword of the last of the Mogul Emperors in the midst of a multitude of his followers, grieving for the downfall of the house of Tamerlane, and the ruin of their own race.

G.

Appendix, p. 206.

THERE is an interesting episode connected with the siege of Bednore, in the life of one of the many French adventurers who during the last century sought their fortune in India, which is worthy of notice. When the chevalier St. Lubin appeared in the Mahratta camp as an ambassador from Louis XVI., he was accompanied by a youth of the name of Louistannau, who eventually rose to great distinction in the Mahratta army. Belonging to the French force which assisted Tippoo Sahib at the siege of Bednore, he had the misfortune to lose his left hand, though it subsequently proved quite the reverse. Louistannau had an artificial hand made of silver, to replace the one he had lost; and on the first occasion of his appearing in the field with this new hand, an Indian priest fell on his knees before him, declaring that the will of God was fulfilled; for an ancient prophecy had foretold that the Mahratta confederacy would attain its highest degree of power when its armies should be commanded by a stranger from the far West with an invincible *silver* hand. This was supposed to have been accomplished by the great victory of Khurdiah, March 11th, 1795, when the Mahratta army, 130,000 strong, entirely defeated the Nizam, ruler of the Deccan, at the head of an immense army, disciplined likewise by a Frenchman, M. Raymond.

The subsequent adventures of General Louistannau were of a most romantic nature, until his death in Syria, A.D. 1837, when sheltered under the roof of the celebrated Lady Hester Stanhope. Dr. Thomson, an American clergyman, who buried Lady Hester, gives the following account in his work, entitled "The Land and the Book," of the scene which he witnessed on that occasion:—

"The British Consul at Beyrout requested me to perform the religious service at the funeral of Lady Hester. It was an intensely hot Sabbath in June, 1839. We started on our melancholy errand at one o'clock, and reached this place about midnight.

After a brief examination, the Consul decided that the funeral must take place immediately. The vault in the garden was hastily opened, and the bones of General Louistannau who died here, and was buried by her Ladyship, were taken out and placed at the head. The body, in a plain deal box, was carried by her servants to the grave, followed by a mixed company with torches and lanterns, to enable them to thread their way through the winding alleys of the garden. When I entered, the first thing I saw was the skeleton of General Louistannau, having a lighted taper stuck in either eye-socket—a hideous grinning spectacle. It was difficult to proceed with the service under circumstances so bewildering. The Consul subsequently remarked that there were some curious coincidences between this and the burial of Sir John Moore, her Ladyship's early love. In silence, on the lone mountain at midnight, 'our lanterns dimly burning,' with the flag of her country over her—

> 'She lay, like a warrior taking his rest,
> And we left her alone in her glory.'

There was but one of her own nation present, and his name was MOORE."

H.

Appendix, p. 56.

MAJOR-GENERAL STRINGER LAWRENCE, Clive's earliest patron, who greatly distinguished himself by his victories in India, is buried in Dunchideoch Church, a small country village near Exeter, and adjoining Haldon House, the seat of Lord Haldon, whose great-grandfather, the first Sir Robert Palk, was the firm friend both of Hastings and Lawrence. He erected a handsome marble tomb in honour of the latter, which bears the following inscription:—

MAJOR-GENERAL STRINGER LAWRENCE,

WHO COMMANDED IN INDIA FROM 1747 TO 1767,

DIED 10TH JANUARY, 1775, AGED 78.

The desperate state of affairs in India becoming prosperous by a series of victories endeared him to his country.
History has recorded his fame.

THE REGRETS OF THE WORTHY BEAR TESTIMONY TO HIS VIRTUE.

Cui Pudor et Justitiæ soror
Incorrupta Fides, nudaque Veritas,
Quando ullum invenient Parem.

Curious to relate, very shortly after General Lawrence's death, Haldon House was the scene of a conference held by the friends of Hastings, in order to make some terms with the British Government during the administration of Lord North. And Col. MacLeane, Warren Hastings' agent in England, in order to show the speed with which travelling was accomplished in those days when there was a special call for despatch, mentions with pride that he "left London for Haldon House, and returned to London on the *fourth day*." Seventy years after, the journey from London to Exeter was accomplished in *four hours!*

INDEX.